worship

renewal
to practice

worship

renewal
to practice

Mary **collins** OSB

The Pastoral Press

Washington, DC

Acknowledgments

Acknowledgment is gratefully made to the publishers and others for granting permission to use again, sometimes in edited form, the following: "Liturgy in America: The Scottsdale Conference," *Worship* 48:2 (March 1974), pp. 66–78; "Who Are the Hearers of the Word?", *Liturgy* 25:1 (January-February 1980), pp. 5–8, 42–44; "Culture and Forgiveness," *New Catholic World* 227 (January-February 1984), pp. 12–15; "Spirituality for a Lifetime," *Spirituality Today* 34:1 (March 1982), pp. 60–69; "Ritual Symbols and Ritual Process: The Work of Victor W. Turner," *Worship* 50:4 (July 1976), pp. 336–346; "Liturgical Methodology, Cultural Shifts, and Worship in the U.S. Church" which originally appeared under the title "Liturgical Methodology and the Cultural Evolution of Worship in the United States," *Worship* 49:2 (March 1975), pp. 85–102; "Critical Ritual Studies: Examining an Intersection of Theology and Culture," *The Bent World: Essays on Religion and Culture*, ed. by John R. May (Decatur, GA: Scholars Press, 1981), pp. 127–147; "Critical Questions for Liturgical Theology," *Worship* 53:4 (July 1979), pp. 302–317; "The Public Language of Ministry," *The Jurist* 41:2 (1981), pp. 261–294; "The Baptismal Roots of the Preaching Ministry," *Preaching and the Non-Ordained: An Interdisciplinary Study*, ed. by Nadine Foley, O.P. (Collegeville: The Liturgical Press, 1983), pp. 111–133; "Naming God in Public Prayer," *Worship* 59:4 (July 1985), 291–304; "Obstacles to Liturgical Creativity," *Concilium* 162 (Edinburgh: T & T Clark Ltd., 1983), pp. 19–26; "Eucharist and Justice," an address given at the Institute on Pastoral Ministry at Boston College; "Ritual Symbols: Something Human Between Us and God," *The Living Light* 12:3 (Fall 1975), pp. 438–448; "Is the Adult Church Ready for Liturgy with Young Christians?", *The Sacred Play of Children*, ed. by Diane Apostolos-Cappadona (New York: Seabury Press, 1983), pp. 3–17 [reprinted by permission of Harper & Row].

ISBN 0-912405-32-5

The Pastoral Press
225 Sheridan Street, N.W.
Washington, D.C. 20011
(202) 723-1254

The Pastoral Press is the publications division of the National Association of Pastoral Musicians, a membership organization of musicians and clergy dedicated to fostering the art of musical liturgy.

Printed in the United States of America

Contents

Introduction

The essays collected here reflect their author's concern that liturgical study, liturgical activity, and the worshiping church cannot be viewed in isolation from one another. The three elements must always be held in balance. It is the church of Jesus Christ which gathers for worship, always at a particular time and place in human history. Liturgy and culture inevitably inform one another. It is the task of liturgical studies to examine ways the interaction occurs and to assess its consequences for the life of a worshiping people.

A systems approach to understanding a complex symbolic phenomenon like the worshiping church takes it as axiomatic that the inquirer should be able to "enter the system" at any point because any one thing leads to the rest. The classical philosophical and theological traditions recognized this truth under the language of the analogy of being and the analogy of faith. The approach assumes some measure of coherence in the whole. When the point of departure for critical reflection on worship is the culture in which the worshipers live and celebrate their faith, cultural insight must inevitably lead to new questioning of the forms of the church, the forms of worship, and the forms of belief.

These essays reflect the assumptions of a systems approach to liturgical studies. While the topics are varied, some more concerned with culture, others with matters properly theological, and while many of the essays were deliberately occasioned in their original form, they converge always on a single recurring concern: the interplay of culture with ecclesial institutions, most especially liturgical institutions.

Whether concern for an earlier cultural experience or a contemporary one predominates, the essays reflect an underlying judgment that all institutional arrangements make good sense to the generations involved in shaping cultural institutions. All critical study of the liturgical tradition must begin with an effort to understand each form or expression on its own terms. The next step is to ask the dialectical question whether the ecclesial or liturgical achievement—its deepest truth—expresses the fullness of the Gospel of salvation in Jesus Christ. This is the theological question. The posing of both cultural and theological questions makes the continuing renewal of worship necessary and critical liturgical studies interesting and valuable for the life of faith.

worship

renewal to practice

THE RENEWAL OF WORSHIP

Introduction

The reform of Roman Catholic worship was mandated in 1963 and the structures for effecting the mandate established almost immediately. Subsequently, friendly and hostile critics inside and outside the church have expressed doubts about the wisdom of the deed. The reform of liturgical books and their immediate translation into popular languages, precipitous as it might have been, is a tangible achievement of the twenty-five years since the 1963 proclamation of *Sacrosanctum Concilium*. A less tangible achievement is the growing pastoral and theological insight that the reform of the structures of worship is neither co-extensive with nor the equivalent of the renewal of worship. The set of rites and texts are always brought to life only in their celebration. And public performance of liturgical rites is always a cultural event, one in which the ritual participants interpret the texts they are using in the very way they use them.

The essays gathered under the heading "The Renewal of Worship" speak to different aspects of the complex culture of the U.S. church which has taken up the mandate for liturgical renewal. The program for liturgical renewal immediately intersected—and at times collided—with late twentieth century cultural agendas: the social ascendancy and the rising self-esteem of U.S. Catholics; the growing professionalism of liturgists; the disillusionment with authority in governmental and religious institutions, to name but a few. These essays reflect one liturgiologist's dialogue with selected aspects of contemporary culture. The liturgical renewal so recently begun will be achieved only when the celebration of the paschal mystery of salvation in Jesus Christ is adequately enculturated, that is, human grounded in the culture and in evangelical tension with it.

1

Liturgy in America:
The Scottsdale Conference

JUST A SHORT DRIVE THROUGH A WELL-POPULATED ARIZONA DESERT separated the Franciscan Renewal Center, site of the 1973 Scottsdale conference on American liturgy, from the workshops of architectural futurist Paolo Soleri. Many of the participants in the invitational conference made a side trip to see Soleri's scale-model archology, the attempt of a visionary to structure humanly and ecologically harmonious environments so as to make possible new ways of our living together on planet earth. Juxtaposed to Soleri's environmental futurism, the American liturgical future being envisioned by the liturgical professionals evidenced their commitment to a familiar tradition. Ten years after the early December promulgation of the Second Vatican Council Constitution *Sacrosanctum Concilium* on the Sacred Liturgy the Scottsdale conference participants clearly reaffirmed the structures and the stuff of the received tradition: Christian initiation, the eucharistic assembly, rites for the dying, people, bread, water, wine, words proclaimed, songs sung. Just as clearly was it evident that the conferring liturgists shared a broadening understanding of that tradition and were committed to creative development of it for the American liturgical future. But there was no evidence that some unimaginable future for Christian worship was being planned in the Arizona desert that winter day in 1973.

However, such judgments about what is thinkable and what unthinkable are quite subjective. Is it or is it not startling to proceed to discuss the future of American worship from the premises of ecumenical openness and the primacy among sacramental symbols held by the community of the baptized? Those two premises shaped the direction and the results of much that the six working groups produced in their sessions, whether they talked about the ambiguity of the faith experience, constituting the faith community, ministering to it, celebrating the service of the word, or the meaning and manner of Christian initiation.

The identification of controlling ideas within the community of American liturgists has only begun, however. The keynote speaker for the conference, Walter Burghardt, asked the liturgists to take on this task among themselves. Calling the group "men and women of uncommon power," the Jesuit editor of *Theological Studies* continued: "But one of the perils of power lies in ignorance. I dare, therefore, to urge on you a profound self-examination." None of the proceedings that issued from the conference working groups shows that the liturgists took up at once the challenge of examining their own presuppositions. Rather, they continued to work within them and with them. Such a course of events was inevitable, given the brevity of the conference (two full working days) and the nature of the group. Despite apparent homogeneity—fifty-five of the seventy-six "persons with liturgical credentials" were Roman Catholic priests—the persons gathered had distinctive pastoral, historical, theological and cultural understandings, all of which shaped their approaches to liturgy. The interaction of these perspectives within the working groups was at times productive and at other times immobilizing. Even where it resulted in a consensus statement, like that produced by the working group on Christian initiation, members of the group spoke of the need to be wary of facile agreements.

At the end of the meeting, Burghardt's three-part keynote question remained to be dealt with formally: how transformative may liturgical reform be? how theological is the reflection of liturgists? how responsive is developing ritual to the faith of the church? Nevertheless, the reports and proceedings from the conference working groups may constitute good preliminary data for considering the issues Burghardt raised. The present essay is no more than an attempt to offer one participant's interpretation of the way such questions might be answered, based on reflection in retrospect on what the working groups did and said.

How Transformative May We Be?

In explicating his first question, Burghardt drew upon J. W. O'Malley's analysis of six concepts of reform operating concurrently within the contemporary ecclesiastical consciousness: reform as excision or suppression, as addition or accretion, as revival, as accommodation, as organic development and as transformation. Transformational reform, in this series, is reform in which discontinuity is more evident than continuity.[1] It is not difficult to make the judgment, on the basis of the proceedings of the various groups, that all forms of reform are on the minds of American liturgists when they reflect together. Transformational reform may be on their minds least of all. In fact, the trumpet sounded significantly for transformation very few times in the ears of this hearer. Most of what was proposed could, I think, be interpreted as the attempt to work in continuity with the 2000 year tradition of Christian worship—excising, suppressing, adding, reviving, accommodating, developing organically, in all manner of combinations. A necessarily selective report on some of the conference proceedings may substantiate this.

Two groups found themselves, in the course of their deliberations, asking what to do with the fraction rite in the eucharistic liturgy. In one discussion suppression of the rite was proposed, since it is nonfunctional if there is no bread to be broken in a land where small, thin wafers nourish. To the contrary, the second group maintained that small, thin wafers feed the eucharistic community poorly precisely because they are too impoverished to bear great meanings. The ritual action of breaking bread, done with real bread, has in addition to its traditional sacrificial significance the power to recall the story of how the disciples perceived the Lord's presence in the breaking of bread, and how the breaking and eating of the one bread was represented to the Corinthian Christians as the antidote to the factions among them.

1. J. W. O'Malley s.j., "Reform, Historical Consciousness and Vatican II's Aggiornamento," *Theological Studies* 32 (1971) 573–601.

Such meanings are fundamental to the life of the church today and should be augmented in the consciousness of the people. Shouldn't American eucharistic liturgy rather restore genuine bread? Why not develop the rite, perhaps by expanding the number of chants to accompany the rite? Why not also sing, on some occasions, some variation on Luke's words: He broke the bread and handed it to them, and their eyes were opened and they recognized him? Or Paul's: Anyone who eats the bread or drinks without recognizing the body is eating and drinking unworthily towards the body and blood of the Lord?

Continuity or discontinuity? There is no established precedent in the liturgy of East or West for using a chant other than "Lamb of God" for the rite of the fraction. Yet the fraction is capable of embodying many levels of meaning; the possibility of allowing now one and now another level of meaning to predominate seems to correspond to what Burghardt identifies as liturgical reform by development, i.e., "Keep what you have, but let it expand and mature to its final perfection."

The reduplication of a penitential rite within the eucharistic liturgy also came under some serious scrutiny. Its placement in one form as an opening rite was widely but not universally rejected. Historical foundations for the rejection came from conceding authority to the more widespread and earlier practice, in both the Eastern and the Western liturgical traditions, of giving ritual expression to the need for God's forgiveness and mutual reconciliation through the ensemble of the Lord's Prayer with its embolism culminating in the kiss of peace in anticipation of eucharistic communion. Theologically, the insertion of a preparatory penitential dimension at the opening of the liturgy of the word was alleged to distort the focus of the action. "It is the word itself that convicts and purifies."

Lack of awareness that the Lord's Prayer ensemble is the appropriate form of penitential rite in the eucharistic liturgy, or ignorance that "It is the word that convicts and purifies" were judged to signal a failure in catechesis, not a justification for having an opening penitential rite. Similarly, the prospect of eliminating the kiss of peace from the rite because some Americans find it offensive or of moving the kiss of peace to another position in the liturgy because "it distracts people before communion" were ruled out on the grounds that the antiquity and near universality of this ritual unit for forgiveness and reconciliation made it virtually inviolable. A double reform dynamic was implicit in the discussion: "Keep what you have by removing threats to it"—namely, the opening penitential rite. "Keep what you have by breathing new life into it" through better catechesis. Excision, revival.

Other discussions on ritual ventured farther from the historical tradition, even while they were hardly discontinuous with it. Rites for the dying, characteristically included as a subsection of the rite for the anointing of the sick, are so treated in the new ritual promulgated by the Congregation for Divine Worship in 1972. Does the very traditional liturgy for the commendation of the dying suffice in twentieth-century America? The group which talked about the ministry to the dying and to the survivors of a death asked whether such a ministry needed the support of ritual in some new way.

The cultural conditions which occasioned their question are, of course, those pointed out by many American psychologists and culturally responsive American theologians like John Dunne, who have identified the great spiritual malaise we suffer as a people who more easily accept death through violence than the human act of dying. What of rites for the commendation of the dying and the consolation of the survivors? What bearing does the work of Dr. Elizabeth Kübler-Ross have on any American liturgical adaptation of the commendation rites and the funeral liturgy? Should either or both rituals reflect the five psychological states through which, according to Kübler-Ross, the dying person passes and with which he and the family must cope? Is there room in the Christian rites of death for giving fuller expression to negativity: for attending to the humanly necessary denial of the reality of one's own or another's impending death, to anger, to the attempts to bargain for continued life, to depression in the fact of the inevitability of death, and only then to acceptance? In the words of the working group's report, "the efficiency of our theology of death" and the abundance of our words about the afterlife warrant evaluation vis-à-vis the rites for the commendation of the dying and the rites of Christian burial.

Whatever the outcome of the probing of cultural conditions and liturgical rites together with the theology of death and resurrection called for here, there was little evidence that the working group intended to be revolutionary. The mode of reform envisioned for the American liturgy of death and dying was the mode of accommodation—"making adjustments for differences in times and places," in Burghardt's terms.

A note of ecumenical openness was sustained throughout the meeting, although only nine of the participants spoke from a liturgical tradition other than Roman Catholic, and only one of these from the perspective of Eastern Christianity. Robert Taft, S.J., professor at the Pontifical Oriental Institute in Rome, remarked on the normalcy of the collaboration of Protestant and Roman Catholic Christians in matters of liturgical reform. Viewed from the East, differences in initiation and eucharistic practices among American churches are not fundamental differences but variations of the one Western rite. Where these variations are in conflict, emerging from the great Western schism of the four-teenth-fifteenth centuries, they remain local problems, not problems for the church universal. Taft himself stressed the need for maintaining continuity between East and West in dealing with the most ancient liturgical units, those traditional elements found "everywhere and at all times," such as the Lord's Prayer in anticipation of communion in the eucharistic liturgy.

Clarence Joseph Rivers illustrated the "one Western rite" approach to liturgical development and adaptation endorsed by Taft while discussing his work as director of the department of culture and worship for the Office of Black Catholics. Although there is no culturally authentic tradition of liturgical worship among American black Catholics for reasons rooted in the history of the American nation and Western Catholicism, a vital black American worship tradition developed among black Protestants. This tradition is a living source in the search for humanly expressive ritual forms for American Catholic liturgy. Rivers was direct in his recommendation to American liturgists to be responsive to the black perspective in worship, the dimension of "soul," not only for the welfare of black Catholics, but for the life of the whole American church.

This attitude of openness to all the resources of the Western liturgical tradition, both Catholic and Protestant, was evidenced also in the efforts of the working group on Christian initiation rites. In presenting their consensus statement on the nature of

Christian initiation to the conference, Ralph Keifer noted that the consensus was possible primarily because only inadequate patterns for Christian initiation exist anywhere in American Christianity, Protestant and Catholic alike, and the unsatisfactory nature of the situation made the issue easier to deal with.

The consensus statement dealt with fundamental principles and presuppositions and broad structural considerations, not with details of the ritual forms for initiation. Among the prominent points of consensus reached in a working group with Lutheran, Episcopal and Roman Catholic members were the following:

1. The rite of Christian initiation should normally consist of the unified sacramental event in which the three now separated moments of baptism, confirmation and eucharist are integrated. The full rite is to be used at any age when a person is initiated.

2. Within the economy of the sacraments, adult initiation should be the practical norm.

3. Infant baptism derives from the adult form. It places specific responsibilities upon the adult community.

4. The entire Easter season from Lent to Pentecost is derived from the public practice of adult baptism. The meaning of baptism is best demonstrated when it is celebrated within the Easter season.

5. For children of responsible Christian parents, two different patterns of initiation might well coexist: the celebration of the full rite of initiation (baptism, confirmation, eucharist) shortly after birth, to be followed by catechesis appropriate to succeeding stages of development; or enrollment of the infant as a catechumen, with initiation to be celebrated at a later age after catechesis.

6. The development of viable and visible catechumenate structures on a parish, interparish or diocesan basis is essential to the renewal of the sacraments of initiation.

7. Penance is a process culminating in a rite of reconciliation. Each year at Lent and Easter the whole initiated community reenters the conversion process, hears the word of God with renewed attention, waits in mutual prayer and support, and finally renews its dying and rising in the sacrament of reconciliation.

8. What is said here about the sacraments of initiation is based

on overriding theological principles. Sacraments form a continuum; the manner or time of celebrating one sacrament dictates the practice of others.

The consensus statement on Christian initiation, were it to be implemented in American churches, would call for major adjustments in the liturgical life and religious education of all American Christians, Catholic and Protestant. But the liturgists proposing this reform of Christian initiation rites are not revolutionary. Wisdom about Christian initiation is recognized as lying in a past on which the American community might well draw for its own spiritual strengthening. An assumption is made that Christian initiation in the pluralistic American culture will be best reformed by devising structures comparable to those which once supported Christians living in the culturally diverse and hostile ancient world.

The sharpest note of discontinuity, a genuinely revolutionary movement toward the unprecedented, came in the form of the declaration from a working group probing the liturgy-life tension as this evidences itself in actual eucharistic celebrations of the American church ten years after the promulgation of the Constitution on the Sacred Liturgy. The declaration stated: "Women are obviously part of the sign of the gathered community. This will not be evident until this bald fact is allowed full expression in the exercise of ministerial responsibility which is their right through baptism. Consequently, at the present time there should be no obstacle whatever to their concrete exercise of all nonpresbyteral ministeries. Thus the community can also be prepared for a positive solution to the urgent question of the presbyterate for women."

The opening sentences of the declaration are not revolutionary but rather call for a restoration to women of ministeries held by them at other times in church history. There is well-documented precedent for the exercise of virtually all ecclesiastical ministeries by women in the West. Joan Morris's *The Lady Was a Bishop* cites evidence to show that the only ministry for which there is no clear historical precedent for women is that of presiding at the eucharist. Further investigation of what Morris calls "the hidden history of women who have held the jurisdiction of bishops" may or may not modify historical understandings.

Nevertheless, even when the ministry of women as deacon-nesses was a vital ministry in the church, the conferral of the office was regularly deferred until well after menopause, on the unchallenged assumption that there was an inherent unclean-ness which lingered in mature, adult baptized women. Further-more, being a woman, whatever her age, was considered a de-cisive impediment to presiding at the eucharist of the Christian community. Thus the final sentences of the declaration, in noting that there should be "no obstacle whatever" to women's exercise of non-presbyteral ministeries now and the presbyterate in the foreseeable future, explicitly depart from the mainstream of Christian tradition which has always made natural biological functions more decisive than faith, baptism and the gifts of the Holy Spirit in ordering ministeries in the community.

The implications of the working group statement deserve ex-plication. But even without it the declaration is revolutionary by Burghardt's criteria, for it clearly implies "at least a partial re-jection of the past in the hope of creating something new." There is no attempt to justify the "no obstacle whatever" stance on the basis of history. The stand reveals the premise of its formulators that the liturgical past does not control us and that the Christian church is free to work out its own future.

Behind this declaration lay as a controlling theological idea the understanding that the whole community of the baptized is a constitutive element of each sacramental sign. The idea, drawn from recent ecclesiology and sacramental theology and endorsed in the teaching of the magisterium, clearly shaped the judgment that women, as part of the sign of the community, must be visible in the community's expression of itself. The influence of the idea was widespread. In a discussion on the nature of suitable open-ing rites for liturgical celebration it was noted that while the gathered community is a basic sacramental sign, it does not yet perceive itself as this sign. Thus the purpose of the opening rite was judged to be that of assisting "in constituting the people as this sign." Since there is no existing ritual unit which gives expression to the conviction in faith that the living Christ is already present within the congregation by the very fact of its gathering, prior to the proclamation of the word and the cele-bration of the eucharist, it becomes a task for local communities to explore ways they can express their own being this sacramental sign of Christ's presence. Space, light, incense, posture, orientation may be factors in symbolizing this mystery.

The power of this concept of the community as a constitutive element of the sacramental sign showed itself in other ways. One working group noted that the clergy's wearing of baptismal robes in a eucharistic concelebration is a commendable idea in itself. But at concelebration with a congregation, albs actually become a countersign of separateness within the covenant community, a sign inconsistent with the meaning of life in the church. Elsewhere the premise of Christ's primary presence within the sign of the gathered community provoked inquiry into the possibility that the eucharistic prayer should have a more obviously dialogical form. Such musings are potentially though not necessarily revolutionary for the future shape of liturgy. If historical precedent is retained as the overriding norm, the musing will come to little.

All manner of tension is to be found in the presuppositions and premises, historical and theological, invoked by the liturgists in their conversations on particular problems of reform. The data was there to bear out Burghardt's thesis of the need among liturgists for profound self-examination on their pattern of historical consciousness. "Whether you like it or not, at this moment you do have a style of historical thinking (perhaps unreflective); this style of historical thinking affects your theology of reform (perhaps unreflective); this reform theology dictates what you are ready or willing to change in today's liturgy, how far you are willing to go, where you believe you must say, 'Thus far and no farther.' " Classicism, providentialism, primitivism, and evolutionism, as well as contemporary historical consciousness (O'-Malley's categories) were all in evidence in Scottsdale. In what proportions and in what relationships was never clear, in any given working group or in the whole conference.

What Theology Shapes Our Thinking?

What theology did shape the liturgists' thinking? This was the second question Burghardt put to the liturgists participating in the Scottsdale conference. Again, no direct answer to this question was forthcoming from the working groups. For the most part, they worked within their theological horizons without examining them. Yet one clear theological position emerged in the conference proceedings. It came in developed form in the major address of Langdon Gilkey to the conference, "Symbols, Meaning and Divine Presence: A Wayward Protestant Shot at a Sacramental Theology." It appeared again prominently in the report of a working group discussing the central and crucial importance of authentic human signs. It appeared implicitly in much that issued from other groups.

Gilkey's paper attended to three fundamental meanings of symbol in Christian theology. The fundamental and primary meaning of symbol has reference to the creature as creature, for the Christian doctrine of creation means that each creature as *itself* is symbol of the presence of the holy. Human being becomes its authentic self precisely when inwardly in faith and outwardly in action it reflects its creaturely status and role as *image* of God. Therefore when the presence of the holy in our existence is completely unknown, Gilkey noted, then the other levels of religious symbols will communicate little or nothing, because it is the holy as experienced in all of our ordinary life as human which provides the experience to be thematized or shaped by concrete Christian symbols, theological or sacramental.

However, the Christian believes also that God, the true self and the true other have all been obscured, veiled, lost, forgotten. Awareness of the divine presence had to be reawakened and reappropriated by special manifestations of the sacred. So at a second level Christians use the word symbol to identify those privileged media of particular revelations of the sacred universally present yet universally obscured. The originating Christian symbols of special revelation are the history of the community Israel and the person Jesus. The universal fact of alienation required this second level of symbol, the finite and particular medium which incarnates the essential nature of the true *humanum*, human community and the eschatological fulfillment of each.

Symbol is used in a third sense in the Christian tradition to designate those created realities which have again become media to point to, recall, and reintroduce by representation the originating presence of the holy in the privileged revelatory symbols. For Christians these tertiary symbols include communal acts and elements like sacraments, and words spoken and reflected upon, which in turn generate theological symbols like creation and incarnation.

Gilkey proposed that the present inadequacy of both classical forms of Christian worship, Protestant and Catholic, lies not with their selective and almost exclusive emphases on word or sacrament. The inadequacy lies rather with the failure of both to maintain the crucial relationship of the tertiary meaning of symbol to the primary one; "namely, that the divine works in and on *us* as creatures, too, and that awareness of this our role as "symbols"—in our being, our meanings, our decisions and our hopes—lies at the heart of any experience of the holy that is to be relevant to and effective in us." Gilkey continued: "Our argument is that unless the symbols of our tradition in word and sacrament are brought into relation to the ultimacy that permeates our ordinary life—unless traditonal symbols reawaken in us our role as symbols of the divine activity—there is no experience of the holy."

A comparable theology of man as God's primary symbol shaped the work and results of the group considering authentic human signs. In its report, "Conclusions to our Conversations Concerning Symbol, Symbolic Action and Christian Liturgy," the group took a clear position which was nowhere countered in the conference and was frequently implied in much that issued. On the matter of the starting point and the meaning of Christian rites, the group stated: "The purpose of Christian liturgy is to celebrate and empower the growth of man toward his true humanity; toward becoming more fully a symbol of God's power and love in all his ordinary existence."

The report took further note of the fact that while eucharistic liturgy is a symbolic action of eucharistic meal in the context of the prayer of the community, nevertheless the long-standing stress within Roman Catholic worship on the isolated element submerged the community's awareness of the way in which liturgical action symbolically mediates the divine. Moreover, the isolation and sacralization of the priest in the liturgical action also diminishes the full meaning of the holy covenant community making eucharist as the mediating symbol of Christ's presence.

This working group also confronted the problem noted earlier—namely, that "the community does not yet realize it is this sign"—though it seemed to focus unnecessarily and unfairly on the lack of awareness among the Christian laity, as though the narrow vision were embedded only in the consciousness of the unordained masses but had already been excised from the consciousness of the clergy and replaced there by a transformed theology of symbol. As an antidote to the limited vision of sacrament which does not recognize the human as the primary symbol, the group noted a need for a renewal of the preparatory rite in liturgical celebration and a new catechesis.

The tension between this emerging theology of symbol and liturgy among American liturgists and the authority of the church's liturgical and theological past will undoubtedly shape the dialectic of American liturgical reform. Much of the tradition of rites and ministries was molded by another theology, another understanding of sacramental presence. Much of that other theology and its liturgical manifestations perdures. Will the emerging theology of symbol be the criterion for selecting among new things and old in liturgical expression? Will old or not-so-old-but-familiar forms remain in possession, even when they are distortions within the new theological vision, primarily or exclusively because they are old and familiar?

Keynoter Burghardt also posed the question whether the liturgists had a conscious and consistent theology of prayer and were ready to say what manner of prayer liturgy is? Again he pointed out that presumptions about the nature of liturgical prayer determine the ritual shape, whether wittingly or unwittingly. "The liturgy will not corrupt if you challenge my approach to prayer. It may well corrupt if you have no theology of prayer, if that theology is perverse or if, as Jerome said about Scripture, you do not even know what you do not know." No talk of sacrifice of praise, or sacramental sacrifice, of proclamation of the wonderful works of God, or *ex opere operato* efficacy entered overtly into discussion. But there was insistence that liturgy is kerygmatic, that man discovers himself in proclamation and praise of God in whose image he exists. That clarity was overshadowed by the chairman's summary remark that in the community of faith which is American Catholicism, "people believe in different Gods." What, then, of a theology of liturgical prayer as proclamation and praise which both expresses faith and molds it?

How Responsive Is Our Liturgy?

The final issue raised for consideration in the keynote address was: how responsive is your ritual? A working group explored the problem of the ambiguity of the faith experience and in its final report testified to its inability to offer an integrated and integrative statement about the contemporary American experience within which Christian faith lives and grows. But Langdon Gilkey's address offered a firmer foundation on which liturgists might build. Gilkey observed: "Ours is . . . an age fortunately reawakened to the intimacy of the relations of body to spirit, of the spirituality of the bodily and the sensual, if you will. The sensory and the aesthetic are thus for us again, after centuries, possible media of spiritual insight." He contended that the emerging cultural reevaluation in the United States of the earthy, the bodily, the natural and the human was disposing people to new openness toward sacramental worship which celebrates the presence incarnate in the world of a transcendent power to save.

The University of Chicago theologian surmised that a Catholicism forced by twentieth-century historical consciousness to abjure the temptation to absolutize the relative and thus sanctify the ambiguous could discover a vast strength within its sacramental form of religion—"namely, the divinely granted capacity to allow finite and relative instruments to be media of the divine and so to endow all of secular and ordinary life with the possibility and so the sanctity of divine creativity; and thus, more than Protestantism, to bring Christianity alive, well and active through the turmoil of the modern world." Gilkey was clearly more sanguine than the working group.

Nevertheless, in regard to this matter of the responsiveness of ritual vis-à-vis the faith experience in all its ambiguity, there was broad consensus among liturgists Catholic and Protestant, Eastern and Western, white and black, that the liturgical reform efforts of the past ten years were too exclusively verbal, not sufficiently sensory. As Gilkey suggested, when the liturgy presumes to mediate ultimacy through words alone, either the mediating speech claims to be absolute, a reflection of clear and distinct ideas, or the words are acknowledged to be simply the opinions and preference of the presiding minister. Neither approach, Gilkey pointed out, is in our day a possible or happy solution.

Echoes of this outlook were found throughout the conference: the liturgy of the word must again become ritual proclamation of the word. Homilies and responsories must "dance around the word," not presume to say authoritatively what the word means. People must be given the human skills to celebrate in song and gesture, in the rhythms of sound and silence. Clarence Rivers, in a final response to the conference at its closing session, clarified further the need to deal liturgically with the ambiguity of faith in ways other than the verbal. Styling himself an artist rather than an academician, Rivers observed that analysis of words and their meaning frequently leads to polarization, because analysis does not exhaust reality at any time, least of all when persons attend to the incarnate presence of the holy in creation. The ambiguity of the faith experience in a diverse community can find its unity in the act of celebrating the divine mystery which eludes every attempt to analyze it.

If one can speak conclusively about what emerged at the Scottsdale conference on American liturgy ten years after, perhaps it is not too little to say that the liturgists' program for future reform is this: better ritual celebration of the Christian mystery of redemptive incarnation by the baptized who themselves constitute a fundamental part of the symbol. Gilkey in his "wayward Protestant shot" called the liturgists to consider going even further, to consider a possibility wholly discontinuous with the past understanding of sacramental liturgy. As presently and historically celebrated and understood, word and sacrament are directed to the covenant community. Is it possible, he wondered, to retain the special tie of sacramental action to special revelation, Christology, redemptive grace and ecclesiology and at the same time widen the scope of sacramental meaning to give it reference to our life as human in the world, so that rebirth in the covenant community is in no way separate or divorced from being human, from living humanly in the world, at one with God and neighbor? In Gilkey's thinking, such wider reference in liturgy to our life as human in the world may represent a discontinuity with tradition necessary in our situation. "It is this reference to the sacred quality of the secular that our liturgy desperately needs for its realization and validity—in order that it may fulfil its task of sanctifying and liberating the world's life."

Gilkey's "shot" in his concluding remarks traveled faster than the speed of sound, apparently. There was no evidence that his words struck any auditory nerves, for there were no outcries, no return volley from the members of the conference while the conference was in session. That may well not be the end of the matter, however. So many items of unfinished business, unexplored ideas and unexamined presuppositions remained at the conference's end that the participants with one voice agreed to the early constitution of a professional society for American liturgical research. John Gallen, convener of the Scottsdale conference, was empowered by the group to take preliminary steps to accomplish this goal. In January, 1975, the North American Academy of Liturgy appeared.

The Scottsdale meeting could well prove to be an important event in the maturing of American Catholicism and of all American Christianity. All Christian churches need initiation, reconciliation, eucharist and other rites rooted in the worship tradition of the universal church yet responsive to the faith experience, however ambiguous, of American Christians. More than once at Scottsdale reference was made to a prophetic moment in the infancy of the American Catholic Church when Archbishop John Carroll secured and held for almost two decades a rescript authorizing English language liturgical celebration among Roman Catholics in Protestant America. It may be that the conditions for proceeding with liturgical renewal and cultural adaptation will vanish in the American Catholic Church at the turn of the twenty-first century as they did at the turn of the nineteenth. Nevertheless, the present moment holds promise.

2

Who Are the Hearers of the Word?

IT IS T.S. ELIOT WHO GIVES US THE SENTENCE: HUMAN KIND CANNOT bear very much reality. Undoubtedly that is why our human kind normally shuns too much association with artists and poets and prophets. They deal in heightened presentations of the real. Flannery O'Connor, short story writer, novelist, and letter writer, was one of our human kind who regularly looked at the real and named it.

In a letter written twenty years ago to a writer friend who had earlier questioned her about the Catholic Church, O'Connor had said: "Human nature is so faulty that it can resist any amount of grace and most of the time it does. The Church does well to hold her own: you are asking that she show a profit."

Many of us are probably like Flannery O'Connor's correspondent, crypto-capitalists, people who want the church to show a profit. Perhaps it is because we would like to have our life investments yield dividends at least annually, if not quarterly. But O'Connor offered a warning to her friend and then to the rest of us crypto-capitalists working in church circles: "To expect too much is to have a sentimental view of life and this is a softness that ends in bitterness. Charity is hard and endures."

Who are we, the hearers of the word which we believe is in our midst? The question seemed theoretical, moot, an academic exercise during the 1979 visit of Pope John Paul II to the United States. For a week, the prospective and the real hearers of the word were faces and forms lined up in television camera lenses—

ten or twenty or thirty million people gathered on streets, and circles and squares, in parks and parking lots and fields. They have been all manner of U.S. citizens, believers and unbelievers, come to see the Polish Pope named John Paul, who as one child said, appeared in a white dress and red cowboy hat. In the words of one journalist, writing at the high point of papal enthusiasm, "His presence tells us that God is like him, only better, and this helps us to receive his blessing whether we have any theology to go with it or not." Every manner of human being—leaders of states, and also, handicapped adults called for the opportunity to serve the church and society and not to be in its custody. Boisterous students turned docile, prelates and clerics, cynics and skeptics and enthusiasts among the affluent and the poor, the workers and the unemployed, the old and the young, women and men, Catholic and non-Catholic loyalists and the loyal opposition turned out for the Bishop of Rome.

Whatever ministry of the word is to be exercised in this church in the next decade, it is a ministry to be performed by those people and for those people. They are both the hearers of the living word and the ones who will utter it, not by their own power, but by the power of the Holy Spirit who rests where it will. Whatever form that ministry of the word will take, it must begin and end with the conviction in faith that the word of God in our midst comes in the address and the response we extend to one another as human beings. Short of that conviction, we believe neither in the grace of the Word Incarnate nor in the mystery of redemption by the power of the Spirit of Jesus.

Who are the hearers of the word? This is a complex question which needs response at several levels. At one level, it is a question about theological anthropology. At another level it is a question about the Catholic Church in its institutional form. It is an historical and cultural question. Reflection at each level would require extensive investigation and some detailed analysis; my response will be preliminary, exploratory, suggestive of some themes that may merit further consideration.

When Karl Rahner developed his essay in foundational theology a number of years ago, he talked about the human person as a hearer of the word in history. Rahner's foundational theology saw within the human person the possibility of limitless receptivity to the mystery of God's presence throughout a lifetime. In fact, said Rahner, "mystery in its incomprehensibility is what is *self-evident* in human life." When it manifests itself as the mystery of *love*, it is embraced as *holy* mystery, even if it is a knowledge of God that is unrecognized, unthematized, and without a name.

The foundational theology of the American systematic theologians like David Tracy and Langdon Gilkey also looks at concrete persons living out personal and social history as the place where the living word of God breaks through. So, too, story theologians like John Shea and Rosemary Haughton and storytellers like Flannery O'Connor look for the working of grace and the effective presence of divine mystery in the daily life of ordinary people.

When you look out at your liturgical assembly, the gathering together in prayer of Mrs. Goehegan and Mrs. Gutierrez, the Santinis and the Stendebachs, Barbara and Ralph Wolski and Teddy and Tammy and Pammy and Todd, or you recall some of the millions who gathered to hear John Paul, you are faced with concrete persons whom the systematic theologicans have raised or reduced, depending on your viewpoint, to the abstract category of hearers of the word in history. Ordinary people in their ordinary lives: this is the setting for the experience of holy mystery.

But the presence of divine mystery, the sounding and re-sounding of the living word of God, is diffuse in ordinary life. It is often inaudible or unattended to precisely because so many other dynamics and forces are also making their claims on ordinary people in ordinary life. In fact, ordinary life in the United States today is the human experience which has given rise in popular culture to the ritualized world of disco. That world presents ordinary life experienced as immediate, noisy, relentless, disconnected, cavernous, momentarily and erratically brilliant, but always pulled back toward darkness.

In this cultural cacophony, not every experience is revelatory of holy mystery. So, according to the viewpoint of biblical faith, the presence of holy mystery, the presence of the one who is, YHWH, has been concretized and thematized and named. We believe that if our human kind in history are to recognize holy mystery in their own lives, they must come to know the story of the presence of divine love in the midst of a chosen people.

Christian faith says that story of saving love culminates in the story of Jesus. Christians believe that in him the holy mystery of love and its consequences is fully embodied, if not completely understood. So believers tell the stories of Israel and Jesus, trusting that here they have the mystery of God's loving presence disclosed to them. Believers proclaim that story in their assemblies for worship, trusting that they will recognize in it their own story.

But we hearers for whom the word is spoken inevitably face a double obstacle. First, the word sounded in our lives is only one voice among many others. Second, the word sounded in our Scriptures always speaks in the strange language of another age. So while the scriptural story is privileged and authoritative, it always needs transposition into later cultural keys if it is to fit with the living word of love experienced in the midst of ordinary life. The living word thus needs an active ministry. It needs ministers who are filled with great reverence for the hearers whom God is addressing in their lives. It needs ministers filled with great awe for the wondrous and unexpected story of death and life in Christ Jesus. The ministers of the word are also our own human kind. There are no other kind. But they are nevertheless the mediators of an intended meeting of the hearers and the word in history.

The liturgical assembly is the ritual culmination of all that activity. Ordinary people assemble, embodying the ambiguous experiences of their ordinary lives. A part of the story of Israel and the story of Jesus is ritually announced. The homilist who knows and loves the people and also the scriptural word of God provides the interpretations and so mediates the meeting of God and the people. The ordinary people and the mediator together make eucharist and return to ordinary life nourished by the word and by the body of Christ eucharistic and ecclesial. This is, of course, an ideal description. In reality, there are the obstacles.

The principal obstacle is the ambiguity of human experience. This ambiguity of human experience wears historical dress. So I would like to recall some shared history of the Catholic Church in the United States. My focus on the hearers of the word will be an inquiry into our corporate experience, based on the theological premise that we are called not singly, but together, as a people. As a people we are a church of immigrants. That experience has shaped our hearing of the Gospel message and given institutional form to our responses. There are the middle-class American Catholics, with their relative readiness for dis-covering the word of God in their/our midst. And there are the neglected Native Americans and Black Americans, as well as the new immigrants to this nation and to the Catholic Church in this country. Middle-class Catholics—we ourselves—are what has become of the immigrant church of the late nineteenth and early twentieth century. Our successful passing into the dominant American culture at the close of the twentieth century—or the aspiration to accomplish that passing—is the historical situation in which the word of God is being heard or obscured in the heart of American Catholics.

That passing has been remarkably successful in this century. When we gather in liturgical assemblies we do so as the pros-perous or upwardly mobile grandsons and granddaughters, sons and daughters of immigrants. We are in fact, children of refugees who have become people of privilege. Andrew Greeley's 1977 research on *The American Catholic* reported some hard data. "In terms of mobility, Catholics are the second most mobile group in the society educationally, and the most mobile denomination in annual family income." The church has indeed shown fiscal profits of substantial proportions in this century.

The nineteenth and early-twentieth century Catholic Church poured its energies into getting our European immigrant fore-bears to this point. Church leadership made a decision in the late nineteenth century to pour out the abundant human and the limited financial resources of the Catholic Church for the well-being of its own. It recruited workers—it recruited *us* as workers—to build the buildings, to staff the schools and par-ishes, the seminaries and colleges, to champion workers' rights, to promote their health, to guide and discipline their behavior.

Having come to this point of development, at the close of the century, a growing number of middle-class Catholics in the United States suspect, borrowing T.S. Eliot's words, that "we've had the experience but missed the meaning." In any case, upon arrival at this point, some of us are comfortable and satisfied, but some others are guilty, others bored, others confused and questioning about what it means religiously to belong to the Catholic Church in the United States today. Is it as effective for salvation as it has been for socialization?

Again, it is T.S. Eliot who focuses the scene with a few words. His God in "Ash Wednesday" looks out on the twentieth century Western world and asks:

O my people, what have I done unto thee.

Then Eliot the poet questions the situation:

Where shall the word—be found, where will the word Resound?

And he answers with unsentimental realism:

Not here, there is not enough silence . . .
For those who walk in the darkness
Both in the daytime and in the night time
The right time and the right place are not here.

He concludes the stanza with a judgement:

No time of grace for those who avoid the face
No time to rejoice for those who walk among noise
    and deny the voice.

I would like to borrow Eliot's image to characterize our corporate historical situation. As a church, we are indeed among those in the Western world who "avoid the face" and who "walk among noise and deny the voice."

What face? And what voice? It is our own younger face we are avoiding. As a middle-class church we have muted the memory of suffering. We have become willful amnesiacs, protecting ourselves from the only recently eluded misery of poverty, the indignity of social inferiority, and the humiliation of exclusion. Our conscious everyday identities do not now want to deal with the insistent demands of the human suffering of others. We are seeking a respite from our own struggles and a measure of respect. As a church, middle-class Catholics have become somebodies, and we would like to enjoy the fruit of our labors—the television cameras on us approvingly, and the eyes of the church in Rome.

If it is our own younger disreputable faces we are avoiding as a middle-class church, what voice are we denying? Nothing less than the imperative of our one baptismal consecration to Christ, our many eucharistic communions and the ecclesial commitment of which we have been the beneficiaries all our lives. It is the voice which calls: *your life for the life of the world.* Like other generations of the chosen, we deny that election ends in mission.

Other stories are being superimposed regularly over the story *Exodus,* the story *Paschal Lamb,* the story *Calvary,* the biblical stories which have given burdened peoples a sense of meaning and destiny for generations. We do not comfortably think for long about our lives as episodes in those tales, tales which have us leaving the familiar for the unknown, the secure for an uncertain destiny. Why? Flannery O'Connor has her post-Christian preacher Hazel Motes put it in words one night when he is street preaching:

> If you had been redeemed, you would care about redemption, but you don't. Look inside yourselves and see if you hadn't rather it wasn't if it was. There's no peace for the redeemed, and I preach peace. I preach the Church without Christ, the church peaceful and satisfied.

Hazel Motes' gospel was an overt attempt to make enough noise that he could avoid the face and deny the voice which threatened him. His posture was deliberately self-protective. He had grown up, O'Connor says, with a grandfather who had "Jesus hidden in his head like a stinger . . . ."

Our shared preference as a middle-class church for another story than the story *Calvary* is not necessarily so self-conscious. It might almost be said that other stories have found us during our immigrant century than that we have deliberately sought them or created them.

Consider the number of middle-class Catholics, we ourselves perhaps, who live comfortably within the American cultural tale of hard work and self-reliance, without any reference to a religious or ecclesial ambiance for their lives or any advertance to the suffering of the many who gave their lives so that this generation might prosper. Consider also those who live within a classic non-Christian Mediterranean myth, the tale of Narcissus, of whom Ovid wrote: ". . . he desired himself, and was himself the object of his own approval." Consider how many are absorbed in these tales while they also maintain allegiance to the Catholic Church still institutionalized as a church of dependent immigrants.

These readily available cultural tales are capable of swallowing us up, of estranging us from our own past, of washing over and obliterating almost every trace of the basic Gospel message, even among peoples whose forebearers had been baptized for generations. Why? Again, the reality is complex. I ask you to look at it through a single prism: the immigrant church in the United States is a church of cradle Catholics. This is true of both the leadership and of the membership, the old and the young. But that fact has had tangible consequences for our corporate history as a local church.

A moment ago I said "other stories have found us." Let me pursue that statement.

I have in mind the text in which the risen Jesus Christ of the Gospel speaks to the church of Matthew:

> When an unclean spirit goes out of a man, it wanders . . . looking for a place to rest and cannot find one. Then it says, "I will return to the home I came from." On arrival, finding it unoccupied, swept and tidied, it then goes off and collects seven other spirits more evil than itself and they go in and set up house there, so that the man ends up by being worse off then he was before. That is what will happen to this generation.

Is it not close to what has happened to ours? A full seven other stories have found us and moved in.

We were once marked with oil and the sign of the cross as home for the indwelling Spirit. But we have taken our indwelling guest for granted from infancy. We were all family, after all. So we did not become particularly attentive to the presence of the inner voice calling us to a new future: *your life for the life of the world.* Was it indifference or complacency? No matter. Being cradle Catholics in a church of European immigrants, we took Christian faith for granted both in its substance and in its historical forms. It was American we had to become. So the spirits of this age have moved in one by one and have crowded the Spirit of Jesus. Now we are finding it hard to be hospitable to everyone. There is tension in the house. Not every spirit is compatible. Each is demanding our undivided attention, and we are not fully present to any of them. Are we to listen to the church of immigrants in the form of institutionalized dependency? to the church as an agent of socialization? to the voice addressing us from God's future?

The Spirit of our baptism still abides in most of us, speaking quietly if persistently: *your life for the life of the world.* We attend often enough that we cannot be accused of total neglect. But in some corners of the household of the immigrant faith, members have been either pre-occupied or re-occupied by other spirits, most of them fully American, so that the living Spirit of Jesus has effectively been silenced. Abraham Heschel's writing comes to mind: It is God who is looking for us, not we for God.

If this is a true description of our condition as a church, what is to be done? Some of those spirits who have moved in on us and camped for a while may have to be evicted. The language of the Gospels speaks both of repentance and conversion and of confrontation with evil spirits and exorcism. We once learned to think of those as pre-baptismal events. We are having to learn all over again by testing the Gospel against our experience.

Not only the gospel but also the early liturgical tradition knew of the tension laden household of the faith. For example, a relatively unknown sixth-century document, the *Ecclesiastical Hierarchies* of Psuedo-Dionysius, depicts a liturgical community which is composed not only of catechumens and initiates and hierarchs. Among the initiated, some he designated "the possessed." The language of Dionysius suggests the Matthaean church. It also provides an image world in which we recognize ourselves: the post-baptismal possessed.

The Gospel tells us that the confrontation with alien and destructive spirits takes place always dramatically and painfully. "What do you want with me Jesus? I implore you do not torment me." The Risen Christ Jesus responds by asking the question: "Who are you?" The truth of the situation is unexpected: "My name is Legion." Jesus prevails in the life of the tormented man. But the Gospel shows us a startling consequence of Jesus' intervention: There is no rejoicing in the community. The people, in fear, ask Jesus to go away. We are not likely to be any different.

To this point I have talked of our historical and cultural situation in the Catholic Church of the United States as a circumstantial case of inattention to the radical demand of the indwelling spirit of our baptism. Having been elected from our youth and cared for by the church, we presumed that "was the meaning." Earlier I mentioned the ambiguity of experience, but did not discuss evil or sin. This last Gospel image reminds us to look for something more culpable to explain the persistence of our situation. "The people were afraid for themselves and asked Jesus to leave them."

We should not fool ourselves that we want a more lively ministry of the word within the church in the United States. We who are baptized, ordained, vowed in marriage and in religious community may just as likely be intent on protecting ourselves from discovering the word in our midst with its insistent sting: *your life for the life of the world.* This imperfect immigrant church is, after all, our home. Like the home of every childhood, it has fostered dependency and resisted the move to the mature interdependence of all the members of the household. It has been a place for belonging. Nevertheless, after a time, the best of childhood homes must be left behind.

When Dr. James Fowler of Emory University reported to a research seminar about work he was doing: collecting and analyzing and classifying the personal stories of believers, what struck me was the way the stories he has gathered fall into two characteristic patterns. In most personal stories, believers have aligned their lives with more-or-less theologically sophisticated but already-available answers. In others, believers have responded to the questions in their lives. I report this here, because I believe it has bearing on our concern for understanding the hearers of the word.

It is in the nature of institutions—families, schools, governments, corporations—to reward persons, leaders and members, whose stories respect available answers. It is in the nature of institutions to isolate or even to punish those—leaders and members—whose lives are shaped by questions about institutional answers. The church shares in this characteristic behavior of human institutions. They are always organized to protect and to promote values already available in the group. But the century-old church of immigrants is not a self-serving institution. It exists to serve the living and life-giving Word of God, Christ Jesus. In that sense, the church is always also an historical movement. Movements are more likely than institutions to be alive to questioners and questioning. Movements explore and promote emerging values within a community.

The hearers of the word, our human kind, have these characteristics as answer-gatherers and question-raisers long before they gather in liturgical assemblies. So a well-ordered ministry of the word which culminates in the liturgical celebration of the word must deal with the full reality of human experience. The church of immigrants does have some answers to hand on, the corporate Christian wisdom drawn from the experience of centuries of living faith. Yet it has fifty million living members today who must also be present to the mystery of love claiming them today. It is obviously true that the raw experience of these fifty million lives is ambiguous, and not easily interpreted in the light of the Gospel. But either we believe that the word is alive and active among us today, or we do not believe at all. We cannot rule out the new discoveries about God's ways with us and claim to believe in a living God. How are we to deal with all this ambiguity of undifferentiated spirits? In the Gospel according to Matthew, we see the Risen Christ come to the bedeviled believer with the gift of a question: Who are you?

That is the question addressed to all prospective hearers of the word, all our human kind. It is put specially to those hearers who are also ministers of the word in history. It must be put particularly to us who were attracted to and recruited for the service of the immigrant church. Who are you? Of what spirits are you possessed? Is your own believing characterized by aligning your life with available answers? Is your believing a matter of questioning all answers, even your own? Can you be minister of a living word?

The ministry of the word served primarily to provide information, to confer identity and to give answers in this first century of an immigrant church. Such a ministry has had its legitimate purposes. Such a ministry by itself is no longer adequate, when

so many people who have come to this moment with the church
question all answers, both for the substance and the form, and
so many others come looking still for easy answers.

We cannot suppose that the post-immigrant generations of
American Catholic women and men at the close of the twentieth
century have a disinterested or dispassionate attitude toward the
announcement that Jesus is good news, freedom, light and life.
Some, ordained and lay, wonder whether they have outgrown
the answers that they once learned about life in Christ in an
immigrant church. That Gospel they have judged to be boring,
if not oppressive or irrelevant. Others, ordained and lay, leaders
and members, want to cling to a familiar and comforting world
of youthful certainty—now without the pain—as the only sane
alternative to our cultural cacophony.

Furthermore, in this generation Jesus' judgments about our
human kind are just as liable to be judged themselves. Who is
he to say: you are the light of the world and the salt of the earth?
Who is he to say: you are a worthless and evil generation, un-
profitable servants? Who is he to say: *your life for the life of the
world!* The only way now to engage both the disengaged cultural
Catholics and the narrowly engaged institutional Catholics of
every stripe is, it seems, to turn the tables and ask the question:
who in the world are you? If you are Legion, show your several
selves in turn.

That word, the evangelical question, still has the power to be
heard in any momentary silence in the din of ordinary life. Furthermore, it has the power to turn everyone who hears the question into a storyteller—everyone: the bishop of Washington and
the bishop of Rome, the fearful and the peaceful, women and
men, the aging and the poor. What will their stories tell? Always
and inevitably, they will describe our human kind, wounded
and broken, graced and looking for wholeness. And only this
human kind, wounded, graced and searching, really recognizes
the inbreaking good news of active love in their own lives, can
hear it resound in the biblical story, can discern its demands as
it is proclaimed, can interpret its challenge in the liturgical assembly, can give thanks with the whole church, and be nourished for life by the Incarnate Word Jesus. The German theologian Gerhard Ebeling points out: Not every word about God

is the word of God, but only that word spoken in our hearing which sets us free to love.

What are some of the emerging values recognized in life experience, the signs of the inbreaking of the mystery of love, which have to be responded to and thematized in a post-immigrant Catholic Church? I would suggest that their substance was already identified during the council in the Pastoral Constitution on the Church in the Modern World. The inbreaking of the mystery of love in the lives of people everywhere on earth is tied to the human experience of the desire for greater personal dignity, for genuine human community, and for greater justice.

These universal human experiences of people living at the end of the twentieth century always have particular cultural forms. We do not experience the possibility of greater social justice or more genuine human community as abstractions. We experience them in our lives. For example, through a century of life as an immigrant church we have seen some peoples thrive spiritually and others languish because their gifts, their leaders, their ethos of religious expression was affirmed or rejected by the whole community. And we have seen the revitalization of the faith and the hope of peoples when the church did accord them, their gifts, their methods, their spirituality some recognition. We know the way in which uniformity can crush the human spirit and we know the excitement, the joy, the surprise, and the saving grace of meeting the Spirit of Jesus—our Holy Spirit—in unexpected forms. Can we speak a prophetic word to the world and to our own church from our experience as a post-melting-pot people? It is not just a Teilhardian hypothesis that genuine union of peoples differentiates and, paradoxically, that uniformity alienates.

Our roots are in a world of monarchy and empire. Can we now call relative those forms of social ordering that we had learned to see as absolute? Can we proclaim new forms of genuine human community and call others to affirm these without at the same time calling ourselves?

Further, the post-immigrant Catholic Church in the United States has a unique opportunity to thematize the universal experience of the call for genuine community as a call to the reconciliation of the churches. We were prepared from childhood to expect the worst from non-Roman Christians. We know to the contrary, from our experiences of collaboration with other Christians, and from the dialogues of our theologians, that we Christians—Lutherans, Episcopalians, United Methodists, Roman Catholics, the many others—are indeed all one in Christ and form one Body. A defensive church of dependent Catholics cannot risk attending to that voice within our American experience. A ghetto church cannot speak a prophetic word to every Catholic hierarchy and to every Christian communion. A dependent church cannot sound the call for mutual forgiveness, reconciliation, and recognition. Can we risk our life—are we yet mature enough to risk our life—for the life of the world? If we speak this word, the church we know and which has shaped us would have to die. We may yet need to cling to the ghosts of the past.

Likewise, the post-immigrant Catholic Church in the United States has the opportunity to thematize the universal human experience that justice, dignity, and community are all better served when the needs and the gifts of women and men alike are valued and used for the good of all. The post-immigrant Catholic Church in the United States is in a position to relate to the Gospel its century-long experience that women are indeed full participants in the mystery and ministry and mission of the local church. It has the opportunity to point out the obvious: that women are natural sacraments of the mystery of divine love. Every human being born has come to life because some woman first offered her blood and her body for the existence and the nurturing of human life. Our church has the opportunity to relate this universal human experience to the mystery of the eucharist, Christ's gift of his body and blood for the life of the world.

Can we risk announcing to the Catholic Church universal the Gospel foundation for the genuine human aspiration of greater justice, fuller personal dignity, and more human community? This is not an hypothesis we entertain, but a reality we know. Should we keep still and deny our experience? If we announce it, the church and the society we know and which has shaped us would have to die: *your life for the life of the world.*

Who are the hearers of the word? In the Catholic Church in the United States, the hearers are the immigrant church of women and men who have a corporate memory of human suffering from injustice and persecution, a corporate experience of election and ecclesiastical guardianship, and a corporate vocation to mission in a post-immigrant posture of mature conviction. The hearers of the word in this church are women and men who have distinctive life experiences which have unfolded throughout a century and which are awaiting thematization in the light of the Gospel. Further, they await proclamation to the church universal.

In a letter written twenty years ago to a friend who had questioned her about the Catholic Church, Flannery O'Connor wrote: "Human nature is so faulty that it can resist any amount of grace and most of the time it does. The Church does well to hold her own: you are asking that she show a profit. . . . To expect too much is to have a sentimental view of life and this is a softness that ends in bitterness. Charity is hard and endures."

3

Culture and Forgiveness

"HIS TRAGEDY WAS I SUPPOSE THAT HE DIDN'T KNOW WHAT TO DO
with his suffering." The Georgia-born short story writer and
novelist Flannery O'Connor penned these words in comment
on the suicide of an acquaintance. O'Connor herself died in early
middle age after a long struggle with a debilitating illness, better
able in her judgment to live with suffering than was the man
who took his own life. Two Georgia lives and deaths pose the
question well: what do we do with suffering? He annihilated it
by annihilating himself too. She lived into it and with it and
through it, discovering herself and humanity on the way. Many
take a third course; they ignore suffering, anesthetizing themselves against it, perferring numbness to feeling. If his tragedy
was that he didn't know what to do with his suffering, the
world's tragedy may be that his problem is our peculiar cultural
problem: what do we do with suffering?

Embracing and valuing suffering is not our cultural style. Viet-
nam veterans know that. We cannot forgive them. They cannot
forgive us. They lost. We made them lose. We failed them because we abandoned our nerve, our will to win. They failed us
by exposing our vulnerability to the whole world. Now the Viet-
nam Memorial in Washington, D.C. confounds us all, tapping
into tears and memories. Whoever moves within close range of
its two long wings, which gently set out the names of the dead,
hears a quiet insistent question: what about this suffering? A
young Asian-American woman Maya Lin dared us, through her
memorial design, to look at suffering, to come close enough to

37

see its human scale, and to see our own faces dimly reflected in the highly polished marble wall. The place is dangerous. In its ambiance, we could all be moved to forgive one another.

Forgiveness requires awareness of human vulnerability, requires compassion, requires a readiness to admit we're all in this together. Our public cultural style generally denies this, telling us it's every man for himself. So self-actualization is valued and pursued as achievable without self-denial; competitiveness is pitted against cooperation; aggressiveness is praised and human weakness masked by posturing. Actualizers, computers, tough aggressors are winners, he-men. Deniers, collaborators, the vulnerable are losers, wimps, wo-men. What do we do with suffering?

Sufferers are not easily forgiven their lot. A decent priest friend tells a tale of how he once stomped a leprous street beggar in India. The beggar had laid a claim upon the healthy, well-dressed American who presumed to visit his city. Whenever the priest went out from his lodgings, to shops, to homes of acquaintances, to libraries, the beggar followed and waited. He waited even outside the restaurant where he took his meals. The ugly beggar's very existence steadily became too much a meeting with truth. One evening after a fine dinner the priest suddenly found himself kicking, pushing, stomping and shouting angrily. The beggar fled. But the city was filled with leprous beggars who could not forgive him his existence as he could not forgive them theirs.

The whole world is filled with people who make claims on us, who cannot forgive us our existence as we will not forgive them theirs. The unborn want to live and crowd our world. The old refuse to die. The hungry put out hands for food. The palsied flail their limbs. The mutilated expect access to public places. People who have lost their minds from fear or disease or who never got good ones to begin with, babble and ramble as if they deserved to be listened to. "It's not our fault," we protest. "Leave us alone." We kick, punch, stomp and shout. Get rid of one, somebody else shows up, always dogging us. Where are there enough polished marble memorials to powerlessness that we could all come closer, see the human faces of pain and defeat, recognize our own faces dimly, and risk forgiving one another?

The stakes are really higher than one priest and one leper in a stand-off, or two perceptions of the national good in conflict.

But the ugly leprous beggar trailing the comfortable American is a useful image of the spectre which haunts us. If the scale is different, the root of the conflict persists. A way of life which accuses and threatens us has no right to exist; it invites annihilation.

As a people, we will not or cannot see the Soviet peoples as anything other than evil stalking us, asking to be stomped. But even as we shout and threaten, other infested peoples are moving in on us, terrorizing us from the south. The spasms of violent reaction which have seized us are symptoms of a soul sickness as virulent as the disorder we resist. Here is mortal sin to fit the name! It can destroy us and the whole planet with us unless we can get our seizures under control. But how?

For Christians, the way out of this mortal peril of self-annihilation is not to be found within the familiar resources of the political process. One group of Cambridge, Massachusetts citizens worked to get a resolution on the November, 1983, ballot to declare the city a nuclear-free zone, a community which prohibits nuclear weapons commerce and industry, research and development. Another group raised money to defeat the resolution as contrary to the great cultural traditions of academic freedon and free enterprise, preferring abstractions to a compassionate look at the face of suffering. Whether it's Reagan in 1984, Glenn or Mondale, Jesse Jackson or Barbara Jordan, the nation's soul will not be touched deeply by party platforms and public debates. The public debate will operate on the only publicly acceptable premise, namely that the noxious Soviets are the sole danger that threatens. It will not do to advance the notion that the evil we see and fear in the Soviet Union is a mirror image of evil which is deeply rooted in our own hearts too.

Ann Sexton's poem "The Sickness Unto Death" comes to mind. Written in reflection on a period of mental illness, a time of inability to function in ways acceptable to "normal" 20th century Western society, she acknowledges her incredulity over the claim of God's love in the face of radical evil.

The priest came,
he said God was even in Hitler.
I did not believe him
for if God were in Hitler
then God would be in me.

That God could forgive and love a loathsome Ann Sexton or Adolf Hitler were equally incomprehensible. The shock of the discovery of radical human ugliness had immobilized her. (Most of us function better with a measure of certitude about our own innocence, our basic goodness.) But the theologians tell us that breakdown is also a moment of grace for people with faith in God. In this moment of near despair there also occurs the possibility of hearing the good news, accepting God's forgiveness, living with less trust in one's own goodness and with great confidence in God's power to make things new.

If Ann Sexton was immobilized by the magnitude of human evil and her share in it, her case is the exception. The norm among U.S. Catholics is more typically what I met in a visit several years ago to a women's group in a Washington, D.C. parish. I had identified the parish many months earlier as the home church of several prominent administration and career government officials who exercised considerable influence on both domestic and foreign policy. I had accepted the invitation as an opportunity to comprehend better how Catholics in this city understand and live with the demands of faith.

The group had requested an update on the sacraments, so we talked about the church's new awareness of the ethical imperative in every Sunday eucharist. I called it ironic that in a century of unprecedented social evil—Auschwitz, Nagasaki, and Hiroshima standing as symbols of a cultural madness—Catholics had learned to present themselves routinely for eucharistic communion each Sunday and to present themselves less and less frequently if at all for sacramental reconciliation. I invited their observations on the situation. Was it true? Was it significant?

Someone informed me that a priest giving a parish mission had assured them they were hardly capable of serious sin, so demanding were the traditional requirements for judging a sin to be mortal, that they ought not to worry about confession before communion. I pressed them: what did they think themselves? Was there any culpability anywhere for the world's suffering? No one seemed to know. The confusion was genuine. The response was a far cry from traditional Catholic sensibilities, where guilt abounded. Here were adult Catholics who in good faith had no reason to seek God's forgiveness.

In this shift of sensibilities, the church has become genuinely

American. The myth of innocence is bedrock to our cultural self-understanding. Almost twenty years ago, in his *Conjectures of a Guilty Bystander*, Thomas Merton had reflected on the formative character of the earthly paradise motif for the American psyche. The opportunity to begin life again in a new land had meant leaving everything behind, including the sin of the old world, even original sin. Merton was confident, in the midst of the civil rights struggle of the mid-1960s, that the sin of the nation was indeed being revealed to it and that the age of innocence was over. Repentance, confession of sin, reconciliation, and forgiveness were requirements of the moment.

Contrary to his expectation, a different development has occurred in the past two decades. The old Catholic sensibility of personal sinfulness with its cult of personal guilt has been discredited and the emerging moral sensibility, more complex and more subtly attuned to social evil and complicity with it, has had a hard time establishing itself. There is no place in the cultural imagination for such a possibility, namely that Americans as Americans are implicated in the sin of the world. Pastors and catechists who have tried to advance such an understanding and to form conscience toward a new moral sensibility have been accused of introducing politics into religion. The very charge indicates the certitude that all is well with our participation in the public realm. There is no need for God's forgiveness where there is no perception of sin.

A new kind of pastoral program is required to deepen and strengthen Catholic moral sensibilities so as to contribute to the renewal of a national moral consciousness. Efforts to get Catholics "back in the box" could be regressive if the broader question of the moral demands of this age are not faced. (Sincere Catholics who are beginning to feel guilty about not feeling guilty are prime candidates for participation in such a regressive movement.) The tradition itself has resources to help believers come to terms with our violent spasms of rage at the rest of the evil world and to recognize our common humanity. Recreating the past is not the issue. But the best of the past can be used in new ways to allow the Gospel to be heard, believed, and acted upon even in the public order for the sake of humankind's survival.

Imagine the following national pastoral program to come to terms with cultural obtuseness about our innocence as a people and so our need neither to forgive nor to be forgiven. This risk in the approach is that it takes seriously the commitment of the baptized to walk in the way of Jesus, takes it more seriously than many take themselves. Given the stakes, the risk seems necessary.

A rhythm of regularity is crucial in the development of conscience. Regular time for confession was part of the effectiveness of the system which sustained an earlier private moral sensibility: every Saturday afternoon, before First Friday, before Communion Sunday. If slower rhythm seems necessary for establishing and maintaining a social moral sensibility, the quarterly intervals at which the now-dormant ember days recurred provides a more natural time: spring, fall, summer and winter seasons of repentance. The natural times coincide with Advent and Lent, and the post-Labor Day new start in a school culture. What is an early summer moment? When should the people expect to be summoned to hear the good news of forgiveness for those who believe?

Sufficient time to become disposed to the message is a second factor in developing an effective pastoral program. Our experience with communal penance celebrations tells us it is worth looking for a better way to form a people committed to the mystery of the reign of God at work in the world. Elements of the old parish mission can be reinterpreted or reintroduced into the quarterly seasons of repentance. A full week should be designated for the work at hand.

At the Sunday eucharistic assemblies which open the week, the Gospel of forgiveness should be preached with clarity and conviction. Here the people can come to know in a sustained way the story of sin and God's way with it, culminating in the story of Jesus, in memory of whose sacrifice for the sin of the world the church makes eucharist. Further, offer good biblical preaching in the context of celebrations of the word. Song, meditation, litanies, dance, whatever supports the people's capacity to internalize the word of God with devotion, should be part of these proclamation and preaching events.

Not everyone can reassemble midweek. Invite the people to fast and abstain during the week. Propose a concrete program, since the younger among them have no awareness of an ecclesial tradition of fast and abstinence and the elder may need to reconstruct what has fallen into disuse. Recall religious reasons why people fasted in earlier generations and encourage them to discover new reasons for this one. To aid the discovery and the recovery, invite them to a week-long program of scripture study and faith-sharing, when possible, in their homes. (What should they read? The lectionary for the sacrament of penance has ninety-nine biblical texts on the mystery of sin and forgiveness.)

On the last days of the week, have ample opportunity for private confessions for people who wish to present themselves. Many such confessions will now be informed by several days of corporate and personal reflection. Few people will be involved in all the activity. Most will have committed themselves to something. But an ecclesial environment will be taking form to support repentance, conversion, confession of God's goodness and our own complicity in the world's sin. The eucharist of the following Sunday will be an occasion of thanksgiving for God's work begun in Jesus and continuing into this generation. The assembly can be encouraged to recognize where relationships in their own lives and in their world have broken down—among family members, at work, at school, with neighbors, racially—and to imagine how in the spirit of the Lord's prayer they might effect reconciliation immediately or over a period of time. When they are dismissed, they can live with whatever measure of conversion the event has brought to them until the next season picks up and deepens the inquiry into the mystery of sin and forgiveness. Formative structures do not guarantee conversion, but they can support and prepare the way for God's action in God's good time.

Such a pastoral program aimed to counter the cultural myth of innocence and the projection of evil outward will have a disorienting effect on Christian peoples who have learned to protect themselves against pain and powerlessness. The Gospel preached in Jesus's name has the power to expose demons as well as to effect conversion. The Gerasene demoniac of Mark's Gospel, chapter five, shrieked to be left alone when Jesus approached him; the townspeople asked Jesus to leave before he interfered further in their lives. Peace is not the only outcome of the preaching of the Gospel. Peace and compassion are its blessing for those who repent and believe. The Georgia suicide, devoid of such resources, chose self-annihilation.

4

Spirituality for a Lifetime

THE WRITINGS OF AUGUSTINE OF HIPPO AND T.S. ELIOT COME QUICKLY
to mind at the start of a reflection on the human meeting with
God in the passing of time. Readers of this essay might do well,
before going further, to promise themselves to return to the
Confessions of Augustine, the *Four Quarters* of Eliot, his "Ash
Wednesday" and "Choruses from 'The Rock.' " Each of these
searchers sought the meaning of the human lifetime within history, and both recognized in time remembered a mystery within
which humans might discover the living God. But their reflections have distinct orientations. Augustine's long autobiograph-
ical account of the remembrance and recollection of the divine
presence in his lifetime is counterbalanced by Eliot's sharp poetic
crafting of words to capture our more typical contemporary experience; time is opaque; time is a surd.

Culture indeed mediates the human perception and apprehension of time. A culture which invented daylight saving time—
and which can manufacture clocks with switches to make the
transition from standard to daylight time and back again the
concern of a fleeting moment—knows that it controls time. Not
for this culture the slow rhythms of the tides and phases of the
moon, the turning of seasons and planetary orbiting, gestation
and maturation. Our culture, which is characterized as an era
of historical consciousness, fails to comprehend time and history
as the staging ground for divine/human interaction. Rather, our
time, to be made useful, is levelled, routinized, and measured

in equal segments for easy manipulation. Such is the time we have to manage. More than 10,000 minutes are at our disposal each week, some to kill, some to save, some for work, some left over to spend with friends or family if we plan well.

In this culture we inevitably allocate time for God, too. Sixty minutes a week "for the old guy" is still a minimum for conscientious believers. From the devout there may be sixty a day. Good people struggle to fit God into the heavy claims on their time. But the time-management business tends to overwhelm many who are searching for spiritual depth. Abraham Joshua Heschel made familiar the image of God within Jewish mystical piety which represents him as wandering the earth in search of his beloved humanity. The image can be accommodated for our time-controlling culture. Imagine God alone in a waiting room hoping for an appointment.

The caricature only exaggerates; it does not falsify. Nevertheless, the apprehension and use of time as measured segments is only part of our human perception of time. We also know that this routinized time is liable to be disrupted by unrepeatable events. In our century we have known the time of the First World War, of the Dust Bowl, of the Papacy of John XXIII. Ours has been a time of great death agonies and of the birth struggles of millions. We have known the time of the annihilation of the North- and South- and Meso-American Indian nations. Such times are not able to be calculated in terms of minutes spent or lost or saved. Such times have their worth not from duration but according to the character of the events that mark them: good times or bad, hard times or brutal, bittersweet or ebullient. These eventful times, too, are part of a human lifetime. Network managements report, unfortunately, that presentations of such unique events, whether live or as documentaries, are poorly received by the masses who do not welcome disruption of their "prime-time" expectations.

Liturgical Time

Christians and Jews also know of something designated liturgical time. It is neither public nor private time in the ordinary sense; but it has an aura of facticity about it, and it can crowd available time. Such liturgical time is often conceived of as the time of God, an overlay superimposed on the time segments we manage and the eventful times that disrupt. Christian liturgical time has in cycles, as it were, its own segments of hours and Sundays and seasons and feasts casting interesting Christological shadows over other times passing by, whether in the steady measure of minutes or the irregular measure of rising and receding events. Whatever time it is, it seems always time for the church to acknowledge God's time. So during the Easter season, whether the year is 1914, 1944, or 1984, the church will ordain new ministers. At sunset each day of each year, whatever is struggling to die or to live, it is time for vespers. Alternately, someone might conceive liturgical time as a massive grid of God's time. Just as the ecclesiastical scheme of dioceses allocates all known earth space and puts every human person within the embrace of Christ through the agency of a local bishop, so liturgical calendars chart all personal time and social history on a map of feasts and seasons and occasional rites, the times of God's visitation.

The problem with these images of liturgical time as God's time superimposed on our times is that they, too, are caricatures. The truth, however disconcerting, is that the liturgical time cycle is not the starting point for understanding the second-level reflection of "God's good time." Understanding the latter requires taking a look at the foundational experiences of God in time which gave rise to time's schematization in worship. A Christian seeking an authentic liturgical spirituality, spirituality for a lifetime, must be rooted in the common ground shared by Augustine and Eliot and the Scriptures. It is from this rich ground that the church has distilled that essence of the mystery of time which is put forward in liturgy.

Augustine caught a complex insight and crafted it into simple language which has made it accessible to many Christian generations. "I have learnt to love you late, Beauty at once so ancient and so new! I have learnt to love you late! You were within me, and I was in the world outside myself. . . . You were with me, but I was not with you,"[1] The mutual presence of God and humankind is indeed at the heart of all concern with spirituality and appropriate spiritual disciplines. The presence of God is

---

1. *Confessions*, X, 26, trans. R.S. Pine-Coffin (New York: Penguin Books, 1961) 231.

hidden but able to be known, so Augustine learned, in retro-
spection, in attentiveness in memory to his early delight with
the world and to his experience of life's gifts of food, wisdom,
compassion, mercy, love, forgiveness, and humility as counter-
points to his own avarice and arrogance.

Augustine's personal account of memory as a way of access
into the mystery of God's saving presence is a classic in spiritual
literature. T.S. Eliot might well have had Augustine in mind
when he wrote:

> . . . But to apprehend
> The point of intersection of the timeless
> With time, is an occupation for the saint—
> No occupation either, but something given
> And taken, in a lifetime's death in love,
> Ardour and selflessness and self-surrender. . . .
> For most of us, there is only the unattended
> Moment. . . .[2]

The greatest Christian classic, the writings of the Old and New
Testaments which comprise the Bible, returns again and again
to the theme of remembrance as the sustaining force of biblical
faith. According to one motif dominant in the Old Testament,
God and Israel are drawn together and irrevocably united in a
symphony of remembrance.

Remembering

In all Old Testament literature God's remembering always implies God's movement toward whatever he remembers; his remembering always has its effect. When the people flourish, when
the poor are fed and sheltered, when the long-awaited child is
born, or the rains fall and the grain yields an abundance, God
has clearly remembered his people for blessing. God also remembers their injustices, their mutual exploitation, their worshiping idols. And so remembering, God may punish to bring
them to repentance and change of heart. On the other hand,
God may choose to forget their deviance. God's forgetting, too,

2. *Four Quartets,* "The Dry Salvages," V, 1. 200ff. (New York: Harcourt Brace
Jovanovich, 1971) 44.

has its effect. Whatever God forgets ceases to exist; it is no more. So sins are forgiven.

Summing up his study of this theological viewpoint in the Old Testament, Brevard Childs concluded that the essence of God's remembering lies in his acting toward the world and everything it holds because of a previous commitment to it. The fourteenth-century English mystic Julian of Norwich sums up the nature of that previous commitment revealed by Christ: what is true of everything that is, is that "God made it, God loves it, God keeps it." Within this perspective all of human history is simply the story of God's remembering, the working out of the one continuous movement in which God is creating and gathering the world to himself.

Israel's remembering is another matter. The record is mixed. Israel forgets much: the Rock which bore them, the covenant which keeps them. But the people's forgetfulness is not decisive. As the chorus proclaimed in Leonard Bernstein's *Mass*, in which he is at his Jewish best, "No, you cannot abolish the Word of the Lord." The forgetting does have consequences, however. When Israel forsakes the covenant, the aliens suffer, the poor go homeless or are imprisoned, wages are withheld, and the rich lord it over others. On the other hand, the great temple hymns collected in the Book of Psalms show that the deeds of God were often celebrated with joy and gratitude in Israel—their passage through the sea, the gifts of manna and quail and the land flowing with milk and honey, the planting of the vine of David, the beauty of Zion, deliverance from enemies, forgiveness of sin.

Teachers in Israel rescued that remembrance of the great deeds from becoming a recital of ancient history by showing the people that the great deeds of God were constant, extending into each new generation. The deeds and their known consequences themselves contained the evidence that God had taken the initiative in establishing a beneficial relationship with this people and that his intention had never changed. His presence was abiding. But it was left to each new generation to decide whether it would honor the relationship with clear expressions of its mutuality.

According to this viewpoint, the present claims on the people's lives were direct extensions of a movement of God that had its foundations in the decisive events of the past. "You shall not wrong an alien, or lay hands upon him; you were yourselves alien in Egypt" (Exod. 22:21). The key to insight into the present is a good memory. For these teachers in Israel, as Childs puts it, memory serves a critical function, properly relating the present with the past. But the prophets also knew that a good memory of God's historical commitment could give the people a vision of the future with God. Present, past, future—God has one single purpose. Remembering the past, anticipating the future, believers would have ears to hear and hearts to obey the call of God in the present.

Reminders for Remembering

Structures for remembering the living God were thus necessary and integral to the world of the Old Testament faith community. Some structures, many of the earliest ones, were physical. Stone altars and markers were constructed on sites where the patriarchs interacted with God. The problem with such structures was that intensification of remembrance and of readiness to obey was tied to the durability of the marker and the ability of the people to travel to the site of God's visitation. Gone today is the oak of Mambre; pilgrims still go daily to the holy places in Jerusalem and to the Sinai desert. More commonly, especially in the later biblical period, the structures for remembering were tied to time. At the time of the full moon, blow the trumpet! "Observe the month of Abib . . . for it was the month that the Lord your God brought you out of Egypt" (Deut. 16:1).

The times of the world of creation—the times of the moon and the stars, the sun and its seasons—were available structures on which to pin the public remembrance of God's saving deeds. "Seven weeks shall be counted: start counting from the time when the sickle is put to the standing grain" (Deut. 16:9). The human use of those times for sowing and harvesting underscored their usefulness as structures for remembering both God's present and future and his historical deeds. The human lifetime with its seasons provided another available time frame on which to fix community remembrance of the God who was always remembering his own. Childbirth, puberty, marriage, the fact of death, and its wake of bereavement all bore traces of the hand of the living God. Each of these moments was a memorial (Hebrew: *zikkaron;* Greek: *anamnesis*), an available point of access into the continuing truth of God's creative, sustaining, healing, and redeeming deeds. Furthermore, such timely memorials were witness to God's own effective remembering of the people he made. If Israel kept periodic festivals and performed recurring rites in order to remember God's saving deeds, it was because God had already provided the world with structures for remembering when to remember! A marvelous deed in itself.

The young Augustine, enamored of his professional life of teaching and public speaking and convinced by the Manichees of their objections against Scripture, had no inclination to look into this classic for wisdom concerning time remembered as a point of access to the living God. Augustine set off on his own, virtually unassisted by the living tradition of memorials in time which had been maintained from Judaism and reinterpreted by the Christian faith community. The Christian times for remembering were still tied to the same times as those which structured Jewish faith, for Jesus had been arrested, executed, and glorified by God at the time of the spring festival of Passover. But what dominated Christian remembering at every subsequent memorial time—annual, seasonal, weekly, daily—was the greatest deed God had done in Christ Jesus, namely his remembering the world by sending his own Son to open up the way of salvation. If Augustine did not join with the Christian community from one season to the next to contemplate the self-emptying of Jesus and his exaltation by God, God remembered the isolated Augustine nonetheless. The concluding book of the *Confessions* begins, "I call upon you, O God, my Mercy, who made me and did not forget me when I forgot you." Augustine finally found the living God—the hard way, he might well have agreed. "You were with me, but I was not with you."

Christian Time Today
Most Christians before and since the young Augustine have made use of the structure of a liturgical calendar and a sacramental system to support their remembrance of the decisive events of redemption and their continuing power to save. The central day of Christian remembrance, the Lord's Day, is the principal weekly memorial of the Easter event of the death and glorification of Jesus. Within this day there is an intensification

of remembrance, when multiple memorials coalesce in the Sunday eucharist. First, the Christian people, who are the body of Christ in all epochs and cultures, assemble. They are living stones, tangible markers of God's having passed by this way. In their assembly they proclaim the story of salvation which has Christ Jesus as its center. They give thanks for this Christ-event, offering with Jesus the memorial of his body and blood given as he directed for the life of those who gather to put on the mind of Christ. Because that, too, is a gift from God, the assembly intercedes, asking God to remember the church and to pour out the Holy Spirit on it for its own benefit and for the salvation of all the world. The prayer is answered immediately in the gift of the meal which is the body and blood of Christ Jesus by the power of the Holy Spirit.

This weekly time of Christian remembering is caught up into the macro- and micro-cycles of a liturgical calendar. The macro-cycle sweeps through the year in strong whorls which pull time toward them, sometimes in less than orderly configurations. The Easter whorl sweeps together the days from the beginning of Lent to Pentecost into an annual festival of the resurrection, looking now at one aspect and then another of the mystery of Christ and his church. It is a special season for reconciling and baptizing, for First Communions, ordaining, and marrying. The Christmas whorl sweeps more widely through the year. It gathers together and neatly ties the weeks of Advent through the twelve days of Christmas to the feast of the baptism of the Lord. But it has undercurrents that reach out to pull in whatever is related to the historical events of the coming at Bethlehem or to the second coming of the Lord Jesus: a celebration of the annunciation to Mary nine months earlier, the birth of John the Baptist six months before. The Christmas cycle plays with light and dark. The darkest days of the year reveal the light to the nations, whereas the brightest days of the year mark the birth of one who is less than the least born into the reign of God.

The micro-cycle of the twenty-four hour day also uses the structures of light and darkness to remember God's great deed done in Christ Jesus. When the dark comes, the candle for evening prayer is lighted, and the Easter light in Christ Jesus is proclaimed every day with thanksgiving. At the light of dawn, it is time for daily praise for the light of creation, the light of revelation, and the light of redemption, which are all one in Christ the Lord.

The majesty of the scheme is indisputable. Nevertheless, observing a liturgical calendar is not an end in itself. The reality it is meant to serve is the mutual abiding presence of God and humankind. Paul, who was proud of his Jewish heritage, was also aware that a liturgical calendar could become an obstacle to awareness of the living God. He counseled the Colossians, "Allow no one to take you to task . . . over the observance of festivals, new moon, or sabbath" (2:16). Rather, he advised, "Let Christ's peace be arbiter in your hearts. . . . And be filled with gratitude. Let the message of Christ dwell among you in all its richness" (3:15–16). A liturgical calendar and the occasional sacramental celebrations of the Christian people are a useful, indeed God-given, means to the rich indwelling of Christ in his body which is the church. But indwelling demands openness to the one who comes. And openness comes with trust that the message of Christ is indeed good news. How can anyone be sure?

The Scripture and the saint are both reliable guides to learning trust. Grounds for venturing trust lie in the long history of God's dealings with the world he created, sustains, and clearly loves. Evidence lies also in the remembrance of one's own lifetime with gratitude, from infancy to the present. The liturgical calendar, honed and polished through centuries of use, celebrates the great historical evidence. However, T.S. Eliot warns us of what we know to be true in our day, namely, that the evidence of the biblical narrative may not be cogent even for those who once called the church home:

> . . . it seems that something has happened that has never happened before: though we know not just when, or why, or how, or where.
> Men have left GOD not for other gods, they say, but for no God; and this has never happened before
> That men both deny gods and worship gods. . . .[3]

Eliot was keenly aware of the fragmentation of the human community and its loss of common memory. But for Eliot, perhaps

3. "Choruses from 'The Rock' " in *Selected Poems* (New York: Harcourt Brace and World, Inc., 1964) 120.

thinking of Augustine, the breaking of the impasse which blocks awareness of the living God must come always through the way of memory. He wrote:

> This is the use of memory: For liberation—not less of love but expanding of love beyond desire, and so liberation from the future as well as the past.[4]

Memory can nurture spirituality for a lifetime. Moreover, even the journey in memory which for some people must start as a solitary passage through their own lifetime does not end alone, so Augustine discovered. It ends eventually in the recurring public assemblies where the believers who know the living God present in all his graciousness in their own lifetimes, in that of the people of God, and that of the whole race, join their voices in chorus to remember together.

4. *Four Quartets,* "Little Gidding," III, 1. 156ff., p. 55.

THE STUDY OF WORSHIP

Introduction

Liturgical studies is not so much a single academic discipline as it is a field for inquiry. Liturgy can be studied historically, anthropologically, sociologically, linguistically, legally, dramatically, architecturally, psychologically, theologically. The sources for the study of liturgy include the whole of the church's liturgical tradition. Documents—especially official liturgical books, narrative accounts of liturgical events, and homiletic and catechetical interpretations of them—are important witnesses to the tradition past and present. But liturgical rites, like all ritual activity, is relational activity. One can, and should, recognize that the field of liturgical inquiry involves the relationships and roles expressed in the transaction and interactions which occur in ritually defined sacred space. Further, liturgical activity is symbolic activity, public activity which draws upon a repertoire of verbal and non-verbal symbols to express God's way of saving the world in Jesus Christ.

Symbols, verbal and non-verbal, are elusive vehicles of meaning. Unlike the public language of contracts and scientific inquiry which intends to delimit meaning—ideally, one word, one meaning—the symbolic language of religion welcomes and embraces multiple points of reference, multiple meanings, within a single form, word, or phrase. Liturgical rites bring many such symbols together into relationship, creating a veritable thicket of possible meanings. Ideally, nothing means just one thing.

The study of liturgy has benefited in the last two decades from a broadened approach to the determination of meaning in liturgical celebration. Studies of the interpretation of language, the interpretation of symbol, and the interpretation of culture have given liturgiologists new questions. The gift of a new question is a rich bequest for those who engage in the work of the mind. Copernicus and Einstein twice turned the scholarly world on its ear because each saw the system of relationships in the physical universe in a new configuration. They provided more questions than answers; and they created challenging work for new generations of scholars. The field of liturgical studies is at such a turning point. Scholars are recognizing new configurations of meaning. They are slowly formulating the new questions to be asked.

5

Ritual Symbols and the Ritual Process: The Work of Victor W. Turner

HOW DO SCHOLARS STUDY LUTURGICAL RITES? HOW DO SCHOLARS study anything? Often the work is done by methods learned from one's own teachers. Regularly these ways of studying reflect well-established assumptions and techniques in the field; they rely upon the ordinary tools used by experienced investigators. If the work is literally a dig, whether for archeological or architectural or dental purposes, the tools are tangible and learning to manipulate them is part of apprenticeship in the field. When the work is primarily intellectual, as is the case with liturgical studies, the tools are less tangible; most often they take the form of suitable questions.

Whenever investigators become aware that the tools they are using are not adequate to their task, they begin to look around for more adequate tools. If they do not find something handy in their collection of traditional tools, they borrow or redesign or invent something that is fitted to the task before them. This step requires, of course, that the investigator is well aware of the nature of the thing being investigated. Liturgical investigators have recently come to new awareness that their tools must be refashioned as they recognize that the matter that they are studying is a living tradition undergoing a growth spurt stimulated by two realities: an ecclesiastical mandate and massive cultural shifts.

Liturgical studies have been complicated in recent decades as liturgiologists come to terms with both these factors. Even as the Roman See writes down normative ritual texts and specific directives for the celebration of the Mass, for example, the churches gathered for the eucharist in Manila, Managua, Boston and Buffalo inevitably interpret the directives in the course of their regular Sunday worship. While it has always been the case that local churches interpreted what Rome promulgated, the situation has been intensified since 1963, when the Second Vatican Council mandated the revision of all the liturgical books, and one of the characteristic features of the revision was to provide for what was then called local adaptation.

Even before the revision process was completed, it became apparent to liturgiologists (as well as to officials responsible for liturgical discipline) that local liturgical practices often do more than adapt or interpret what is proposed in the official texts. Sometimes (wittingly or unwittingly) they supplement and sometimes supplant the official liturgy promulgated in the revised liturgical books of the Roman Catholic Church.

Liturgical historians, taking the long view, have been able to point out that this development should surprise no one. The history of the Western liturgy before the sixteenth century Council of Trent is a long tale of the interaction between the Roman Church and the church among the non-Roman peoples of Europe, each teaching and learning from the other about helpful ways to celebrate faith in the saving mystery of the death and resurrection of Jesus Christ. Dioceses and regions regularly borrowed and rejected one another's ideas for liturgical worship. Rome was commonly in the center of the exchanges.

The Council of Trent made an effort to stabilize a dynamic liturgical situation; it did so by requiring that revised Roman liturgical books prepared after that Council should become the official books for the universal church. But the historical record shows that western liturgical practice was never uniform for very long. Now, after another church council that promulgated new liturgical books, the churches outside the city of Rome and the Roman center are once again interacting. Each is committed to maintaining the faith tradition by celebrating it well. Interpretation, adaptation, and more—innovation and even genuine creativity—are inevitable. These processes prompt liturgiologists to want to ask new questions.

Only a small part of the work of contemporary liturgical study is done when the history of the officially revised liturgical books is set forward and the intended theological meaning exposed. These texts are the work of ecclesiastical scholars with vast sensitivity to the Western liturgical tradition, mainstream, tributaries, rivulets and stagnant backwaters. Their work was genuinely conservative—attempting to retain the best of the living tradition and reviving what had become dormant. Their work was just as genuinely the work of diplomats, making compromises and concessions in one area for the sake of gains elsewhere.

The most vast undertaking of contemporary liturgical studies is to attend to the actual local practice, the customary usage of particular churches. These practices have not been shaped by the ecclesiastical experts. Sometimes the experts' work was too slow in coming. A decade is no time at all in the lifetime of the Catholic Church. In the lifetime of the local worshipers assembling regularly, a decade means 520 performances of a weekly rite, 120 performances of a monthly celebration, 3650 performances of a daily rite, or the all-important celebration of those rites like marriage which have impact for a lifetime. Sometimes the experts' compromises satisfied the negotiators at the conference table or the Roman Congregation to whom they were accountable, but estranged the local churches whose spiritual life was either coerced by or simply untouched by the official resolution of controverted issues.

Local worshipers have often fallen back on their own resources. They have worked with greater or lesser knowledge of the wider liturgical tradition and the official liturgy, past and pending. They have drawn on the depth or superficiality of their experience and understanding of the paschal mystery, the mystery of dying and rising which is celebrated in every liturgy. They have been more or less successful in distinguishing the truly archaic ritual symbols of the Christian liturgical tradition still capable of embodying living faith, from the merely antiquated ritual forms of other eras. They have combined these archaic forms in new ways, or they have juxtaposed them with the cultural forms of this era. Sometimes local worshipers have created ritual forms of sufficient vitality that they warrant inclusion in the public repertoire of the Roman Catholic Church. At other times, the banality of the forms or their esoteric qualities invite conscious repudiation and even banishment from the ritual repertoire of the Catholic community.

Acceptable criteria and methods do not yet exist for evaluating the popular tradition which is developing alongside and in dialectical tension with the official ecclesiastical tradition. Historical canons are not always applicable, even though this very pattern of development through mutual interaction has ample historical precedent. The canons of pontifical authority or episcopal jurisdiction, quite intelligible—though never fully effective—in an autocratic age and under cultural conditions of popular illiteracy and mass ignorance of the tradition, are antithetical to the contemporary self-understanding of church as the people of God, the community of those baptized in the Lord Jesus and sharing the one same Spirit, who are served and guided but not coerced by responsible authority.

Nevertheless, U.S. liturgiologists recognize that some criteria and methods are needed for evaluating the popular American liturgical tradition of the Catholic Church. The Western church woke up one day and found itself Arian, according to Saint Jerome's famous dictum, because the church was not watchful. Serious distortion of the Catholic faith tradition is a real possibility in every age and culture, including our own.

Integrity in liturgy is not a matter of indifference in the Catholic community. Liturgy is a major communicator of the faith tradition of a people. As *leitourgia*, the work of the whole people, it is not simply the provenance of the Roman congregations or those with canonical jurisdiction. But the American church may need deliverance as much from the encroachment into liturgy of the going philosophy, "You do your thing and I'll do mine," as it does from the autocratic philosophy of a passing ecclesiastical ethos. The church needs to regain its capacity for spiritual discernment in the area of liturgical practice just as it does in other areas.

The problem for contemporary liturgical studies is, then, to find appropriate and effective ways for interpreting and evaluating those indigenous liturgical changes generated by the living faith of the local churches in touch with their own experience of the paschal mystery and with the living tradition of Catholic liturgy as well as with their own cultural experience. The concern is to find ways of uncovering what is happening in these events and why; what religious understanding is being heightened and what discarded in the ritualizing activity. What is the doctrinal and ecclesiological content of the indigenous forms? For want of new methods of liturgical study, both the dross and the gold of popular liturgical adaptation are just as much in danger of being kept indiscriminately as of being discarded. In the meantime church officials and bureaucrats pursuing the promulgation and implementation of official liturgy may continue to experience the frustration of apparent popular ignorance or rejection of their efforts.

Structural Analysis and Beyond

How do you study liturgical rites in the very moment of their development? Social anthropologists have developed several methods of studying rites, either in their structure or in their performance. Two theoreticians of ritual study whose work dominates the field of social anthropology are Claude Lévi-Strauss and Victor W. Turner. Their approaches are distinctive but not mutually exclusive.

Lévi-Strauss, the father of structuralism, has developed an analytic method which establishes the principle of binary opposition as the key to symbolic communication and so the key to religious ritual.[1] Since the effectiveness of symbolic communication is dependent on the actual human communicators, it is all known versions of a given rite which constitute the data for study. For it is likely that some forms of the rite will not accomplish their intent, and the message will be distorted.

According to this theory, structural study of multiple performances of a given ritual or multiple versions of a given folktale or myth should disclose those which are "correct" and expose the inadequacy of those which are "incorrect" or distorted versions. In an unpublished study of the rite of religious profession among American Benedictine women from 1969–74 I analyzed the textual materials for 67 separate profession liturgies celebrated in

1. Claude Lévi-Strauss, *Structural Anthropology*, trans. Claire Jacobson and Brooke Grundfest Schoepf (New York: Basic Books 1963) 206–231. See also E.A. Hammel, *The Myth of Structural Analysis: Lévi-Strauss and the Three Bears* (Reading, Mass: Addison-Wesley 1972).

24 priories and compared this information with available textual materials from the pre-Vatican II period in order to explore the implications of the structural method of Lévi-Strauss. The disciplined inquiry yields certain kinds of useful data.[2]

Using synchronic and diachronic patterns of scoring, the researcher should theoretically be able to expose clearly the basic ritual structure and those elements which are "structural zeros." She should also be able to judge which performances were structurally inadequate to accomplish the intent of the ritual.

The field of the social sciences is divided on the extent of the usefulness of the tool of structural analysis to deal with dynamic social reality. Its purpose is limited. It presumes to deal with the fundamental nature of human cognition and communication, and has little interest in the communicated or perceived meanings themselves.[3]

By contrast, Victor Turner's methodology reflects his interest in dealing with ritual meanings and the way in which the ritual effects its intent through the use of multivocal, condensed or "thick" symbols, both dominant and secondary. For Turner, the data for investigation are found in the particular performances of a given ritual. The root metaphor which underlies his approach to ritual is the metaphor of the drama, specifically social drama involving a community sharing a common set of values, a functioning social structure, and a common set of natural and cultural symbols.

In contrast with the strict structural analysis of the Lévi-Strauss variety which is interested in the instances of structural consistency rather than instances of deviation or "error," the critical

2. Only case studies can, I think, help establish the liturgical researcher's control over the theory and verify its actual usefulness as a tool for analysis and interpretation. Good procedure would demand actually doing field studies, recording what is seen in some detail, and then proceeding with orderly analysis and interpretation. I have one such case study in draft form, the one noted above. The early stages were done in consultation with Turner, and some aspects of it were discussed with Turner and his graduate students in a seminar in comparative symbology in early 1975 at the University of Chicago.

3. In "Structuralism and Biblical Studies: The Uninvited Guest," *Interpretation* 28 (1974) 133–145, Robert Spivey reports on the recent exploration of structural analysis in New Testament studies. Condensed in *Theology Digest* 22 (Autumn 1974) 219–222.

approach developed by Turner focuses on the idiosyncratic processes of choice and on the way in which persons deal selectively with options from among operative values, structures and symbolic forms according to the requirements of a situation. Turner's approach has been distinguished from Lévi-Strauss's structural analysis by identifying the former as situational analysis. The issue, according to colleague J. Van Velsen, is not one of radical departure from the structural framework but of amplification through a different emphasis.[4] The poststructuralist interest is in understanding the particular concrete ritual rather than in showing the abstract universal principles underlying all ritualized behavior.

Turner's analytic methods and ritual theory were first devised during his studies of African tribal societies and the ritual process operative in them. Subsequently, he expanded his own field of inquiry to include the study of ritual forms in larger, more complex societies and the study of the symbol systems of major world religions. He has refined and developed his conceptual framework in this process. He has not himself studied the liturgical rites of the Western church. Extensive exploration is needed to determine the applicability of Turner's analytic tools for the development of research methods for contemporary liturgical studies.[5]

Four Analytic Tools
Specifically, four conceptual areas developed by Turner need to be tested for their usefulness in dealing with the current liturgical situation. The first of these is his use of the metaphor of dramatic interaction or *social drama* as a key to social reality. He proposes it as more apt, less misleading, than either the mechanistic metaphor of behaviorists or the organic metaphor of evolutionists. In making this choice of root metaphors, he

4. J. Van Velsen, "The Extended-Case Method" in *The Craft of Social Anthropology*, ed. A.L. Epstein (London: Tavistock 1967) 129–149.

5. Margaret Mary Kelleher did a major theoretical inquiry and an extended case study testing the applicability of Turner's method for ritual study to Roman Catholic liturgy. See *Liturgy As an Ecclesiastical Act of Meaning: Foundations and Methodological Consequences For a Liturgical Spirituality* (Ann Arbor, MI: University Microfilms, 1983).

intends to focus on the reality of people interacting and the consequences of their interactions for the maintenance and meaning of a cultural system.

Implicit in pursuing a study of the current liturgical situation from Turner's perspective, using his social drama concept, is the judgment that the ecclesiastical institution that embodies the ecclesial reality, at once "human and divine" in the words of the Constitution on the Liturgy 2, is understandable as a human cultural system. It does not exclude the understanding that this cultural system is religious, that its existence is rooted in transcendence and that its interacting members are touched by this transcendent reality.

The second conceptual area which dominates Turner's thought is his *processual view of society*. A colleague, noting the centrality of this theme in Turner's works, said of him that Turner assigns a role in human history to the tension between structure and community as comprehensive as the one Freud attributed to opposition between the life and death instincts.[6] For Turner, society is a process rather than a timeless entity. It is created again and again out of the effort to resolve the tension between *structure* and *communitas*.[7] By Turner's definition, structure refers to everything in society that defines differences, constrains people's actions and holds them apart. Communitas or "anti-structure" refers to the essential and generic human bond without which there could be no society.

It is Turner's position that hierarchic social structures symbolically affirm communities in periodic rituals in which the social roles of the lowly and mighty are reversed.[8] It is likewise true, maintains Turner, that marginality and structural inferiority—whether expressions of voluntary separation from the hierarchical structure or of alienation from them—are the cultural conditions that most frequently generate the myths, symbols, rituals, philosophical systems and works of art for that society.

Implicit in a liturgist's judgment that these ideas of a proces-

6. Charles Leslie's review of Turner's *The Ritual Process*, in *Science* 168 (1970) 703.

7. *The Ritual Process* (Chicago: Aldine 1969) 92.

8. *Dramas, Fields, Metaphors: Symbolic Action in Human Society* (Cornell University Press 1974) 53.

sual view of society are pertinent for contemporary liturgical study is the prior judgment that ecclesiological issues are a fundamental part of liturgical form, and that the sense of church manifested by the participants is an integral part of liturgical reality. Turner's structure/communitas dynamism has significance in the light of Avery Dulles' discussion of the inadequacy of the dominant model of the church as institution and the contemporary reemergence of the models of the church as people of God, mystical communion, sacrament and servant.

Turner's ritual inversion theory also suggests that liturgical rites which effectively affirm communitas can and do simultaneously affirm structure in the continual process of becoming church. His third premise, noted above, on the latent power of marginality, structural inferiority and communitas, suggests that the sources for ritual adaptation and development are not likely to be found in the "structure" equivalent to the institutional experience but rather in the "anti-structural" experience equivalent to communitas or the quest for it. According to this premise, one might hypothesize that the churches of Asia Minor and Africa will be especially creative in their efforts to celebrate the Roman liturgy, and that in the Western churches, assemblies of women and the poor will struggle most creatively with the form and content of the official Roman liturgy.

A third area of ritual investigation of which Turner has refined analytic tools is that of *ritual symbols*. Turner himself identifies this as the distinctive mark of his own work, the basic difference in emphasis which distinguishes his approach from that of Lévi-Strauss. He remarks that Lévi-Strauss is more interested than he in the role of ritual and mythical symbols as factors in cognition and less interested in their role as instigators of feeling and desire.[9] Turner has characterized the properties of ritual symbols, identified their modalities, pointed out the multiple dimensions of their significance, and established basic semantic principles and methods for interpreting them. For Turner, and for social anthropology generally, a ritual symbol is the smallest unit of ritual behavior—whether object, activity, relationship, word, gesture or spatial arrangement in a ritual situation.

The three properties of ritual symbols, he suggests, are [1]

9. *The Ritual Process* 42.

their multivocality or condensation of many meanings; [2] their power to unify their disparate referents; and [3] their tendency to attract or to absorb meanings around two semantic poles, the one having affective or emotional value and the other pointing to structural or moral norms. The two modalities of ritual symbols, in Turner's analysis, arise from the distinction between dominant symbols and instrumental ones. Dominant symbols, says Turner, represent axiomatic values in the society and have this referent regardless of their ritual positioning. Instrumental symbols, on the other hand, are employed to attain the specific goals of a given ritual. Their signification is shaped by their incidence in the system of symbols in a given rite.

According to Turner, ritual symbols do have multiple dimensions of significance, since they can be considered operationally, positionally and exegetically. Operational significance is discovered by noting who does what. Positional significance is acquired as the relationship of one ritual symbol to another or others is determined within the rite. Significance is established exegetically through verbal explanations as systematic as doctrine or dogma, as subtle as myth, or as piecemeal as explanations based on appearances or normative "common sense" cultural perceptions.

Through his extensive field research and analysis, Turner has established basic semantic principles for interpreting ritual symbols: namely, [1] that there is no single hierarchy of classification of ritual symbols, that is, that a recurring symbolic form does not always have the same valence; [2] that a single symbol may be a point of intersection for many symbolic relationships manifested in ritual pairing or clustering; and [3] that what is symbolically visible in the ritual is made accessible for the purposive action of the society or community.

Finally, Turner has established a method for inquiring into the system of meanings the rite presents. He advises the researcher to note [1] the explicit and the implicit reasons the rite is performed; [2] the form or profile of the rite, for example, diachronic or processual; [3] the details of the site where the rite is celebrated; [4] the identity of the subjects of the rite and the identity of those excluded; [5] what things, natural and cultural, are used and why; [6] how things are used in relationship, that is, what is the structure of the rite, the structural dyads and triads, the opposed values set in binary opposition in distinct planes of ritual space; [7] what is submerged or present only in veiled form and what is the effect of this concealment; and [8] what emotions are portrayed or evoked.

Turner's theory of the nature of ritual symbols was shaped in his early work with the Ndembu of central Africa. It is at least plausible to consider whether these ideas do not have more general applicability for the ritual symbols of Christian liturgy. It is just as plausible to anticipate that the ideas will be refined or modified should liturgists begin to bring them into confrontation with Christian liturgical forms. Yet the researcher using these analytic and interpretative tools for contemporary liturgical studies is conceding the likelihood that all ritual symbols, as human expressive forms, share many traits in common with those Turner has identified.

In the fourth major area of conceptual clarification, Turner has offered an hypothesis about *how rites work,* why they don't work at times, and what effects they produce. He proposes that they work when communitas has some measure of reality to support the ritual action and the ritual intent. He suggests that in the course of ritual action there is an interchange between the affective and normative poles of meaning of the ritual symbols, so that the obligatory is made desirable and the conflict between personal aspiration and social necessity is reduced. This interchange is effected through a dominant symbol that encapsulates the total ritual process to bring the ethical and jural norms into close contact with the strong emotional stimuli. On the other hand, he maintains that rituals break down when the meanings associated with either the affective or normative poles of the dominant symbol no longer obtain, for whatever historical reasons. Such breakdowns make impossible the dynamic exchange in which norms and values become charged with emotional power and basic emotional impulses become disciplined through contact with social values.

Ritual Studies and Sacramental Theology

The liturgical researcher who explores these ideas of ritual efficacy at a human level concurs with the patristic judgment, *sacramenta sunt propter homines.* Such a position does not negate or obviate theological reflection on sacramental efficacy. In fact, such considerations as these may help strengthen the impact and expand the meaning of the theological category *ex opere operantis*, which makes human liturgical activity count for something. It also provides meaning at another level for the classical theological judgment that sacraments are effective for salvation when no obstacles have been placed by the human participants. That classical dictum continues to echo in the contemporary judgment that good celebration can strengthen faith while bad celebration weakens it. The analytic method of Victor Turner suggests where to look for the source of ritual breakdown, a genuine obstacle to ritual power. Conversely, it identifies the locus of ritual vitality and of all liturgical development past and future.

A Basic Annotated Bibliography: Victor W. Turner

The major conceptual framework Turner employs is presented and shown in operation in four basic works. There is development in them chronologically, since Turner began to work his ideas out in tribal society and subsequently explored and refined their applicability in complex societies. In both contexts, Turner proceeded from the premise that ritual action cannot be studied independently of the social group which is engaged in the ritual behavior.

The Forest of Symbols (Cornell University Press 1967) The early pages of this work (1–47) offer a resumé of many theoretical issues which have engaged Turner because of his work with the Ndembu: [1] life crisis ceremonies; [2] the properties and structure of ritual symbols; [3] the distinction between dominant and instrumental symbols; [4] the function and the effectiveness of ritual symbols; [5] the limits and possibilities of psychological interpretations of ritual symbols; [6] the limits and possibilities of anthropological interpretation of ritual symbols. Other chapters treat of the relation of ritual symbol, morality and social structure, and of the character of the liminal period.

"Forms of Symbolic Action: Introduction" in *Forms of Symbolic Action*, ed. Robert F. Spender; Proceedings of the 1969 Annual Spring Meeting of the American Ethnological Society (University of Washington Press 1969) 3–25. Among the areas Turner considers in this address are: [1] multivocality of ritual symbols; [2] social conditions for ritualization and deritualization; [3] the three major dimensions of ritual significance, namely, the exegetical, the operational and the positional; and [4] the three semantic foundations for the meaning of the ritual symbol. A summary of his theoretical work to date.

The Ritual Process: Structure and Anti-Structure (Chicago: Aldine Publishing Company 1969). Half the book deals with Ndembu rituals and the analysis of them which shaped Turner's categories. A necessary introduction to his conceptual theoretical framework. The second half of the work distinguishes and relates liminality and communitas as phenomena in the social process and discusses rites of liminality in religious groups.

Dramas, Fields, Metaphors: Symbolic Action in Human Society (Cornell University Press 1974). In an opening essay Turner identifies the five concepts basic to his own interpretation of the field data on ritual symbols: [1] social drama; [2] the processual view of society; [3] social anti-structure; [4] multivocality; [5] polarization of the ritual symbols. The subsequent essays are specific inquiries into the effectiveness of dominant symbols (here called *root metaphors*) in the social process in diverse cultural settings in complex societies.

6

Liturgical Methodology, Cultural Shifts, and Worship in the U.S. Church

IN 1973 WALTER BURGHARDT, EDITOR OF *THEOLOGICAL STUDIES*, AD-
dressed North American liturgiologists on the various ways historical data can be put to pastoral use within the church.[1] He
provoked the academic community to explore their conscious or
unconscious approaches to handling the data of history as they
worked within the movement for liturgical reform and renewal.
In his presentation he flattered those he addressed, calling them
men and women of uncommon power. That judgment, if accepted uncritically as a normative description of the professional
liturgiologist, is both self-deceptive and unsound. The work of
academicians committed to liturgical studies is more modest; it
is only in the absence of sounder purpose and clearer procedures
that scholars can present themselves and be accepted in the
Christian churches as religious shamans.

De Facto Power and That Power Examined
Burghardt's observations, however, invite us to consider the
liturgiologists' special access to and use of the data of liturgical
history. The present generation of liturgical scholars has benefited from the major liturgical research of the past century which
clarified the fundamental structures of Christian worship and
the patterns of structural development and deformation. In the

1. Walter Burghardt, "A Theologian's Challenge to Liturgy," *Theological Studies* 35 (June 1974) 233–248.

1970s, academic liturgists, whose training gave them a special competence in interpreting the tradition, experienced an ecclesiastical vote of confidence in virtually all mainline Christian churches. These churches authorized scholars to become involved in the reform of official rites and the production of new liturgical books. As a result of their contributions to this activity, the impact of historical liturgical research on contemporary pastoral liturgy has been far reaching.

In the course of their reform and renewal activity, liturgiologists advanced official and personal proposals to develop the tradition. They called for the revival of what had long been dormant; they argued for the suppression of elements which historical research showed to be later accretions to an originally simpler liturgical structure. They sometimes endorsed the addition to a liturgical rite of an element that was without precedent; and they framed proposals that would accommodate the traditional to new cultural realities. Some advocated fostering the organic development of possibilities long latent within the tradition of public worship; they proposed letting things as yet unknown or unimagined in the historical tradition appear within the liturgical assembly.

This influential role of professional liturgical scholars as active reformers has been a new one. Previously, the liturgiologists' work was limited to historical research and publication and theological reflection, either alone or in combination with classroom teaching in seminaries and occasionally in universities. Their novel and unprecedented power to shape reform—officially authorized and even mandated within the churches—invites critical reflection, as does every other development in church life in the post-conciliar period. Murmuring from the pews and sanctuaries against professional expertise might be too easily dismissed as an outcry of yahoos. It is not so easy to dismiss the criticism of professionals who also study religious rituals from the viewpoint of the social sciences: it is unheard of, so say cultural anthropologists, that religious rites expressing living belief should be devised and decreed either by bureaucrats or by academicians.

Liturgy is not only a didactic enterprise geared to shaping belief, although it does have a formative function for the church's faith. It is also an event in which the living church gives expression to the faith, hope, and love which is in them. Technically "correct" liturgy may stifle what the Spirit is saying to the churches. Nevertheless, it is possible to find some positive significance in the efforts of the 1970s, when the bureaucrats and academicians in good faith paternally suppressed and added, revived and accommodated, and at times even advocated radical transformation of the church's liturgy. It is also important to take note of the limits of our present approaches to liturgical studies and to suggest new foundations and directions for liturgical investigation in the third decade of the post-conciliar era.

Perhaps it was inevitable that liturgiologists should be cast into the roles of strategists, shamans, and technicians immediately after the Second Vatican Council. The restriction of liturgical possibility within the Roman Catholic Church since the Council of Trent and within the Protestant churches by their own reactive inhibitions meant that liturgical imagination had all but dried up. Academic liturgists were initially the only members of the conciliar-era church who could lead the churches through exercises in liturgical memory and imagination. They were the only ones who could offer a coherent account of the familiar liturgical world by providing excursions into other actual and possible liturgical worlds east and west. They were also the only ones who could invite the church to consider an initially unfamiliar liturgical future by showing that Christian faith had already found liturgical expression in more ways than most twentieth century Catholics and Protestants had ever dreamed of.

The Present Situation

The work of intensive liturgical education and actual experience with reformed rites is beginning to have results in the church. Liturgical historians and theologians are no longer the only ones capable of leading the church to discover the full possibilities of public worship. We are at the end of an era. What Burghardt called the liturgiologists' "licenses to uncommon power" were indeed only temporary and are now being returned to the communities which issued them, if they have not already been recalled. Insofar as liturgical professional are members of local worshiping communities—indeed, members with a special gift— they will undoubtedly participate in the church's efforts toward continuing renewal and enculturation. But scholars are not, simply by virtue of holding academic degrees and appointments, the sole or the best judges of how living Christian faith will find its most authentic expression ritually. Nevertheless, it should not be forgotten that it is because of the efforts of many dedicated historians and theologians of liturgy that the notion of liturgical enculturation is taking hold in the churches.

After the professionals have returned their licenses to uncommon power, much inquiry into and interpretation of the historical tradition remains to be done. And some new research problems have yet to be addressed. We do not yet comprehend the full implications of the liturgical tradition for our present situation as churches. Yet this meeting point of past and present is an important juncture for theological reflection, so important that it has its own tag in classical theology: *lex orandi lex credendi*. The norm for prayer is the norm for belief, and normative belief finds its expression in public prayer.

Just at this point new research problems are arising in the field of liturgical studies. Liturgical scholars surely had an easier time establishing ritual meanings when all texts, movements, and gestures in actual use were uniformly prescribed and the prescriptions almost universally honored in practice. In stable periods, when there was little history-in-the-making to contend with, it was fairly easy to establish methods of inquiry to determine what the late Alexander Schmemann called the "liturgical coefficient" of each formula and gesture within context of the total repertoire of rites.[2] But in our post-conciliar era both the *lex orandi* and the *lex credendi* are in flux. Even after, and also because of, the promulgation of new liturgical books in the churches of the West, the church's patterns of public prayer are more fluid. Equally fluid are the ways, in a period of massive cultural change, that the faithful are understanding their relationship to God and its implications for their worth and destiny within and beyond history.

This period of liturgical and cultural fluidity has enabled liturgiologists to recognize the need to go beyond the investigation of printed texts in their search for theological significance within the liturgical event. This might seem a discovery of the obvious,

2. Alexander Schmemann, *Introduction to Liturgical Studies* (London: Faith Press, 1966) 11–23.

since Roman Catholics never perceived worship simply as a matter of words. Yet the bias of the rational, linear culture which persists in the West and which is fostered in the academic world served to conceal the obvious. The verbal code within a liturgical event continues to be perceived as the soundest expression of the faith horizon of the church, and texts are credited with being privileged sources of meaning in liturgical studies. But the new question has been raised: what more is being expressed in nonverbal ways? Increasingly liturgical scholars are agreed that not all the serious data about a liturgical celebration of the church's faith are to be found in the texts provided for or used in the particular liturgical event.

As a result, liturgiologists are feeling their way forward methodologically, learning what new questions to ask about a liturgical event as a ritual act with both religious meaning and theological expressed in nonverbal as well as verbal codes. In this project, they are drawing upon a broad range of cultural theorists whose ideas are helping to provide foundations for future liturgical research. Four scholars who have written thoughtfully about human ritual activity will be identified here and commented on briefly for the bearing their work has on the development of method for the study of the nonverbal domains of the church's liturgy and the coherent interpretation of the verbal and nonverbal elements: philosopher Suzanne Langer, cultural anthropologists Clifford Geertz and Gregory Bateson, and ritual studies specialist Ronald Grimes.

Suzanne Langer explores how and why ritual activity begins in motor attitudes. She notes how rituals are presentational rather than discursive embodiments of people's insights into life. She develops the notion that these ritual or presentation embodiments of people's insights are disciplined rehearsals of right relationships with reality whose forms are first devised in play. Clifford Geertz shows how a people's system of sacred symbols not only synthesizes that people's ethos but also contains, expresses, and affirms a general order of reality.

Gregory Bateson, a geneticist and communication theorist, shows that presentational communication in rites, what he calls iconic expression, invariably deals with patterns of relationships. Bateson also elaborates on the economy of the human brain, which harbors in the unconscious the bulk of what humans *know* about the profound relationships of existence. He also traces the way these unconscious perceptions of relatedness find expression in nonverbal codes, through a redundant system of such things as nonconscious and intentional movement and nondiscursive uses of language, sound, silence, and dramatic action.

Ronald Grimes' contributions to the analysis of ritual as a complex form of human communication are also several. He distinguishes and then elaborates on the meaning of six modes of ritual sensibility or embodied attitudes which are inevitable or "necessary" in the complex event every religious ritual is: ritualization, decorum, ceremony, liturgy, magic, and celebration. This schema provides one comprehensive frame for investigating liturgical behavior. An alternate frame for reflection on the liturgical even comes from Grimes proposed reduction of a liturgical tradition to its central kinesic features—the bodily style that constitutes it.

I will consider Langer, Geertz, Bateson and Grimes in somewhat greater detail, offering as I go some personal observations on the pertinence of the insights into the dynamics of ritual for the field of liturgical research. Liturgiology is in an era of flux, when neither traditional historial methodology or traditional sacramental theology is capable of providing integrated and comprehensive interpretation of the phenomenon of public worship. Scholars must turn to other disciplines for methodological assistance.

Langer: Symbolic Transformation of the Data of Experience

Langer's work is historically earlier and provides a general conceptual foundation for the two cultural anthropologists.[3] Langer establishes theoretically what the liturgical scholar, the anthropologist, and the grammarian know, even when they cannot or do not deal adequately with that knowledge: that the elements of any expressive system do not mean or express of and by themselves. They participate in the meanings of the larger whole. This is equally true of words in a sentence and objects or movements in a religious ritual like eucharist or Christian initiation.

3. Suzanne Langer, *Philosophy in a New Key* (New York: New American Library, 1951).

The whole pattern or configuration of words in the sentence or of objects and movements in the rite is a complex symbol that points to a situation. The words of the sentence do so discursively, the stuff of the ritual presentationally. However, whereas the situation which the sentence transforms conceptually may be either mundane or profound, religious rituals share in the tendency of all things religious to envisage the essential and ultimate patterns of reality.

Christian liturgy, of course, consists in a union of the verbal and the presentation. (The use of language in rite is a distinction question that also needs to be attended to.) In view of the didactic propensity of much of the language in contemporary liturgical events, the nondiscursive uses of language in ritual need to be rediscovered, for we do not always use language, even our mother tongue, to make statements. Yet since ritual begins in motor attitudes, as Langer shows, and so is more archaic than discursive language, the systematic study of liturgical rites might properly concern itself with the more archaic level of nonverbal domains.

Grimes: Modes of Bodiliness in a Worship Tradition

The nonverbal domain of liturgical events has begun to yield some of its significance under the critical scrutiny of Ronald Grimes, who shows that "overt bodily actions are not mere punctuation marks" for verbal activity in a ritual event. Rather, verbal activity (or its absence) is but one channel of ritual communication; human bodiliness is another. It is the combination of bodiliness and verbal activity that gives rite to the ritual style characteristics of any given religious tradition.[4] Christian public worship, which characterizes itself as sacramental activity, readily invites inquiry into its bodily style.

To establish his point, Grimes has explored and contrasted the fundamental bodily styles of Christian public worship and Zen meditation. He proposes that the two distinctive styles, *eating* and *sitting*, constitute the two traditions in such a way that they are unmistakably and irreducibly distinct expressions of reli-

---

4. Ronald Grimes, "Sitting and Eating," in *Beginnings in Ritual Studies* (Washington, DC: University Press of America, 1982) 87–100; see in the same collection "Modes of Ritual Sensibility," 35–51.

gious vision. If a Zen person *is* as he or she simply *sits*, so it seems that Christian engagement with the sacred presence is tied to bodily orality: eating and drinking and proclamation. What goes into and what comes out of the mouths of Christians at worship provides contact with the divine. Grimes' investigation of the basic modes of Christian ritual embodiment underscores from the viewpoint of the human sciences an ancient dictum of early Christian eucharistic spirituality, that Christians become what they eat.

This reduction of a ritual tradition to its central kinesic feature provides a paradigmatic center for understanding a religious horizon and the aspirations of a religious tradition. In the case of Christians, the aspiration is to fullness of communion in the Body of Christ through word and the sacrament. According to this perspective, all elaborations in a ritual system through further bodily and verbal activity are so many modifications in the ritual grammar which serves to refine, to reinforce, to prepare for, or to heighten the meanings already expressed in the irreducible bodily mode at the heart of the ritual tradition.

Geertz: Congruence and Incongruity in Ritual and Reality

Clifford Geertz has developed the notion that the patterned symbol system of a religious or cultural community not only embodies its general ideas of reality but also affirms and promotes them.[5] He notes that a symbol system is a construct of and also a program for the intersubjective world of common understandings into which people are born and live and in the light of which they die. Geertz concurs with Langer that the most characteristically human activity is symbolic transformation of the data of experience into alternate forms of expression. For Geertz, the symbolic transformation includes the ability to perceive a structural congruence between one set of process, activity, and relations—such as liturgical rites, for example—and another set of processes, activities and relations for which the first acts as a program—ordinary life as it is understood by the ritualizing community.

This question of congruence or the lack of congruence between

5. Clifford Geertz, "Religion as a Cultural System," in *The Interpretation of Cultures* (New York: Basic Books, 1973) 87–125.

liturgy and life can be illustrated with reference to a 1973 essay by the German liturgiologist Klaus Gamber under the title "Mass *versus populum* Re-examined."[6] Gamber noted that German priests were suffering from dissonance and confusion between renewed liturgy and their ecclesial formation. He argued that some compromise was needed in the 1970 Order of the Mass in order to reestablish architecturally and ritually what earlier generations knew to be the correct relation of priest and people: let the priest face the assembly during the liturgy of the word, but in the eucharistic liturgy all should face in the same direction, so as to be "oriented toward God." To support his sense of ultimate order he presented approvingly the image of the patriarch Moses at Sinai leading and representing the people, taking the message of the community to God and in turn receiving and relaying God's messages to them. Gamber and those for whom he served as advocate "knew" that God dwelt beyond the assembly and that the priest mediated between them. They did not (yet) have an existential sense that the gathered assembly was itself a manifestation of the divine presence, despite the fact that both the 1963 Constitution on the Sacred Liturgy (par. 7) and the 1970 General Instruction on the Roman Missal (par. 7) asserted that to be the case.

In his discussion Gamber ony hinted at the even greater measure of structural inconsistency and incongruity between the set of processes, activities, and relations which are embodied in the reformed liturgical books and the processes, activities, and relationships which find expression in ecclesial life in the local churches at the approach of the twenty-first century. This is by far the greater liturgical and ecclesiological problem.

Why? Suzanne Langer talks about the human brain as a tremendously powerful transformer of the data of experience, and she and Bateson both agree that whenever the data to be transformed is primarily relational it will tend to be transformed into presentational rather than verbal symbols. Liturgy rather than doctrine or theology will become the place where the whole community of believers will attempt to give expression to its experience of saving relationships. Some contemporary Christians are struggling to find ways to transform the patriarchal

6. *Theology Digest* 22 (Summer 1974) 153–57.

model embodied in traditional ecclesiology and liturgy into patterns which express their experience of the mutual giftedness of
the church as the people of God. Others are working as hard to
maintain the patriarchal pattern of relationships both in liturgy
and in life. It is no wonder that liturgical assemblies of every
configuration have the power to alienate some who gather.

What the believing community strives to express presentationally in its liturgical assemblies about saving relationships the
church's theologians work to put into words. Gregory Baum's
theological accounting for the experience of grace as an experience of dialogue and communion comes closer for many of our
contemporaries to the truth of their own lives than the patriarchal
manifestations presently available in official liturgical rites.[7] These
too narrowly define the whereabout of spiritual gifts in the community, crediting them first to the ordained and then to those
delegated by them in their absence. As a result, even when a
local church may itself be able to name many members of the
community who have the gift of healing the brokenhearted and
binding up their wounds there is no adequate way these gifts
can be formally welcomed, celebrated, and ordered for the good
of the community. An international cartel, as it were, determines
that a certain class of males shall continue its public monopoly
of sacramental healing and reconciliation. All women and unordained men who wish to exercise ministries which express their
spiritual gifts are still treated in ecclesiastical structures and liturgical events as though they and their embarrassing gifts were
invisible. Even where new ministries are being promoted, as
with the permanent diaconate in the Roman Catholic Church or
the appointment of lay administrators for "priestless parishes,"
the men and women approved for these offices learn that, whatever their gifts and training, official deeds of healing and reconciling remain reserved for the clergy.

The same is true of the gift of prophecy, the gift of interpreting
within the community what the Holy Spirit is saying to the
church. Women and laymen filled with spiritual wisdom continue to be muzzled in the liturgical assembly; there is as yet no
official way to order their gift for the life of the body. Lay prophets are suppressed by being ignored or repressed by being sub-

7. Gregory Baum, *Man Becoming* (New York: Herder & Herder, 1971).

jected to tight restrictions over the identity of the liturgical homilist.

Nevertheless, most communities of the baptized in the United States today know that the outpouring of the gifts of the Holy Spirit is not restricted; these are falling on daughters and sons alike for the good of the church. The baptized experience the mediation of the grace of Christ broadly, even when the breadth of this mutual mediation cannot yet find expression in the solemn liturgical assemblies of churches where the ghosts of the patriarchs still preside. And no amount of rhetoric which trivializes this dissonance will eliminate the data of experience.

Humanistic approaches to the dynamics of ritual events as vehicles for religious vision can help us understand why we experience distress in our eucharistic assemblies. The analogy of an international cartel used earlier suggests overt or covert collusion. That gives too much credence to the notion that liturgical behavior is reasoned and conscious, when in fact most of it is preconscious and intuitive. Yet it is the case that the Catholics and Christians in other liturgical churches experience the greatest stress and resistance in their eucharistic assemblies for good—if unrecognized—reason. The eucharist constitutes for these bodies what Clifford Geertz, drawing on Singer, might call a "full-blown cultural performance." When the eucharist is officially designated and existentially experienced as "the summit and source of salvation" (par. 10, *Sacrosanctum Concilium*), it is inevitably the event in which structural and experiential incongruence will coalesce.

What is expressed in the eucharistic assembly is conveyed as the model not only for what is believed but also as the way for believing it. In other words, the eucharistic liturgy intends to set out presentationally the Trinitarian and ecclesial patterns of saving relationships, to celebrate them as God's gift, and to reaffirm them. Believers who have begun to think critically about the limits of androcentric and patriarchal patterns and to want to explore new insights into the experience of grace are experiencing varying degrees of alienation and confusion when they are asked to subscribe to official liturgical forms as expressive of the ultimate truth about salvation.

Meanwhile, emerging insights are struggling to find their expression in the liturgical assembly. It seems to some that as women's liturgical participation increases, based on women's increased participation in the mediation of saving grace in the daily life of the Christian people, men's participation is being threatened, when the truth is rather that the Gospel is being more fully proclaimed. Clerical defense of their liturgical prerogatives increases as laity take their places beside them in the sanctuary and in the church's ministry.

Intellectually, we may know there is room enough in the body of Christ for every person and that there is wisdom in ordering spiritual gifts and ministries. Yet the eucharistic assembly is the ritual territory in which this struggle for spiritual identity and relational significance is being played out. How we are related to one another and to God in Christ and the Spirit, how we all participate in his death for the life of the world is a crucial spiritual issue for committed Christians in this age of church and liturgical reform and renewal. The eucharistic assembly will one day be the place where a transformed Catholic consciousness will present itself, just as it is now the embodiment of our confusion, our resentment, our passivity, and whatever hope, enthusiasm, and new insight the baptized people of God may have.

It is not necessary to make a concession to the inevitability of liturgical chaos or to the hopelessness of critical liturgical study once liturgiologists have begun to draw upon the thinking of humanistic studies of ritual. Suzanne Langer offers the possibility of a constructive interpretation of the presently unstable situation of liturgical reform and renewal.

Langer Again: Play As Prelude for Symbolic Transformation

Because of its importance to any religious system of whatever is its "full-blown cultural performance," central liturgical rites are likely to be the last rather than the first place to give evidence that the community is undergoing a ritual transformation of the data of experience. As Suzanne Langer shows, religion and so religious ritual are the *gradual* envisagement of the essential and ultimate patterns of human life drawn from the data of experience.

Langer also notes that as rites are enacted in the contemplation of holy things, *sacra*, the rites give expression to and record human responses to the supreme realities of life and death. Religious rituals require a community to handle holy things that embody or function as tokens of what is perceived to the life-giving and death-dealing. In its handling of holy things, religious ritual gives a presentational account of life experience. Once removed from life's free emotional responses to life experiences, ritual gradually emerges as "a disciplined rehearsal of 'right attitudes'." The constant reiteration and embodiment of the right attitudes helps people to overcome fears that arise in the midst of the confusion that characterizes personal existence.

If it is true, as the proceedings of the 1973 meeting of North American liturgists argued, that the primary Christian religious symbol emerging in this culture is the human person, and if Langer is reliable about the centrality of holy things, *sacra* in rites, then what occurs ritually between and among the persons who are, in Christ, the primary *sacra* of Christianity is critical. Further, if it is the case, as Langer also claims, that before a symbolic form—a ritually expressed insight—can be put into public religious use to serve the difficult task of representing profound religious ideas, it must be refined in *play* (not child's play, but adult play—play intrinsically solemn even when it appears to some onlookers to be ridiculous) then contemporary feminist liturgies are profoundly significant.

In the United States baptized women have been playing vigorously at ritualizing their Christian religious experience for almost more than two decades. Feminist groups devise women's liturgies which exorcise the demon patriarchy; they remythologize the accounts of their creation in the image of a divine matriarch; they "handle" feminine images of the divine and celebrate feminine mediations of grace. Women have been writing new liturgical scripts—composing prayers, chants, litanies, blessings—and assigning the ritual roles.[8] Sometimes they try to find space in their ritual play for women and men together. Sometimes they give males only bit parts or say solemnly derogatory things about patriarchs to humiliate them ritually, Sometimes they write men out altogether. Ridiculous? To what purpose? The single male student in my 1973 course on Women

8. See, for example, Rosemary Ruether, *Women-Church. Theology and Practice* (San Francisco: Harper and Row, 1985); also Penina V. Adelman, *Miriam's Well. Rituals for Jewish Women Around the Year* (Fresh Meadows, NY: Biblio Press, 1986).

and Religion, a prospective Baptist minister, even then recognized the purpose. "For the first time in my life, I know what it is to be treated condescendingly." The ritualizing women are affirming, "We are indeed whole persons."

Elsewhere throughout the renewing church women being denied parish ministries are playing solemnly with hospital ministries, campus ministries, ministries to the elderly, and ministries to one another. All these are marginal ministerial situations. But in them women lay comforting hands on the sick and the suffering, listen to declarations of guilt and doubt and try to relieve them, preside at prayer and proclaim and interpret the word. Marginal themselves, they mediate the grace of Christ to other marginal Christians outside normal parochial structures. Few of the women playing solemnly with ritual structures and ecclesial ministries have received official authorization for all they do. They *play* at ministering because they are not "qualified" to *work* at it.

Whether academic liturgists like or loathe the solemn symbolic play is not to the point. The point is that professional liturgiologists who have some commitment to study the church's liturgical tradition need to find ways to study the process of liturgical renewal as symbolic transformation of the data of Christian experience. It is not ours to control whether such symbolic transformation *ought* to happen. It is happening. The liturgiologist needs to find ways of collecting data from the ritual assemblies marginal to the official program of public worship, where serious and playful deviance abounds.

Bateson: The Reliability of the Unconscious

In collecting the data about "unofficial" liturgical activity within the Christian community, the theoretic outlook of Gregory Bateson is foundational.[9] Let us agree for the moment that the content of all Christian liturgical rites is the expression of patterns of saving relationships. Christian rites, then, speak not only of the relationship of the church to its Lord Jesus Christ but also of the relationships among the members who minister to one another

9. Gregory Bateson, *Steps to an Ecology of Mind* (New York: Ballantine Books, 1972); see "Style, Grace, and Information in Primitive Art," 128–152; "Redundancy and Coding," 411–425; "Effects of Conscious Purpose on Human Adaptation," 440–447.

and to the world. Bateson, agreeing with Langer, makes the case that the vehicles for statements about relationships are presentational forms other than discursive language. In any given ritual these presentational forms are multiple and redundant. For this very reason, they are much less liable to distort the unconscious knowledge of relationships than is discursive and rational language.

The pertinent data, then, for this new phase of contemporary liturgical study will not be found primarily in the conscious verbal domain of texts.[10] They will be found in the domains of nonconscious bodily reactions and of the worshipers' movements within the ritual space. They will emerge in the domains of the dramatic action of the worshipers as they present for contemplation and hold and use and exchange and interact with other holy things. They will appear in the domains of the expressive, non-discursive use of sounds and rhythms and silence by worshipers. They will be seen in the domains of color and line, texture and architectural form. The pertinent data will show themselves in many ways the disciplined researcher will learn to recognize.

For Bateson and cultural anthropologists generally, these expressive domains are not peripheral but central. In actual ritual events, cultural anthropologists fully expect to find inconsistency among the several domains. These are the expression of the ambiguity and lack of integration present in the actual world of experience. If we return momentarily to Christian eucharistic liturgy, we can explore some of the implications of this viewpoint.

Renewal-oriented, intentionally collegial groups of believers may express their vision in texts, often in locally composed eucharistic prayers. But a liturgist studying from Bateson's perspective the whole ritual event in which the prayer is used might ask: what is the integration of the conscious and the preconscious? What is the congruence between what is expressed discursively and consciously in the prayer and what is enacted and embodied in iconic expression. Bateson argues that every rational discourse about ultimate relationships is accompanied by

10. For a study of the relationship of language and ritual action in liturgy, see David N. Power, *Unsearchable Riches. The Symbolic Nature of Liturgy* (New York: Pueblo, 1984).

a mass of semivoluntary kinesic and autonomic signals that provide a trustworthy commentary on the verbal message. Language may try to conceal what the nonverbal presents clearly.

The potential ritual split may work in either of two ways. Some women's groups, for example, are playing solemnly at a distance from official assemblies because they know they are still really left out despite verbal nods that pretend to bring them in. On the other hand, Catholic and Protestant Christians, clergy and lay, whose religious expectation and self-understanding is dependent upon patriarchal and androcentric expressions of the mediation of divine grace, are finding even the most modest verbal nods toward churchwomen inauthentic. Communities exist whose leaders and members are baffled by and resist having lay readers of the word and lay ministers of communion when "Moses" is available in their midst. What these noncollegial communities *do* is more important than the approved texts and commentaries they may faithfully recite. What they know, their own understanding of the experience of grace, is what they will present liturgically. It will be available for the disciplined observer to record.

Future Directions for Liturgical Studies

Collecting the data: the primacy of the nonverbal domains. If liturgiologists are to function with new effectiveness as researchers in a new cultural situation, we need to observe what is happening presentationally in the solemn play of the rump groups—women's groups, charismatic groups, children's and youth groups. We need also to observe what is happening in the nonverbal domains of liturgical assemblies using officially approved texts. As armchair anthropologists had to move out of libraries and studies to become field anthropologists earlier in the century, so contemporary liturgical study which had its beginning in libraries and seminar rooms must move into the places where Christians are assembling for worship in order to collect the pertinent data.[11]

11. Drawing on the field research methods of Victor W. Turner, Margaret M. Kelleher has developed a method for the collection of data from liturgical performance and tested it in a case study. See *Liturgy As an Ecclesial Act of Meaning. Foundations and Methodological Consequences for a Liturgical Spirituality* (Ann Arbor, Michigan: Microfilm Dissertation Series, 1983).

Interpreting the data: inner congruence of rites and the theological conceptualization of ritualized belief. Once out in the field to observe what is happening in liturgical assemblies, researchers will have to develop the ability to make careful, disinterested observations—observations about cultural adaptation and cultural transformation, not *a priori* judgments as to whether this liturgy or this solemn play is apt or inept by historical or contemporary standards. Liturgiologists will have to learn to listen to participants at various levels of sophistication telling as best they can why they did this and not that. They will have to learn appropriate ways to recognize the domains of multiple presentation, to report what they find, and to establish the fact of congruence or its absence among the several domains. Finally, liturgiologists will have to articulate in the theological symbols of the tradition what they are discovering as the insights into the mystery of Christ that the churches are presently living by. They will also need to recognize and to speak critically of the incompleteness and distortions of Christian faith embodied in our churches and expressed in our rites.

Communicating the Data: Ritual Transformation vis-à-vis Institutional Self-Preservation. In all of this liturgiologists must find ways to establish effective communication with the church's bishops and other pastoral leaders. The leaders need to know what the local churches themselves are saying ritually about their participation in the mystery of Christ. Liturgiologists studying the process of liturgical inculturation in these ways will have some check on the degree of congruence within the whole religious system's various vehicles for expressing what it believes, hopes for, and loves.[12] But institutional leadership will finally determine what use, if any, is to be made of the results of this kind of liturgical scholarship.

Some Concluding Observations

If the method of the cultural anthropologist for studying religious ritual is generally valid also for the study of Christian

12. For a treatment of inculturation, see "What Is So New about Inculturation? A Concept and Its Implications," *Gregorianum* 59 (1978) 207–240; for its bearing on liturgical reform and renewal, see Ansgar Chupungco, *Cultural Adaptation of the Liturgy* (Ramsay, NJ: Paulist Press, 1982) and M. Collins and D. Power, eds., *Liturgy: A Creative Tradition* [*Concilium* 162] (Edinburgh: T. & T. Clark, 1983).

liturgy, it will be possible to identify existing tensions in the local churches as they struggle both for the inculturation of their faith and the renewal of their public worship. If this approach is reliable, the tensions will be recognized as dynamic incongruities within the community of believers that will stimulate creative imagination. It is the creative imagination within the faith community that will lead, in turn, to the transformation of liturgical rites. And that transformation of liturgical rites will mark the disintegration of the earlier ecclesiastical and liturgical systems.

If and when genuine liturgical transformation occurs because communities are responding to a transformed experience of the mystery of Christ, the church as we have known it in recent centuries will have died. But the community called to faith in the Lord Jesus and his coming kingdom will have been reborn. In effecting or impeding that death and rebirth both the institutional authorities and the specialists in liturgy are providentially powerless.

7

Critical Ritual Studies: Examining an Intersection of Theology and Culture

NEAR THE END OF FLANNERY O'CONNOR'S NOVEL *WISE BLOOD*, THE protagonist, Haze Motes, who earlier had blinded himself, has begun to wear three strands of barbed wire wrapped around his chest. His landlady, when she becomes aware of this development, chides him, "Mr. Motes, what do you do these things for? It's not natural."

He simply contradicts her. "It's natural."

She persists, "Well, it's not normal. It's like one of them gory stories, it's something that people have quit doing—like boiling in oil, or being a saint, or walling up cats. There's no reason for it. People have quit doing it."

"They ain't quit doing it as long as I'm doing it," he says.[1]

When we approach the subject of the significance of ritual studies for theology and culture, we are forced to say that, despite all the rational arguments that have been marshalled to explain the impotence, the impertinence, or the insignificance of traditional religious ritual, "they ain't quit doing it." People regularly worship their God corporately and publicly, ritually, in cities, towns, and villages everywhere on this continent and on this planet.

T.S. Eliot had looked at the Western world early in the twen-

---

1. Flannery O'Connor, *Wise Blood* (New York: Signet Books, 1962) 122.

tieth century and grieved that traditional worship of God was fading. He wrote:

> But it seems that something has happened that has never hap-
>   pened before:
>   though we know not just when, or why, or how, or where.
> Men have left GOD not for other gods, they say, but for no god;
>   and this has never happened before
> That men both deny gods and worship gods, professing first Rea-
>   son,
> And then Money, and Power, and what they call Life, or Race, or
>   Dialectic.
> The Church disowned, the tower overthrown, the bells upturned,
>   what have we to do
> But stand with empty hands and palms turned upwards
> In an age which advances progressively backwards?[2]

Whether students of religion and culture are preoccupied with those myriads who have quit or those who keep on with the public worship of God according to traditional or reformed rites, they have reason to ask what the phenomenon of ritual action is about and to wonder what inner dynamic of religious rituals gives them their power both to engage and to estrange contemporary women and men. Nor should it be overlooked that some apparently secular phenomena are either cryptically or residually religious events. The modern Olympic games, for example, had their origins in the explicit intent of their nineteenth century founder to provide a ritual celebration of the new religion of humanity.

Attending to Human Ritualization

Despite the ubiquity of human ritualization generally and religious ritual specifically, ritual studies have had a modest academic existence up to the present. In the study of primitive society and primitive religion, cultic behavior has been an important datum because textual materials were scarce or nonexistent. But in the study of the so-called higher religions, academic interest has focused on the study of religious texts. The

2. T.S. Eliot, "Choruses from 'The Rock,' " in *Selected Poems* (New York: Harcourt, Brace, and World, 1964) 120.

liturgical churches—Eastern Orthodox, Roman Catholic, Anglican, Lutheran, for example—have regularly taught their own ritual traditions. However, study of these traditional Christian rites was often limited to the study of proper performance according to the discipline of the tradition.

Since the nineteenth century, historical studies of Christian liturgy have sought to recover long-buried layers of that received tradition. But it was commonly said in the churches that the glory of liturgical rites was their objectivity. And that claim of objectivity in form and content, so assumed, went unexamined. Meanwhile, throughout the past century, advances in textual criticism and exegetical technique and methods of theological reflection on religious writings overran the world of religious studies. Critical study of ritual activity and religious rituals specifically, to the extent that it advanced at all, has developed in the newly emerged field of social and cultural anthropology. Sociologists examining modern societies have, for their part, bypassed ritual action as insignificant data until quite recently.

Some years ago the Orthodox liturgical scholar Alexander Schmemann had noted that liturgical theology—the theological reflection on the public worship of the believing community—was peculiarly in danger of being arbitrary in its interpretations of ritual data. But Schmemann himself had offered no methodological solution to the problem.[3] It was possible to document liturgical history on the basis of extant texts. It was possible to investigate what had been said by earlier believers about the meaning of the texts and rites. It was possible to provide a phenomenology of a rite. But there was no orderly critical way to uncover the comprehensive meaning of an actual ritual event.

The phenomenon of ritual flux in the Western churches in the latter part of the twentieth century—involving both adaptation and invention—compounded the problem. What has been lost? what discovered? what retained? The historical and phenomenological approaches to ritual studies have been strained by these developments. A new approach to critical analysis and theological interpretation has not yet been clearly refined. But some significant developments are occurring. This essay will identify

3. Alexander Schmemann, *An Introduction to Liturgical Theology* (London: Faith Press, 1966) 11–23.

some of the issues at stake and note what is evolving methodologically, simplifying—though I hope not unnecessarily—what
is in reality complex.

At issue are fresh approaches to the exegesis of liturgical rites[4]
and new methods of critical reflection on the meanings present
in ritual acts. These developments should be of interest to and
have a bearing on work currently being done in the interplay of
theology and culture. For religious ritual, like religious literature,
is a cultural artifact expressing transcendent meaning through
non-verbal limit language—a language of acts which press participants beyond the world of ordinary human existence.[5]

With the use of methodological resources adapted from the
human science of anthropology, it is possible to explore critically
what the rites of church, synagogue, mosque, temple, and sacred
circle express about the faith of the believers. Such investigation
shows that ritual faith is not simply static and objective. Effective
ritual acts celebrate faith selectively, choosing themes and emphases for celebration from questions of ultimacy put to the
tradition in particular cultural and historical situations, and using
symbolic forms that are available within the culture posing the
question.[6]

It is common enough to assume that the meanings available
and operating within ritual assemblies are reducible to those
meanings consciously available within the doctrinal and theological traditions of a faith community. It is also common to
assume that old or archaic ritual symbols convey constant traditional meanings. Anthropological approaches to the study of
religious ritual suggest that these assumptions must be examined. In times of cultural flux, when a living faith tradition is

---

4. Exegesis is used here in its fundamental sense of critical exposition of
meaning. Textual exegesis has established methods; such is not yet the case
with exegesis of the language of rites.

5. David Tracy, *Blessed Rage for Order* (New York: Seabury, 1975). Tracy
explores the concept of "limit language" in some detail in chapter six, "Religious Language in the New Testament," pp. 119–145. He notes that a full
development of theological method has to attend also to the study of ritual;
see p. 15, n. 5. This essay proceeds from a comparable premise.

6. Mary Collins, "Critical Questions for Liturgical Theology," *Worship* 53
(July 1979) 302–317.

tested and strained, ritual assemblies are likely to anticipate the new themes and to attempt the new syntheses which are only subsequently thematized and systematized verbally. They do so non-consciously. The new themes are often experienced as dissonant and even disruptive or incongruous. But it is the work of the ritual action to join into a whole, again and again, what is in fragile relationship and always in danger of disintegration, namely, the future, the present, and the past of a people. It is the work of researchers to observe, to analyze, to interpret, and to evaluate what is set out ritually. If the researchers are Christian theologians, they will examine what they uncover in the light of the gospel.

Ritual assemblies have been and continue to be the point of sustained contact with mystery for most people within most religious traditions. Because of this they constitute a fertile ground for religious studies and ought to evoke uncommon interest. They are a prime, if neglected, theological source.

A single case study illustrates the point that ritual activity warrants more careful scrutiny from persons interested in the interplay of theology and culture. Recently I began a study of Roman Catholic rites for the profession of vows by women religious. First, I considered the received tradition of the profession ritual in the group under investigation, considering texts as well as available historical interpretations of them. Next I studied texts of seventy-two recent performances of the rite of profession in twenty-four communities that share a common liturgical tradition. In doing this I focused on the period from 1969 to 1975, a period when such rites were in flux due to persistent pressures from the larger society, from the larger church, and from the communities themselves. I assumed the role of participant observer in one such ritual assembly and did an in-depth analysis of it, incorporating interviews with a dozen other participants in the liturgical event.

Independent of actual ritual development in such local assemblies, the officially revised Roman rites of religious consecration were promulgated in 1970. These included the rite of religious profession and the pontifical rite of the consecration of virgins. Both continued to set out as a central theme the received tradition of the theology of religious life for women, a theology focused on the symbol of virginal espousal to Christ.[7] However, my investigation of indigenous local celebrations among Benedictine women from 1969 to 1975 shows that the received meaning of virginal espousal and the symbols that expressed that meaning were giving way. The symbols bearing those meanings had been consistently transformed, at times even eradicated. Veiling disappeared, as did a crowning rite; so did the prayers accompanying these, with their references to prudent virgins and nuptials with Christ the true spouse. Less consistently, a new cluster of symbolic themes and actions began to emerge, reflecting a search for new meaning for the vowed life of women in religious communities.

These developments occurred in liturgical assemblies under circumstances in which authoritative ecclesiastical interpretation was suspended. In such circumstances, the ritual action constituted "serious play" related to real life within the Roman Catholic Church.[8] Ecclesiology, Christology, pneumatology, and Christian anthropology as it speaks to the identity of women were all undergoing exploration.

It was evident in this case that ritual reinterpretation of received meanings was preceding systematic theological reflection on that form of Catholic Christian life, and was in fact offering operative new themes to any researcher prepared to gather and to interpret the data and to reflect upon it theologically. Every liturgical assembly is self-expressive to some degree in the ritual choices it makes. Because of this, the liturgical assembly is a public forum in which professionals can consult the faithful on matters of faith. In this forum, however, one must be trained to gather not only self-conscious meanings but also the unthematized, ambiguous efforts at new synthesis.

To state the basic position of this paper succinctly, ritual studies are worth pursuing by researchers interested in the interplay

7. René Metz, *La Consecration des Vierges* (Paris: Presses Universitaires de France, 1954). "Le symbole de la *sponsa Christi* constitue . . . le fil d'Adriane de cette liturgie," 118.

8. That "serious play" about life within the Roman Catholic Church today risked some challenge to patriarchal institutional structures, but in the nature of the case religious profession of women within the church involves some acquiescence to patriarchy.

CRITICAL RITUAL STUDIES 97

between theology and culture precisely because ritual acts constitute a distinctive kind of religious and cultural expression, one which is corporate in its manifestations and bodily and nondiscursive in its presentation of content. These very characteristics make ritual inaccessible to ordinary theological methods, which work with texts.

Ritual acts are fundamentally traditional. But they are always the actions of some particular people gathered in a particular place and time who use the available ritual forms for their own purposes. So a "universal" ritual is always local and contemporary in performance. Participants are touched and shaped by the rituals they celebrate, but they also interpret and elaborate the received tradition as they participate in it. This phenomenon of ritual action deserves more attention than it normally receives in the study of theology and culture.

How can ritual activity be better attended to in the church? What biases must be overcome in the attending? What are the implications for the theological tradition of new attention to rites? These matters must be addressed.

New Ways of Analyzing Liturgical Rites

In the recent past religious studies and theological method have been influenced significantly by researchers attending to questions put to them by the human and social sciences. The impact of sociology, both the sociology of knowledge and the sociology of institutions, comes immediately to mind. A similar influence has come from the field of psychology—from depth psychology, social psychology, and communication theory. In contrast with the established importance of these fields for the work of religious studies, one must characterize as inchoate the dialogue between social and cultural anthropologists on the one hand and theologians of Western religions on the other. The late Urban T. Holmes captured the spirit of the current exchange when he entitled a review article in the *Anglican Theological Review* "What has Manchester to Do with Jerusalem?"[9]

9. Urban T. Holmes, "What Has Manchester to Do with Jerusalem?" *Anglican Theological Review*, 59 (January 1977) 79–97.

Manchester is the home of the Anglo-American school of social and cultural anthropology, a school of thought characterized by its concern for developing empirical methods for the study of cultural systems. In its earliest procedures, social and cultural anthropology operated with a presumption of cultural stability and studied ritual action as a function of that cultural stasis. So much was this heuristic premise of stability in control that social and cultural anthropology looked exclusively at primitive, and presumably stable, societies.[10] Accordingly ritual study was originally identified with and determined by the study of primitive religious cultures, not with the religious traditions of the West.

Presently, cultural and social anthropologists are coming to terms with the role of ritual activity as a function of change. They are increasingly interested in it as a manifestation of the social drama. They come to ritual action to investigate aspects of the symbol formations of a cultural system—whether Roman Catholicism in Mexico or Yemenite Judaism in modern Israel[11]— and to analyze the dialectical interaction between the patterns of symbols and the power relationships operating in that system. According to Abner Cohen, one of the operating premises of social anthropology states: patterns of symbolic action persist from the past into the present not because of inertia or conservation but because they play important roles within the contemporary social setting. As a result, says Cohen, the history of a cultural trait or a ritual unit will of itself tell only a little about its significance within its present setting. Symbolic forms of earlier eras may persist in the midst of changes in meaning and power relationships. On the other hand, meanings and relationships from an earlier era may persist despite a change in

10. Abner Cohen, *Two-Dimensional Man* (Berkeley: University of California Press, 1974) 18f.

11. See, for example, an investigation of the power of religious symbol in public events in Victor Turner's study of Mexico, "Hidalgo: History as Social Drama" and his study of medieval England, "Religious Paradigms and Political Action: Thomas Becket at the Council of Northampton" in *Dramas, Fields, Metaphors* (Ithaca: Cornell University Press, 1974) 60–97 and 98–155. For a comparable investigation of religious symbolism in the Middle East, see Schlomo Deshen and Moshe Shokeid, *The Predicament of Homecoming* (Ithaca: Cornell University Press, 1974).

symbolic forms.[12] New and old meanings and symbolic forms can coexist even when they seem incompatible from a historical or logical perspective.

Accordingly, a Roman Catholic theologian can and should wonder what doctrine of church and church order is intended in the 1968 rite of Roman Catholic presbyteral ordination. The rite offers worshipers a sixth century ordination prayer for priests, which recalls the world of the ecclesiastical hierarchy of Pseudo-Dionysius in which spiritual gifts descend from highest to lowest ranks. Yet this ordination prayer comes after a ritual unit which provides for the community's public endorsement of suitable candidates for ordination to that hierarchy—suggesting either that lower ranks can judge the higher or that the local ecclesial community is the locus and source of all ordering. Ambiguity in the rite provides for interpretation in the performance. And it is in local performance that operative meanings will be evidenced. Moreover, it is most likely that actual interpretations will reflect existing power relationships in the local church.

Because social and cultural anthropology have begun to develop methods of inquiry into the ritual process and into the dialectic between symbols and power in a system, these fields are a resource for religious studies generally and for theological reflection on a living faith tradition itself in process of development.

Reference to the symbol formations and power relations of a cultural system calls for some clarification. Clifford Geertz's 1966 essay on "Religion as a Cultural System" has gained the authority of a classic position statement in the relatively young discipline of cultural anthropology.[13] Geertz's definition of a religion has been cited so faithfully in some academic circles that the words have taken on a creedal quality. Moreover, Geertz's definition has had its authority confirmed by being rendered in short form for the convenience of students, field workers, and

12. Cohen, *Two-Dimensional Man*, p. 3. Feminist criticism, for example, points to the persistence of the patriarchal structuring of society throughout successive political shifts within patriarchy. See Elizabeth Clark and Herbert Richardson, eds., *Women and Religion* (New York: Harper and Row, 1977) 1–14.

13. Reprinted in Clifford Geertz, *The Interpretation of Culture* (New York: Basic Books, 1973) 90.

lecture audiences. Briefly, according to Geertz, a religion is 1) a system of symbols 2) that refer to the problems of ultimate meaning and 3) thereby formulate an existential order.[14]

In his seminal essay, Geertz notes that ritual plays the central role in religion. He writes, "It is in ritual . . . that this conviction that religious conceptions are veridical and that religious directives are sound is somehow generated. . . . Whatever role divine intervention may or may not play in the creation of faith—and it is not the business of the scientist to pronounce upon such matters one way or the other—it is primarily, at least, out of the context of concrete acts of religious observance that religious conviction emerges on the human plane."[15]

Geertz's criticism of anthropologists in 1966 was that they were not sufficiently disciplined in their analysis of the system of meanings embodied in the symbols which make up a religion. Too often they were taking for granted the meanings that most needed to be elucidated through careful ritual analysis.[16] The field of anthropology has developed some disciplined methods of inquiry in the ensuing decade which would support the study of ritual as a theological source. Even in the 1980s, it is easy for interpreters of religion and culture to work with a priori meanings for ritual symbols which have been disembodied from actual ritual events.

Once ritual activity is recognized and acknowledged for the distinctive source of meaning that it is, careful study of ritual data is a necessity, with research techniques appropriate to the data. Because some of that data is ritual texts in particular religious traditions—Roman Catholic, Protestant, Orthodox, and Jewish liturgical texts are all cases in point—appropriate methods of textual criticism, exegesis, and interpretation are in order. But much of the ritual data of world religions, including those just mentioned, is not textual. Other methods of investigation must be found, therefore, to deal with the complexity of the content ritual action embodies—texts, but also gestures, movements, objects, exchanges, rhythms, sounds, which produce a single

14. Deshen and Shokeid 156.
15. Geertz 112.
16. Ibid. 125.

coordinated impact.[17] The single effect is like that created by disparate pieces of clothing, many of them redundant, which are worn simultaneously to produce the layered look, as contrasted with those same pieces of clothing on hangers in a closet.

Cultural anthropologists try to read the data of ritual events so as to uncover the inner coherence and intelligibility of a ritual symbol formation within a total symbol system, whether that system is Catholic Christianity or the culture of the televised professional football game. They aim to identify the root metaphor and the dominant ritual symbols of a cultural system and then to interpret the complex and subtle elaborations of these which operate in the various ritual acts of the performing group.

Social anthropologists look at the same ritual data as liturgiologists, but look at it somewhat differently, namely as a manifestation of political or social process. Geertz's observation that a religion is a cultural system with ritual at its heart will help to concretize this point. Geertz specifies that the investigator should focus on whatever action constitutes a system's fullest public manifestation in order to see its symbolic formation fully elaborated ritually.[18] The point is true for any cultural system; its most elaborate public ritual will set out its dominant symbols.[19] Any number of people have proposed, for example, that the interplay of symbols of youth, sex, money, physical force, male dominance, and consumer goods in the ritual of the televised Super Bowl constitutes the central cultural performance of the United States at the end of the twentieth century.[20] This ritual event is perceived as programmatic. It presents in condensed symbolic form the beliefs and aspirations of a cultural system.

17. See Gregory Bateson, *Steps to an Ecology of Mind* (New York: Ballantine Books, 1972); "Redundancy and Coding" discusses patterned and coded behavior, 411–425. For a judgment on the implications of Bateson's theory for liturgical studies, see Gerald Lardner, "Communication Theory and Liturgical Research," in *Worship* 51 (July 1977) 306.

18. Geertz 113.

19. Victor W. Turner, *The Forest of Symbols* (Ithaca: Cornell University Press, 1967) 20.

20. See, for example, Eugene Bianchi, "The Super-Bowl Culture of Male Violence," in Eugene Bianchi and Rosemary Ruether, *From Machismo to Mutuality* (New York: Paulist Press, 1976) 54–69.

When the social anthropologist takes up the examination of the system of symbols, interest lies in the dialectic between the symbolic patterns and the power operating in the cultural system. This will be reflected in ritual events.

In the Christian ritual tradition as presently restored in all the so-called liturgical churches of the West, the Easter Vigil, the full rite of Christian initiation culminating in the eucharistic meal on the night of the resurrection of Christ is judged to be the fullest elaboration of Christian ritual performance. In that sense, the rite can be expected to be programmatic; that is, it should contain within it the dominant ritual symbols which have borne the beliefs and the hopes of the community from the beginning to the end of the twentieth century. Moreover, the actual use of the symbols may be expected to—and do—say something about power relationships. For example, ritual control over the use of dominant Christian symbols, e.g., water, oils, wine, bread, the word, normally lies with the ordained. Rules for extending this use also originate with power wielders.

It is possible, by considering all known versions of the rites of Christian initiation, to uncover those elements which are basic structure and those which are "structural zeroes." In the case of the rite of Christian initiation, covering the movement from entering the catechumenate to participating in the Easter rites, the dominant symbols emerge: signing with the cross, laying on hands, anointing with oil, transmitting new light, pouring or plunging into water, attending to a living word, sharing bread and wine, and ordering the assembly.

The liturgical units which are "structural zeroes" are not thereby meaningless. They are instrumental and are regularly used to establish, maintain, or clarify power relationships. Postures, for example, can and often do serve such a purpose. So does the conferring of insignia designating role or status—garments, rings, croziers, the pallium, or the veil. Controlling access to certain ritual spaces is another way of ritualizing power relationships.

The dominant ritual symbols and the instrumental ones recur in various combinations and recombinations throughout the total Christian liturgical system, expressing beliefs and hopes and also establishing and maintaining historical relationships. A researcher investigating rites can gather the conscious meanings easily enough, by consulting the participants and the authoritative sources of the living tradition. But the non-conscious meanings are harder to establish. Disciplined observation of the performance of a rite can provide a starting point. What are the external forms and the visible characteristics of ritual objects or ritual transactions? Pursuing this line, the researcher may find iconic significance in the choice of substantial or insubstantial bread, the marking of a "dry" cross on the head of a catechumen and one with chrism on the initiate, the range of physical response or emotion permitted or controlled.

Further, what are the significant contexts in which the liturgical events occur? Pursuing the second line, an investigator should learn what are suitable times and who are suitable subjects and agents for the various ritual actions, what spontaneous elements have been introduced into a performance, what predictable elements omitted, and for what purposes. As with any analytic and interpretative task, the intelligence and disciplined imagination of the investigator shapes and guides the work of identifying significant data.

What will result from critical exposition of the contents of a single liturgical performance, which is only part of the larger symbolic formation of the religious tradition, is a plethora of meanings. Investigation will yield a list of ambiguous, redundant, and often apparently disconnected meanings. But there are ways for interpreting the disparate data. Victor Turner's research has led him to hypothesize that the meanings for any ritual unit tend to cluster around two poles, as in a single magnetic field, one attracting affective meanings, the other normative ones.[21] Ritual participants will be drawn affectively to meanings that have to do with personal identity and destiny, with living within the mystery of a loving God. So, for example, Christian ritual anointings speak of personal transformation by the Holy Spirit of the Risen Christ.

From a theological point of view, one could inquire into the distinctive content of each of the several forms of ritual anointing—during initiation, at the time of illness, and for the consecration of a bishop. Liturgical anointings intend to affirm personal existence in relation to Christ, to his Spirit, and to the

21. Turner, *The Forest of Symbols* 28.

Creator. Yet, anyone who attends carefully to the ritual anointings past and present learns without words of an ambiguously different relationship with Creator and Redeemer for women and for men. Episcopal anointing, which asserts fullness of authority in the Spirit through Christ, is proscribed for women. Liturgical rites intend to make statements about identity which affirm but also constrain.

Accordingly, liturgical rites make normative ethical and institutional statements. They set limits and define. The ritual participant will be caught up in and engaged with all of these meanings simultaneously. Liturgical anointings establish relationships and roles within the community as well as with the triune God. The normative meanings are fundamentally socio-political, ecclesial and ecclesiastical, having to do with authority and power, roles and duties, privileges and obligations.

Turner further hypothesizes that the two poles in the magnetic field of a dominant ritual symbol exert power over those who enter openly into liturgical action. The identity and destiny in God promised in the anointings makes acceptable and even attractive the roles and obligations of life in the community of believers. Effective liturgical rites can transform lives.[22] Esther Ticktin shows an intuitive sense of this in an essay she calls "A Modest Beginning," in a collection entitled *The Jewish Woman*.[23]

Ticktin had come to feel a need, as a Jewish woman, for traditional Judaism to confront the diminished status of women in that covenant community. She proposed ritual confrontation with the dilemma rather than further rabbinic argument. Ticktin suggests: let the men who study Torah zealously and say they can find no resolution to modern women's needs in the face of Torah's obligations themselves participate ritually in the experience of exclusion from the covenant community. Let them do it in three ways, straining and testing their own identity.

First, let them separate themselves from any assembly of God's people which separates and secludes women, even if the women claim to agree with the separation. Second, let them deny themselves their right to read the Torah portion in a synagogue which

22. Ibid. 30.
23. Esther Ticktin, "A Modest Beginning," in *The Jewish Woman*, ed. Elizabeth Koltun (New York: Schocken Books, 1976) 129–135.

denies this to women. Finally, let them exclude themselves from participating in any circle of male dancers who rejoice in Torah if the circle has no place for the dance of women. And as they strain their own religious identity, let them meditate on their experience in the light of the Torah text, "For you were strangers in the house of Egypt, and I brought you out."

Ticktin's sense of the power of ritual tells her that, should the men of Israel ever confront this impasse ritually so that they can feel the issue as well as discourse about it, the community of Israel would move beyond what it now understands of the power and demands of Torah. Rituals are distinctive social and religious actions precisely because they use the human body in disciplined ways to express, explore, and even transcend available human and religious meanings.

But if Esther Ticktin is optimistic about the power of creative religious ritual to press a people beyond the limits of the possible, many more have noted the loss of power of the traditional religious rituals in the past decades. British sociologist Robert Bocock observed that even in the 1970s most Britons still looked to Christian rituals, especially life-stages rituals, for significance, but he contends that they confronted in these rituals elements which contradicted their own basic feelings about themselves. They were not caught up in the identity the ritual offered, but came away further confused. Bocock asserted that the dissonance arose at the level of identity because of the overt and hidden ritual denials of the goodness of bodily existence.[24] He further argued that the ascendancy of rock music and the decline of participation in church rites were correlative developments in Britain, and that rock rituals arose through pre-conscious resistance to operative religious anthropology in church rituals.

Before passing too quickly over Bocock's judgment, we should consider it in relation to some frequently cited research by Andrew Greeley. Both researchers address the question of contemporary women and men rejecting Christian rituals. They do so by looking at different poles in the magnetic field of identity and obligation that Turner hypothesizes. Bocock finds Britons turning away from a God whose worship requires them to reject

24. Robert Bocock, *Ritual in Industrial Society* (London: George Allen and Unwin, Ltd., 1974) 38.

their own bodies while Greeley sees American Catholics dis-
daining a church which burdens them with guilt about their
sexuality when they assemble for worship.[25] In the first case,
personal identity is the issue; in the second, institutional norms
and obligations.

In 1973 Mary Daly wrote in *Beyond God the Father* that women
specially had to say "no" to the false identities, obligations, and
roles set out for them in religious rites. In 1978 she published
an extensive critique of the religious and social rites that have
diminished women physically and psychologically.[26] Inevitably,
the whole religious community has some faith-inspired nay-say-
ing yet to do in the face of conventional religious anthropology.
Basic to such a conversion is critical theological inquiry into the
preconscious cognitive content of the liturgical tradition of the
churches. The resources of cultural anthropology will aid that
task.

CULTURAL AND ECCLESIAL RESISTANCE

Bocock and Geertz offer correlative reasons for stressing ritual
studies among the human sciences: to understand Western culture generally, and to understand also the distinct cultural system which a religious tradition constitutes. But, currently, ritual
studies have only a modest place in the theological investigation
of religion and modern culture. Some of this, Bocock indicates,
can be attributed to the western world's preoccupation with the
primacy of reason and rational discourse as the privileged vehicle
of meaning.

Since the enlightenment certainly, modern culture has been
driven by a pursuit of rationality and has been correspondingly
uncritical of its real limits. As participants in modern culture,
the Christian theological community has been caught up in this

25. Andrew Greeley, *The American Catholic: A Social Portrait* (New York: Basic
Books, 1977) 126–151.

26. Mary Daly, *Beyond God the Father* (Boston: Beacon Press, 1973) 140–146;
also, *Gyn/Ecology: The Metaethics of Radical Feminism* (Boston: Beacon Press, 1978)
on Indian suttee, Chinese footbinding, Africal genital mutilation, and European
witchburning, chapters three to six.

preoccupation even while it talked of mystery. More recently, mere rationality is coming to be recognized as an inadequate foundation for human meaning, whether social or religious. We do not live now and never have lived by head alone. Ritual says this insistently because it requires the human body to articulate human and transcendent meaning. Bocock notes that the very act of bodily presence is the basic ritual action: one must participate "in person." He adds, "The use of the body . . . places ritual at the center of our attention if our concern is with the split in our culture between the body and the mind."[27]

Nevertheless, because of the general cultural bias that persists, there has been a remarkable indifference to ritual study in the Roman Catholic theological tradition, given the functional centrality of liturgical rites for the celebration, transmission, and appropriation of religious beliefs within the tradition. Yet something more than the general bias seems to be operating. Obviously, anthropologists look more readily than theologians at the ways in which rituals employ bodies in limit-testing behavior. Rituals engage humans in movements, exchanges, and transactions which strain to effect an integration of paradoxical transcendent meanings.[28] They do this in ways fully as immediate and imaginative as the limit-shattering language of a religious tradition in its primary expression. Why, then, have ritual studies been relatively insignificant in the study of Western religion and culture?

It seems plausible that the human body's very centrality to ritual action may be the prime reason that rites are judged by academics to be insignificant sources of transcendent meaning. At least two implications of such a judgment warrant investigation. The first is more immediately accessible to view, a cultural truism; the other, more remote.

First, because of the cultural dualism that has pervaded the Western theological tradition, ordinary people—even the baptized and especially women—have been viewed primarily as manifestations of unredeemed humanity in need of salvation, not as icons of the divine. While being bodily present in the

27. Bocock 34.
28. Roger Grainger, *The Language of the Rite* (London: Darton, Longman, and Todd, 1974) xi.

worshiping assembly is indeed the basic ritual act, no one is bodily present in the abstract. Specific postures and gestures required, permitted, or prohibited themselves communicate the participant's attitude toward self. The ritual use of the body makes it a vehicle for integrating positive and negative religious feelings. A ritual assembly embodies whatever self-understandings are active, whether official or unofficial. Whether there are ranks of holiness to be affirmed, or distinctions between groups, the ritual use of the body communicates the appropriate religious feeling.

More subtly, some have argued that the basic Western attitude toward the human person which surfaces in liturgical rites is anti-incarnational. Moreover, the Western Christian theological tradition has effectively rationalized the diminishment and distrust of the body—thus, of historical persons. Reevaluation of ritual studies as a font capable of yielding data for critical reflection on the Christian faith presupposes a certain readiness to discover religious significance in what people do in and through their bodies.

It is doubtful that the attitudinal change required to bring about a new valuation of ritual studies as a theological source can be effected simply by rational discourse while negative Christian feelings about the body is in control. Such feeling has been learned by participation in the very rites that invite analysis. Clerics have imposed their values not by talking about them but by participating in ritual actions that reinforce feelings of clerical separation and superiority. Women have appropriated "womanly" roles by participating in rites that reinforce feelings of inferiority and religious dependency. Because there is a characteristic concealment of emotion operating in ritual activity, it is difficult for participants to recognize the depth of ritual communication and to analyze it critically.

Discussing the problems inherent in the anthropological interpretations of rites, Victor Turner notes among the main characteristics of rites the tendency to stress the harmonious aspects of relationships and to suppress latent conflicts within the rites.[29] This suppression might take the obvious form of elimination

29. Turner, *The Forest of Symbols* 32–41.

from ritual speech of matters about which participants are fully aware; but more complex concealment of what is consciously known is also possible, as Turner indicates:

> It may be said that any major ritual that stresses the importance of a single principle of social organization only does so by blocking the expression of other important principles. Sometimes the submerged principles, and the norms and customs through which they become effective, are given veiled and disguised representation in the symbolic pattern of the ritual; sometimes . . . they break through to expression in the spatial and temporal intersection of the procedure.[30]

The point Turner makes is illustrated by a familiar element within the Jewish Passover ritual.

The shank bone of a lamb is included on the plate of ritual foods used during the Passover Haggadah. Although the narrative tells the story of Yahweh's choice of a people, it omits the dark side of that relationship, manifested in the destruction of the Jerusalem temple. The bone, not mentioned in the ritual narrative, nonetheless calls attention to the end of the temple and temple sacrifice. The matter is frequently more complex and the disguise more effective, though, than selective inattention to one item among ritual foods.

Gregory Bateson, an interpreter of iconic communication, of which ritual is one form, carries the matter of concealment further. He notes that iconic communication regularly expresses much that has sunk to the level of the unconscious, for whatever reasons. Further, what is expressed iconically and metaphorically has its own distinctive "grammar." Among other things, iconic communication about relationships lacks the grammatical capacity for simple negation. So, says Bateson, the actors find it necessary to *"say the opposite of what they mean in order to get across the proposition that they mean the opposite of what they say"* (emphasis his).[31]

Redundancy, the patterning of a message in several codes simultaneously, sustains and reinforces the unconscious data.

30. Ibid. 40–41.
31. Bateson 140–141.

Through ritual redundancy humans participating "in person" both appropriate and reinforce non-conscious messages through their bodies. Quite literally without thinking, participants situate themselves in this space and not that, or move in and out of designated spaces; they wear these garments and not those, or exchange garments, assume these postures and not those, or vary postures and gestures according to sexual and social classifications. Non-reflective participation does not negate the presence of complex symbolic meaning. Moreover, it is possible that what is expressed and represented may be a sustained ritual inversion of the actual state of affairs known by what Bateson calls "primary process," that level of unconscious mental activity concerned with comprehending relationships.

The fact that religious ritual deals simultaneously with religious feelings about the self and about ultimate relationships— some of which are consciously suppressed and some of which are non-conscious perceptions known only at the level of primary process—makes the critical study of rites a potentially challenging enterprise within the Western theological community. Western theology has been historically wary of the images that have expressed the religious feelings of mystics, visionaries, and devotees, regularly eradicating this content from the corpus of significant theological data. Nevertheless, it is unexamined ritual activity which sustains uncritical "religious" feeling about the self and about ambiguous distinctions between the "saint" and the reprobate, between the ordained and the unordained, or between male and female. The power of feeling and the feeling of power reinforced culturally and religiously through ritual acts may be the crucial factor inhibiting serious engagement with ritual studies in both the academic and the theological communities.

Still, persons who study theology and culture critically have reason to inquire into the dynamics that control what meanings are expressed and which remains concealed. Similarly, they have reason to question the theological mode of operation which disregards ritual study as a fertile source of human and religious meaning. The renewal of theological anthropology or the emergence of the practical political theology of the human subject cannot be accomplished in abstraction from the understanding of human persons, male and female, set out in liturgical assemblies.[32] It is here that the investigator can consult the church of any era about its perception of ultimate realities.

For example, the Roman Catholic Church's official promotion of motherhood in contemporary society is belied by its ritual attitude toward the saving power of wombs that bear and breasts that nurse. It is true that there is new-found academic fascination with the mystical vision of Julian of Norwich that Jesus is indeed mother as well as brother. But there is no sign of institutional readiness to introduce into public liturgy biblical imagery that points to the pregnant woman and the nursing mother as a human icon of the One who gives both body and blood for the life of the world. In fact, post-Vatican II reformers suppressed the rite of the blessing of women after childbirth. Having arrived at a judgment that the traditional rite carried a genuine denigration of women's experience in giving birth, they wittingly or unwittingly continued to assume that there is in childbearing nothing positive to celebrate which is revelatory of the paschal mystery. Ritual attention and inattention alike communicate.[33]

Profound transformation of religious feeling and consciousness will be required before the Christian assembly can proclaim the praise of the Creator who has given the world in the female as well as the male an icon of God and the mystery of salvation available in Jesus Christ.[34] The religious imagination is clearly capable of such iconic recognition and symbolic transformation.

32. Johannes Metz, for example, speaks uncritically of "the human subject" when he proposes a theological criticism of middle-class religion without adverting to the clear structural distinction maintained within both middle-class religion and society concerning suitable roles for male and female subjects, and in proposing memory as a basic category of practical critical reason without adverting to the implications of distinct sexual roles for that basic "human" memory. See *Faith in History and Society* (New York: Seabury, 1980).

33. Walter von Arx, "The Churching of Women after Childbirth," in *Liturgy and Human Passage: Concilium 112*, ed. David Power and Luis Maldonado (New York: Seabury, 1979) 62–72. The article, which narrates the history of the rite and the reasons for its suppression, does not take into account the general liturgical status of women. This matter will not be "forgotten" simply by suppressing the churching rite.

34. See Bernard Lonergan, *Method in Theology* (New York: Herder and Herder, 1972) 238–244, for a discussion of religious conversion as the basis for both intellectual and moral conversion. For a related discussion of conditions which block insight, see *Insight* (San Francisco: Harper and Row, 1978) 191–203.

Yet the sole institutionally sanctioned image of the divine savior remains the celibate male, paradoxically set out as the perfect icon of the divine lifegiver and guardian of creation.

But a caution must be sounded against a too facile interpretation of available but disconnected ritual data, whether one is looking at overtly religious or professedly secular ritual events. Meanings are found through a study of the total system of symbols. At the level of theory the social anthropologist hypothesizes that in the dialectic between power relationships and symbol systems minor or temporary shifts in power are seldom immediately accommodated by corresponding changes in symbolic forms.[35] The papacy is a case in point. Only with John Paul II— more than a century after the real change in power had occurred—was there an explicit public eradication of the tiara as a ritual symbol of the papacy and a substitution of the cross.[36] The ambiguity of symbols readily allows for a long-term discrepancy. Moreover, even when changed power relations begin to take a firm hold, symbolic changes are generally seen as idiosyncratic in their first manifestations, as part of the personal biographies of those who are struggling to reorder power relationships. John XXIII, Paul VI, and John Paul I lived with the ambiguity of papal power and the tiara. John Paul II has suppressed the medieval symbol. He has nevertheless revealed his intention to wield the imperial power it symbolized.

Critical students of traditional ritual will learn to analyze the idiosyncratic. Because ritual symbols are characteristically redundant, ritual manifestations of the effort to create new syntheses of meaning and power will be diffuse and can be expected to show varying degrees of creative imagination. They will also embody ambiguity and concealment. Therefore, investigators of

35. Cohen, 36–37. Complexity, ambiguity, density, redundancy, and concealment are all characteristic of ritual behavior. The correlative absence of any transparency of meaning should preclude all hasty judgments about the significance of isolated episodes or manifestations of corporate meaning.

36. John Paul II made prominent use of the cross at the close of his rite of installation in October, 1978. Earlier, he had drawn attention to the suppression of the triple tiara in his installation homily. In his address to Polish workers at Nowa Huta, delivered from the nearby Shrine of the Cross in Mogila on June 9, 1979, he spoke of the power of the cross as a symbol for himself and for Polish workers. *Origins*, 9 (June 21, 1979) 76–77.

the religious meanings operating in liturgical rites must learn to observe, to collect the data, to analyze it within the context of the whole system, and to interpret it in the light of the actual use of power. But they must also learn to ask the critical questions: are these rites congruent with human experience and helpful to human existence? is their expression of relationships the Gospel truth?

The first set of tasks is foundational and their performance can be aided notably by drawing upon the post-structuralist methods of cultural and social anthropology. The second matter is more properly theological; it invites systematic reflection on the Christology, pneumatology, ecclesiology, theological anthropology, and eschatology manifest within the ritual transactions that make up the liturgical event.

Because cultural systems, religious and secular, continuously impinge on one another as part of the social process, the theories and methods of cultural and social anthropology constitute a potentially important resource for the dialogue of theology and culture. Ritual studies may have languished to date because of the cultural-religious bias which split mind and body. It may also be the case, however, that theologians have lacked the proper tools for opening up the many languages of rites. Yet theologians past and present have mastered ancient languages and ancient philosophical systems in their efforts to expose the historical dialogue between religion and culture and reflect upon it theologically. Liturgical studies might well be undertaken now with help from the tools of social and cultural anthropology in the hopes of understanding the contemporary expressions and developments of living religious traditions. Rites are after all as abundant as texts. To date, most students of religion and most theologians have been blind to rites. And the rites, themselves, in turn are mute. What has Manchester to do with Jerusalem? It can facilitate the dialogue between theology, liturgy and culture!

8

Critical Questions for
Liturgical Theology

AS I UNDERSTAND AND APPROACH LITURGICAL THEOLOGY, IT IS AN
integrative activity. Liturgy has trinitarian and christological,
pneumatological and anthropological, ecclesiological and eschatological components. A classic liturgy will manifest a coherence
among all these elements, setting out an integrated vision of the
economy of salvation. Certainly the Tridentine liturgy manifested such a synthesis. What Western liturgical theology was
done during the recent past regularly spoke to the themes of
that synthesis.

We are no longer in that classic moment. Contemporary Western liturgy reflects not a synthesis but our search for one. The
goal of this essay is to advance the discussion of the nature of
liturgical theology in this historical situation. It does so by looking at classical issues in new ways. Part of the task of liturgical
theology will always be descriptive: What is being set out in
these texts and rites? I suggest that the contemporary task of
liturgical theology is preeminently critical: Is the faith vision
being celebrated in the liturgy adequate? Is it congruent with
human and ecclesial experience and expectations of the saving
grace of Christ? The critical questions have gained in intensity
in the past decade. The church's ritual celebration of its faith
and hope takes place today in assemblies which have as many
new questions as they have traditional answers about how they
share in the saving work of Christ.

In order to establish the problematic of the essay, I will set out briefly some aspects of the perspective of liturgical theologians which I take to be axiomatic, that is, nonissues. Subsequently, I will identify some actual issues and probe selectively to illustrate my own point of view. At the end of the inquiry and in the light of it I will prepare an answer to the controlling question: What is it that Christian liturgical action expresses? The answer to that question in turn will point to directions and issues for contemporary liturgical theology.

The Classic Statement

The classic response to the question "what is it that Christian liturgical action expresses" is that liturgy expresses the faith of the church: *lex orandi lex credendi.* Due to the efforts of nineteenth and early twentieth century scholarly inquiry into patristic liturgy, renewed theological precision was given to the meaning of the classic response. That precision is reflected in the Constitution on the Sacred Liturgy. The liturgy of the church sets out the mystery of Christ as the paschal mystery—his *transitus* to the Father "for us and for our salvation." Proponents of liturgical prayer have lauded and still laud the liturgy for its objectivity precisely in this regard: liturgical activity focuses on the mystery of salvation revealed in Christ's sacrificial death and resurrection to new life.

Recent liturgical scholarship has provided additional clarification regarding this phenomenon of the objectivity of Christian liturgical prayer. One important recovery of "forgotten truths" was the insistence that the content of the liturgical books—namely, texts and directives for ritual action—does not exhaust the content of the liturgy. Liturgy is above all the particular and actual celebration of a ritual event. Even with this clarification it is possible to advance the thesis of the objectivity of liturgical action. The structuralist perspective brought to bear in ritual studies has provided analytic tools for mining the fundamental structures, not only those borne through texts but also those borne through transactions and exchanges effected between and among persons and ritual symbols. These nontextual structures also constitute objective data in a traditional rite. Scholars can note variants, transpositions, omissions, embellishments of texts and transactions. They can interpret theologically what they uncover structurally. They can do so with confidence that a structuralist methodology can distinguish between basic structures and "structural zeroes." It is clear that there are both objective structures and objective content in the several rites of the church's liturgy.

The classic statement of liturgical objectivity in content and structure so formulated seems to leave little room or none at all for affirming and interpreting particularity and subjectivity as essential components of the faith of the church. The variants, transpositions, omissions, embellishments which reflect choice have generally been ignored or received negative evaluation in liturgical studies. One has only to recall the conventional treatment of the process by which the Roman books were transformed during an aberrant journey through Western Europe or the express attitude toward baroque extravagance to recognize the bias. Liturgical studies have shown interest in structures, not in the spiritual currents and anxieties which swept in to inform, to transform, and to deform those structures. Nevertheless, the data of variants, transpositions, omission, embellishment are present in abundance. They are testimony that local, regional and cultural particularity in expression are every bit as significant for understanding the church's liturgy and the church's belief as objectivity in content and structure. And perhaps they are more interesting.

Expanding the Focus of Liturgical Studies

To pursue a line of inquiry on the grounds that it is interesting is not to trivialize the academic enterprise. The argument in favor of studying the interesting rather than the conventional is set out by John Dominic Crossan in *The Dark Interval*.[1] It is an argument in favor of recognizing the human fascination with brinks and borders, edges and limits, with the possibility of the experience of transcendence and the desire to give that experience expression. Since liturgical events are assemblies for the purpose of the engagement of the believing community with the mystery at the heart of its life, one might argue that the structural constants function to facilitate that engagement. The reality and

---

1. John Dominic Crossan, *The Dark Interval: Towards a Theology of Story* (Niles, Ill.: Argus Communication 1975) 19–20.

the depth of the engagement desired, achieved, sustained are attended to by the creative choices or "deposits of the spirit." These are the human expressive forms that are testimonials to an active and hopeful faith shaped by available cultural forms and experience. In looking at both of these together we come closer to understanding the phenomenon of liturgical celebration, the event in which the expectation of saving grace is expressed, surrendered to, and appropriated to life. Investigation of living faith is not well served by exclusive attention to issues of objective content and structure. There is need to look at the whole pattern of structure and choice to discover the faith message of the liturgical medium, and so to uncover the data for descriptive and critical liturgical theology.

Recent sacramental theology supports this orientation, although it does not press the point to any immediate conclusions. Sacramental theology acknowledges that sacraments are always the acts of a particular community, a local church, which is itself a sacrament of the saving mystery.[2] That contention considered in its full significance extends the task of liturgical theology. Insofar as the sacramental action is Christian liturgy, it can be expected to evidence the received tradition with respect both to objective structure and content. Insofar as it is celebration of the mystery of Christ as that mystery has been culturally perceived and appropriated, the liturgical event will reflect cultural selectivity in its very celebration.

What methods are appropriate for collecting the data of choice? Cultural anthropologist J. van Velsen has distinguished structural analysis from situational analysis of rituals.[3] That distinction can be useful in pursuing the basic question: What is it that Christian liturgical action expresses? Structural analysis will consider all known and possible performances of eucharistic liturgy, for example, and on the basis of all known and possible cases represent the basic structure of that liturgy. The fact of periodic structural deviance will not invalidate the reality of an objective content and structure. In fact, it can heighten the search for

2. See, for example, Karl Rahner, "The New Image of the Church" in *Theological Investigations* (New York: Seabury Press 1974).
3. J. Van Velsen, "The Extended-Case Method" in *The Craft of Social Anthropology*, ed. Al L. Epstein (London: Tavistock 1967) 129–149.

understanding. Situational analysis is poststructuralist in its orientations. It does not negate the value of identifying the constants, the objective content and structure. But it does find the variables, the manifestations of choice, more interesting; and so it makes difference the object of inquiry. Situational analysis looks to the concrete particularity of any given ritual performance. What does actually occur occasionally or even consistently by way of variant, transposition, omission, embellishment? Does it point to the actual engagement of the participants, their experience, their appropriation of the meaning as theirs? By pursuing this broadened line of inquiry about choice, the liturgical theologian may advance toward an understanding of the faith expressed in liturgical celebration not as an abstract and universal datum but as a living reality culturally expressed and culture laden.

The Bread Sign: Layer upon Layer of Meaning
To illustrate the point of the simultaneity of objectivity and subjectivity in liturgical data, the liturgical phenomenon of eucharistic bread is apt matter for exploration. The element of bread in eucharistic action is clearly a constant in the Christian liturgical tradition. It has a constant use: it is the focus of the great thanksgiving prayer of the church and it is distributed and consumed. It is a bearer of deep symbolic meanings at the human, social and religious levels, meanings which have been caught up and extended radically through the action of Jesus and the responsive faith of the church. At a conventional level of doctrinal understanding the bread consistently bears the meaning of sacramental real presence of the risen and crucified Lord, however this presence is explained theologically.[4]

But bread, even eucharistic bread is not an abstraction nor a generic datum. Bread is a food stuff created from varieties of possible ingredients according to different recipes with a broad range of purposes. Bakers select ingredients according to schemes of use and meaning. There are festive breads and daily breads. What is appropriate for different occasions and uses is

4. The complex subtlety and variety of early theological explanations is set out in Georg Kretschmar, "Abendmahl" (Alte Kirche) III/1 in *Theologische Realenzyklopädie* (Berlin: Walter de Gruyter 1977) I, Lieferung 1, 59–89.

determined according to an operative but generally nonconscious system of cultural meanings which may arise, for example,
according to a principle of abundance or scarcity or according to
a scale of skill in execution.

The phenomenon of eucharistic bread is fundamentally the
same: variant possible ingredients, different recipes, distinctive
finalities and restricted uses. Moreover, what is judged appropriate bread form and use is also determined according to an
operative but nonconscious system of meanings which reflect
cultural experience. The need is for that bread sign which can
effectively symbolize the sacramental real presence of the Lord—
a reality believers hope to experience in their lives. Joseph Jungmann has sketched some of the history of the Western ecclesiastical choices concerning eucharistic bread in *The Mass of the
Roman Rite*.[5] In his treatment he noted the influence of the levitical tradition of the Old Testament in the development of Western liturgical usage which contracted from wide choice to no
choice. But Jungmann did not probe for depth of theological
significance in the particularity of the choice, a task outside the
scope of his work.

The matter is nevertheless interesting in liturgical study—interesting in Crossan's sense. As will become apparent, the significance of the bread choice is heightened by setting it in the
context of other restrictions on choice related to eucharistic bread
use. A convergence of restrictions on choice points to an underlying meaning issue—the stuff of descriptive and critical liturgical theology. Normative decisions about eucharistic bread
which intervene to restrict choice and so to classify some bread
as illicit are possible pointers to expectations about saving experience and the desire to give that experience or its anticipation
expression.

The basic *lex orandi* of eucharistic celebration, bread blessed
and shared, has long been and continues to be refined by juridical decisions. Either they are meaningless and arbitrary or they
mean something. To reject the notion that the particularity of
the bread sign has cognitive significance is to say that the matter
is of no real theological consequence. Such a position is belied

5. Joseph Jungmann, *The Mass of the Roman Rite* (New York: Benziger Brothers
1953) II, 31–41.

by the intense engagement of the community again and again in history up to the present.[6] Bread style and the protocol related to its handling speak from faith to faith. How is the theologian to uncover the meaning?

If the principle of redundancy is operative ritually, as communication theory indicates is in the nature of the case, then the meaning of a particular eucharistic bread form should be reinforced by transactions involving its legitimate use. It is not surprising to note that the historical restrictions placed upon the choice of ingredients and the control of production techniques is replicated in restrictions about licit handling and licit consumption in the liturgical assembly. Choice is controlled through distinctions made, presumably for good reason whether conscious or not. In the configuration of licit choices which have accumulated, distinction itself as a fact in the community seems to be a controlling dynamic. That will be considered further below.

When the inquirer begins to follow the leads set out by situation analysis and communication theory, she begins to get a glimpse, in choices about bread, of things christological and ecclesiological. In fact, the issues underlying licit bread choice and use are fundamentally christological and ecclesiological. The very particularity of the bread sign contains information about the ecclesial body of Christ as the manifestation of the real saving presence of the Lord Jesus. The theological meaning is real, even if it is not immediately accessible to historical and structural methods of inquiry. It is theological meaning that is carried by symbolic forms and patterns rather than by basic structure. But it is, nevertheless, meaning which both expresses and shapes the faith of the believers concerning the present experience of salvation.

Ecclesiological and Christological Content of Liturgical Events

Such an assertion that the bread sign in all its complexity embodies primary theological content needs explication. The basis for that explication comes from the human sciences.

---

6. An unpublished 1978 research report by J. Frank Henderson, "The Problem of Unleavened Altar Bread Today," recently made available to me by the author, sorts out some of the recurring issues.

Fundamental to the discussion about christological and ecclesiological meanings inherent in the bread sign is acknowledgment of the fact that the content of all rituals is an affirmation
about relationships. In the words of Gregory Bateson, ". . . the
discourse of nonverbal communication is precisely concerned
with matters of relationships. . . ."[7] Mary Douglas specifies the
dynamic of ritual behavior similarly; she says it expresses a relation between the physical self and the social self.[8] Christian
liturgical rites, too, speak about relationships, specifically the
saving relationships revealed in the paschal mystery.

"Paschal mystery" is a theological formulation which com-
prehends two salvific moments—the passing of Jesus through
death to transforming union with his Father, and the outpouring
of the Holy Spirit of the Lord Jesus on those summoned to
believe. The people so summoned regularly celebrate the paschal
mystery in a ritual way. Intrinsic to the celebration is the comprehension that the mystery in some way extends to and includes
the participants personally. From the earliest periods, for example, we have evidence of an ecclesial belief that the church
has by the second movement of the paschal mystery become
sacramentally the body of Christ.

Given the structured movement inherent in the paschal mystery we can expect that the bread, which is a focus of the celebration of the paschal event, will symbolically embody truth
about the ecclesial aspect of the paschal mystery. It will do this
just as surely as it sets out symbolically the first phase which
pertains to the *transitus* of Jesus. The eucharistic element of
bread, in other words, intends to express the complexity of the
meaning "body of Christ" in its full extension.

How does the bread symbol refer effectively to ecclesial reality
and ecclesiological structure, "causing what it signifies" in the
traditional formula? I propose that the rite sets out and confirms
the way in which the church is the body of Christ precisely by
the scheme of licit forms and licit transactions related to the
eucharistic bread. The ecclesial issue focuses in the eucharistic

---

7. Gregory Bateson, *Steps to an Ecology of Mind* (New York: Ballantine Books
1972) 411–425.

8. Mary Douglas, *Natural Symbols: Explorations in Cosmology* (New York: Random House Vintage Books 1973) 93–112.

bread because this symbol is the fulcrum of the belief in the reality and the mediation of the saving presence of Christ.

Let us return then to look more closely at the scheme of distinctions regarding what is licit concerning the eucharistic bread sign. Earlier I suggested that distinction itself as a requirement within the community seemed to be a controlling dynamic in the ritual transactions concerning sacramental bread. I would now refine that observation further by suggesting that the issue is not simply distinction but distinction which concerns mediation of the saving grace of Christ. Control or relaxation of control regarding the handling or consumption of the sacramental body of Christ effectively embodies (= is a sacrament of) the church's understanding of the manner and forms of mediation which are proper manifestation of the risen Christ and are effective in the building up of the ecclesial body of Christ. To support this thesis I offer a preliminary inquiry into some well-known liturgical developments of the third to the fifth centuries, drawing upon a pair of Jungmann's classic studies. A thorough investigation of the matter would call for sustained inquiry into key historical moments in liturgical and doctrinal development.

Prepositions and Ritual Transactions As Theological Data

Although Jungmann did not, in *The Mass of the Roman Rite*, suggest depth meaning for the many recorded changes in eucharistic bread and its licit use, he does explore elsewhere, in *The Place of Christ in Liturgical Prayer*, a cognate matter. In the context of the movement from christological heterodoxy to orthodoxy in the third through the fifth centuries he concentrates attention on the debate over which prepositions in the doxology are suitable for expressing trinitarian faith accurately. Syntactically, prepositions are verbal pointers to relationships.

Arian ill-will had led to distortions of the meaning of the traditional doxological formulas of the liturgy. In the early fathers, prayer "through Christ" and "in Christ" had expressed, in the first case, Christ's holy priesthood as the source of effective prayer, and in the second case, the reality of the ecclesial community.[9] During the third century and into the fourth, the for-

9. Joseph Jungmann, *The Place of Christ in Liturgical Prayer*, 2nd rev. ed. (Staten Island, N.Y.: Alba House 1965) 149.

mula "through Christ" was appropriated to substantiate a subordinationist christology. To counter this subversion of the liturgy, orthodox bishops began to refine and to restrict the prepositional choices of the doxology. Jungmann offers the following interpretation of Basil's contribution to the conflict: "*If rank is in question*, then the same rank is due to the Son as to the Father and therefore also the same worship with him (*meta*). . . . Therefore, if the formula with *meth' hou* corresponds to adoration, that with *di' hou* corresponds to thanksgiving."[10] Jungmann clearly recognizes the prepositional issue as christological and as concerned with the nature of relationships being expressed in liturgical prayer.

Later, in his summary discussion of the long-term impact of the Greek prepositional struggle as a theological effort to shore up orthodox understanding of the truth of trinitarian and christological relationships, both absolutely and in the economy of salvation, Jungmann makes other observations which are pertinent to our attempt to understand the eucharistic bread form and transactions as a unified theological statement. He notes as results of the controversy the "suppression, weakening or abandonment of those text elements which make Christ appear as Mediator" and the new emphasis on "the majesty of the triune God, of the Father and the Son and the Holy Spirit." Then he remarks: "Granted that the Arian assault *has not changed* the faith of the ancient Church, yet it has profoundly influenced, at first throughout the East, the *use made* of different facets of the faith in religious and liturgical life."[11] Purposeful ritual choices was perceptibly operative. Jungmann, as a classic interpreter of the objective, tends to devaluate the impact of the choice.

His qualified "at first throughout the East" is elaborated in a discussion of the distinctive differences in the doxological element of the Latin Mass. At the conclusion of his exploration of Latin doxological development, Jungmann agrees that the Roman liturgy, too, celebrates the divinity of Christ the mediator and high priest. But, says Jungmann, this is done "only to emphasize his dignity. . . . The Roman liturgy is not concerned to change elements of the prayer into formulas of faith, to provide

10. Jungmann, *The Place of Christ* 179 (emphasis added).
11. Jungmann, *The Place of Christ* 200 (emphasis added).

bulwarks against those threatening the faith. These may be built from other materials on the periphery of the holy city. The liturgy itself remains, in its midst, the sanctuary in which, untroubled by the noise of the battle without, one only enters before God—today with the same language and in the same Spirit as was customary in the Church of the third century or so."[12]

Jungmann's commitment is to looking at verbal clues only in order to understand liturgical prayer and the faith it expresses. It leads him to overlook the nonverbal language of ritual elements. Yet ritual transactions are discernible as manifestations of the same doctrinal tensions. Moreover, they assert themselves "in the sanctuary" and not on the sidelines.

In the light of this assertion of liturgical objectivity it is ironic that Jungmann's other major work, *The Mass of the Roman Rite,* had compiled much of the available data which showed how a bulwark of trinitarian-christological-ecclesiological orthodoxy had been fashioned in relation to the central bread sign. The issue in the third to the fifth centuries East and West was indeed relationships and mediation. Orthodoxy was set out in the church by ritual transactions as surely as it was by syntactical deliberations. It is appropriate therefore to consider what was happening ritually during the same era of the third to the fifth centuries when the refinements of doxological syntax were intense. But what constitutes data?

It is necessary to recall that during this time the human mediatorial role of Christ had been displaced by an anti-Arian emphasis on his divine majesty. Into the vacancy created by the dislocated priesthood of Christ there appears the mediating hierarchical priesthood. According to Jungmann, "it is noticeable that up to the end of the second century the overseers of the Christian communities were content to be known as *episkopoi, presbyteroi, hegoumenoi* and the like, but not priests. . . ."[13] Jungmann's own explanation of the clearly perceptible shift in the third century remains enigmatic. He writes, "Only a closer look at the organism of the body of Christ distinguishes those organs that have a special share in the priesthood and the mediation of Christ, in virtue of their particular services and powers." He

12. Jungmann, *The Place of Christ* 212.
13. Jungmann, *The Place of Christ* 148.

infers that the "special" share was a fact of the church's experience; its conceptualization in terms of hierarchical orders was subsequent to that experience.

Distinguishing and ordering relationships in the body appears in the same epoch in which trinitarian and christological relationships are being examined. And the distinguishing of relationships surfaces prominently in the liturgical assembly. The *Apostolic Tradition* of Hippolytus is one witness to the phenomenon.

Before attempting to interpret the several parallel developments, it is instructive to look at the kinds of distinctions within the body which emerge, which become the preferred ritual choices in eucharistic action, and ultimately survive as the sole licit choices. Using a formula of equation, we can recognize that the following christological issues were being distinguished and correlated in the church of the third to the fifth centuries:

$$\frac{\text{Christ's divinity}}{\text{Christ's humanity}} = \frac{\text{Christ's majesty}}{\text{Christ's priesthood}} = \frac{\text{Christ's eminence}}{\text{Christ's lowliness}}$$

When the priestly mediatorial role of Christ was deemphasized under the pressure of christological controversy, the presbyterate rose to prominence as priestly mediators. As a result a whole range of ecclesial relationships necessarily underwent readjustment. "Through Christ" came to have a new referent: the priestly office understood as effective power conferred on the *episkopoi* and through them on the *presbyteroi*. As a share in Christ's priesthood, it was sacral in character. It was necessary for it to reflect the eminence and divine authority of Christ from whom it derived.

In order to have some members of the assembly—"in Christ"—signify Christ's eminence, others were required to signify Christ's lowliness. To have some function as sacral mediators, others were required to function as receivers of the divine power. I am suggesting, then, that the formalized distinctions of roles and the absolutized hierarchical ordering in the ecclesial body which gained authority in this era was structured and included as a response to christological heterodoxy. Orthodox christological faith demanded ecclesiological expression in the

liturgy. Fifth and sixth century neoplatonic theology would refine the idea of an ordered hierarchical priesthood. The *Ecclesiastical Hierarchy* of Pseudo-Dionysius is the obvious example.
But this theology was subsequent to the more basic liturgical
effort east and west to order correctly all those "in Christ."[14] The
later neoplatonic theology effectively sustained the development
and refinement of a sacerdotal order by providing a rationale for
it in the medieval church.

In the ecclesial body, the counterpoint message of Christ's
eminence and power conjoined with lowliness and powerlessness received ritual expression in the ordering of the eucharistic
assembly. Divine/human distinctions and functions in Christ
were manifested through human/human distinctions and functions in the ecclesial body of Christ gathered for worship. Females were distinguished from males. Female nature was
perceived and defined as bodily, carnal, *sarx*—a suitable symbol
of lowliness. Male nature was designated a manifestation of
spirit, rationality, *logos*—a suitable symbol of eminence. In the
theological anthropology of the fathers, the discourse on the
issue of male and female nature is prolix. In liturgy, the same
point of male eminence and female lowliness was made by re-
stricting choices about women's participation in eucharistic
transactions—the sacramental symbol of the eminence of the
risen Christ.[15] Menstruation, pregnancy, childbearing, all un-
mistakable signs of humanity and human mortality, were for a
while the occasion for overt sacramental proscription for females.
Subsequently, to the present, these symbols of lowliness function as subliminal bearers of the prohibitions regarding women's
suitability for sacral mediation.

If the female expressed lowliness in an androcentric world,
the male expressed eminence and so could be the bearer of
Christ's sacral priesthood. Yet even within the community of
males, distinction was in order. For sacral priesthood to mediate

14. See Kretschmar (n. 4 above) especially 77–82, for discussion of the relative roles of christology and neoplatonism in eucharistic developments in the
East in the fourth to the sixth centuries.

15. Kretschmar suggests antignostic and antimontanist concerns in the second and third centuries are at the origins of earliest explicit controls over
women's roles in the eucharistic assembly and in the ecclesial community (see
p. 75).

divine grace, human powerlessness and need have to be in evidence. The order of active mediating priests required an order of receptive *laos*. Thus, some males in the ritual assembly signify holiness or source of divine grace; others, deprivation or sinfulness and the need for divine mediation. The classification received confirmation in eucharistic protocol. While all males may signify eminence and are potentially active, only some, the hierarchy, had conferred on them authority for active eucharistic functions. Others retained receptive or passive ones. Thus we arrive at the body of Christ hierarchically ordered according to the following scheme:

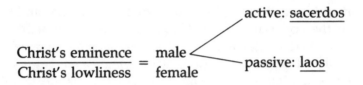

$$\frac{\text{Christ's eminence}}{\text{Christ's lowliness}} = \frac{\text{male}}{\text{female}} \Big\langle \begin{array}{l} \text{active: } \underline{\text{sacerdos}} \\ \text{passive: } \underline{\text{laos}} \end{array}$$

The *sacerdos* came to manifest the eminence of Christ in the ecclesial body by signifying the divine Christ and mediating divine grace present in the divine eucharistic body. Eventually the circle of relations and appropriate transactions coheres in an integrated pattern of ritual ordering. It does so at the cost of deactivating power present elsewhere in the system.

The Shape of the Assembly and the Nature of the Body of Christ

Mary Douglas has written an essay about the relationship of the social body and the physical body which is suggestive for further probing of the issue: what does the liturgy of the church express? Douglas's thesis is "The social body constrains the way the physical body is perceived."[16] Douglas is talking about society and the individual in general and about the vertical relation between social structure and licit personal behavior patterns. It seems plausible to ask whether her thesis can allow for the formulation of a corollary: constraints in the social body also structure perceptions of the body of Christ glorified, ecclesial, eucharistic. Then we can ask: did a social milieu with a Stoic

16. Douglas, *Natural Symbols* 93.

perception of ultimate reality—eminence, lowliness, and mediation—inevitably shape everything in this image?

At a second stage of argument Douglas states, "The scope of the body as a medium of expression is limited by controls exerted by the social system."[17] This thesis presupposes that the scope of bodily possibility always exceeds what is authorized and licit. In every case, then, choices which restrain expression will not be arbitrary, but will correlate with the needs and symbolic structure of the total system. Extrapolating from her thesis and our corollary, we might next suggest: that order achieved in the glorified body and the ecclesial body will be replicated not only in choices about the eucharistic assembly but also in choices about the bread of the sacrament. The licit forms—from ingredients to production to liturgical handling—would predictably come to be whatever is judged to distinguish eminence and lowliness.[18] Only a bread of eminence can function as the symbolic manifestation of the real presence of the divine Christ. Hieratic bread must be distinguished from the human.

This line of inquiry proceeds from the premise of communication theory that a controlling or dominant idea will achieve redundant expression in multiple "language" codes. The human interpretative process of symbolic transformation guides the nonconscious choice of materials and arrangements that adequately express the message. In effect, an integrated christology, ecclesiology, anthropology, and liturgical order will coalesce over a period of time to express the saving mystery of the body of Christ. The integration achieved will, of course, be rooted in cultural experience and expressed in culturally available forms, and so will be liable to erosion under the impact of different cultural experience.

Such a tightly fitted and coherent ritual and conceptual system has the effect of "establishing world," what seems a divinely constituted hierarchical body. What is of interest to liturgical theology is not simply the replication of forms which sustain that "world." Such redundancy is fully predictable. It does not prove divine constitution. Variants, however numerous and in-

17. Douglas, *Natural Symbols* 98.

18. Mary Collins, "Historical Perspectives" in M. Kay, ed., *It Is Your Own Mystery* (Washington, D.C.: The Liturgical Conference 1977) 10–11.

genious, are in fact only transpositions of a cultural perception of christological faith expressed as ecclesial reality.

What is of interest ritually and theologically is what subverts the pattern of hierarchical ordering, what transcends and confounds the known structures of reality. These subversions, characterized by Crossan as "parabolic," point to the possibility of experience which transcends "world" by undermining it.[19] Some experience presses at the edges and limits of the real with the question: what if things are other than what you know and celebrate as the mystery of the body of Christ? other than what you know and celebrate as the ecclesial showing forth of the divine mystery of saving relationships? Such subversive eruptions are not new; they are constants in the liturgical tradition. Liturgical mediations of divine grace by laymen or women who by definition lacked eminence and divine power are also a part of the historical tradition. They were consistently perceived and repressed as deviations, as distorted expressions of saving mystery.

These ritual considerations finally point us to the present Roman Catholic experience of the saving mystery of Christ. Long-established hieratic ritual forms are in tension with—perhaps already in conflict with and under judgment by—contemporary efforts to conceptualize a nonstratified ecclesiological order, a communal eucharist, and a philosophy of the human person which is not androcentric. But solutions to these theological problems are in turn being shaped by what the community already knows or is currently discovering about divine grace and human mediation. This new awareness is already liturgically evident. It is forcing a displacement of the ritual and ecclesiological categories of eminence and lowliness.

Not surprisingly, this expanded awareness of human mediation of the grace of Christ is contemporaneous with a loosening of traditional eucharistic constraints. Ordained and nonordained, women and men, are again perceived as suitable mediators of eucharistic bread. Once again ordinary (that is, using culturally available ingredients and preparation techniques) bread is reappearing as eucharistic bread. Serious debates occur and treatises circulate about whether all of this is licit—that is,

19. Crossan, *Dark Interval* 9, 57–62.

whether an expanded scope of "bodily" expression is to be authorized. Issue by issue, the decisions are in favor of a gradual relaxing of constraints about licit choice. What was "always and everywhere and by everyone"proscribed is now tenable and permissible.[20]

The symbolic shift in the manifestation of Christ's saving power through lowliness as well as eminence, in effect negating the categories, is not simply a conciliar or postconciliar phenomenon. It is one which preceded and precipitated the more recent developments. The shift diverges from and converges with the breakup of the traditional Western sense of hierarchical social ordering, a breakup which gained political credibility through the French revolution. In any case, the absolute identification of the christological meanings of eminence and lowliness, source and deprivation, with particular classes of persons no longer obtains in the licit ritual handling of the eucharistic bread.

It is commonplace among liberal Catholics to dismiss such liturgical developments as trivial, mere ritualization. The emotion engagement and resistance of conservative believers in the face of such ritual and symbolic issues is in fact much more perceptive. An ordered world is indeed being subverted by such ritual changes. It is not yet clear what "more" is coming, nor whether the "more" will be christic or antichristic. From a liturgical perspective it would appear that the eucharistic community has already begun to venture with hope into the unknown "more" of the mystery of saving relationships. What the ecclesial body of Christ already knows in faith to be true, it has begun to explore ritually. This cognition will eventually break through at every level: theological discourse, doctrine, and ecclesiastical order.

20. Subsequent to the original preparation of this paper the Congregation for the Doctrine of the Faith raised questions in a June 4, 1979, letter to the National Conference of Catholic Bishops about both the liceity and the validity of the growing use of "ordinary" bread for the church's eucharist. The very raising of the question confirms the point of this essay, that the bread sign is not peripheral but has significant relationship to the church's doctrinal teaching about salvation. For a canonical reflection on the significance of that letter, see John Huels, "Eucharistic Bread and Wine," in One Table, Many Laws. Essays on Catholic Eucharistic Practice (Collegeville, MN: The Liturgical Press, 1986) 54–62.

What Does Christian Liturgical Action Express?

The liturgy of the church expresses the faith of the church. It is a faith which has trinitarian and christological, pneumatological and anthropological, ecclesiological and eschatological components. The liturgy expresses the faith through a complex world-ordering pattern of ritual symbols, verbal and nonverbal, in the syntax and vocabulary of its prayer and in the scheme of licit transactions associated with the eucharistic species. The liturgy expresses the faith of the church selectively—choosing its themes and emphases from questions of ultimacy put to it by particular cultures. Moreover, it expresses faith in the saving grace of Christ and its mediation to the world in forms that are available within the culture that posed the question.

It is the task of liturgical theology to discern what is being set out in the scheme of licit ritual choices and then to interpret that selective perception of the order of salvation, accounting for what it affirms and what it omits, negates, or rejects as the truth about the present experience of the saving grace of Christ in the church and in the world.

THE WORDS OF
WORSHIP

Introduction

The symbolic words of worship can be studied from a variety of perspectives. The semiotics and hermeneutics of religious language—how language works to express meaning and how it is to be interpreted—are major dimensions of contemporary liturgical study. The essays gathered here all concern themselves with the way in which the language of worship expresses and structures ecclesial relationships.

At issue in the lengthy study of the language of the revised ordination rites are the relationship of clergy to the godhead, of clergy to the laity, and of clergy to one another. The archaic metaphors explicit and implicit in the liturgical text pull the speakers and hearers into an imaginative realm where historical institutions are given sacral significance. The language of the ordination rites has a history. Unexamined, the words the church uses in its liturgical assemblies for ordination exercise divine authority over church life, interpreting the New Testament witness about leadership in a community of disciples without itself being put to the test of evangelical authenticity.

A comparable problem is identified in the essays attending to the language the church uses in public prayer to name God and to remember God's deeds on behalf of humankind. What does it mean that some in the church have begun to call the Christian tradition of God language androcentric? The church has never pretended to be other than androcentric. The traditional norm for gender in God language in public prayer can be established easily enough. Although exceptions to the norm can be found, there is clear preference within the biblical, liturgical, homiletical, catechetical, and theological traditions for male imaging of the triune God.

Do the facts of the liturgical tradition, its words and its prescribed and proscribed transactions, critically examined by liturgiologists, tell the contemporary church anything significant about male and female in human culture, about male and female in the church of Jesus Christ, about the mystery of an ineffable God? The outlook on divine and human personhood and human sexuality embodied in the structures of traditional worship demands examination, not trivialization. When we understand what we are communicating in the many symbolic languages of liturgy, we have to determine in what measure the outlook we proclaim in the liturgical assembly is the gospel truth.

9

The Public Language of Ministry

THE PHENOMENON OF STATUS ORIENTATION IN THE LANGUAGE OF ministry is apparent in the liturgical texts for the ordination of bishops, priests and deacons set out in the 1968 *Pontificale Romanum*. Those texts themselves reflect a long tradition within the church of making status distinctions within the community of believers and among those who serve it. This essay will investigate what is at issue in the phenomenon reflected in those texts. The investigation will have three parts. First, the liturgical texts themselves will raise the human question of ordering and community, and the function of language in the process of ordering. Next, selected historical data will be used to consider sacralization of ministry as an event in the institutional history of the church. This will lead finally to some theological reflection on the present situation of the language of ministry in the Roman Catholic ecclesial community.

LITURGICAL TEXTS

The language of ministry used in rites of ordination can be presumed to express the official self-understanding of the group which uses the language. Public ritual language sets out for all who participate in the rites the relationships which are known and affirmed within the group. Roman Catholic ordination rites are rites of passage according to their structure and function. In typical passage rites, some members of a community enter into

137

a new set of relationship with the group, and in the process, all the relationships within the group are modified and then reaffirmed.[1] The texts of the ordination rites use language which identifies as one of the outcomes of the liturgical action the status-elevation of the *ordinandi*.

The Texts

Each ordination rite in the 1968 *Pontificale Romanum* contains a unit in which the presiding minister addresses the assembly and asks them to focus on the meaning of the event in which they are participants. Language about elevation is prominent. At the ordination of a bishop, the assembly is enjoined:

> Pay careful attention to the position in the Church to which our brother is about to be promoted. (. . . *sedulo attendite, ad qualem in Ecclesia gradum frater noster sit provehendus.*)[2]

At the ordination of a presbyter, the episcopal injunction to the assembly is:

> Give careful consideration to the position to which they are to be promoted. (. . . *attente perpendite ad qualem in Ecclesia gradum sint ascensuri.*)[3]

A similar injunction is spoken to those gathered for the ordination of deacons:

> Reflect thoughtfully on the ministerial rank to which they are to be promoted. (. . . *attente cogitate ad qualem ministerii gradum sint ascensuri.*)[4]

1. V.W. Turner, *Dramas, Fields, and Metaphors: Symbolic Action in Human Society* (Ithaca, N.Y.: Cornell University Press, 1974) 273–275.
2. *Pontificale Romanum. De Ordinatione Diaconi, Presbyteri, et Episcopi.* Editio Typica (Typis Polyglottis Vaticanum, 1968; henceforth *PR*): Ordination of a Bishop, 18. English translations are the author's unless otherwise noted. Those of the International Commission for English in the Liturgy (ICEL) are given in footnotes. ICEL: "Consider carefully the position in the Church to which our brother is about to be raised."
3. *PR*: Ordination of a Presbyter, 14. ICEL: "Consider carefully the position to which they are to be promoted."
4. *PR*: Ordination of a Deacon, 14. ICEL: "Consider carefully the ministry to which they are to be promoted."

The new situation into which the ordinand is moving is in each case characterized as involving an ascent, a step upward, a promotion.

The candidates, too, are addressed with speech about elevation. The deacon-elect is told:

". . . you are being raised to the order of deacon." (. . . *vobis autem, filii dilectissimi, ad ordinem Diaconi provehendi. . . .*)[5]

The candidates for the presbyterate hear:

You are now to be advanced to the order of the presbyterate. (*Vos autem . . . ad ordinem Presbyterii provehendi. . . .*)[6]

The words spoken publicly to the bishop-elect break the pattern in an interesting way:

Beloved brother, keep in mind that you are chosen by the Lord, raised up from among the people, and appointed to act on their behalf in matters related to God. The designation bishop refers to a job to be done, not an honor. Therefore, it is necessary that a bishop should serve rather than rule. . . . (*Tu autem, frater, carissime, electus a Domino, cogita te ex hominibus esse assumptum et pro hominibus constitutum in iis quae sunt ad Deum. Episcopatus enim nomen est operis, non honoris, et Episcopum magis prodesse quam praeesse oportet . . .*)[7]

At the moment of reaching top rank, the one advancing is told, in phrases borrowed from the description of the levitical high priestly role fulfilled perfectly in Christ Jesus (Heb 5:1), that his is an extraordinary mediatorial role. Accordingly, he is cautioned about the paradoxical purpose of his elevated status: to be among the people as one who serves. This theme of service complements the theme of advancement, promotion, upward mobility

5. Ibid. ICEL translation given.
6. *PR:* Presbyter, 14. ICEL translation given.
7. *PR:* Bishop, 18. ICEL: "You . . . have been chosen by the Lord. Remember that you are chosen from among men [sic; Latin: *hominibus*] and appointed to act for men and women [sic; Latin: *hominibus*] in relation to God. The title of bishop is not one of honor, but of function, and therefore a bishop should strive to serve rather than to rule. . . ."

in the rite. However, it is only the latter theme which is the focus of this study.

The ritual address to the assembly and the ritual address to the *ordinandi* are not the only uses of language of ascent. In the consecratory prayers spoken on behalf of the *ordinandi*, God is proclaimed as the one who authorizes and maintains the work of selecting and promoting men for special purposes. The prayer of consecration of the deacon declares:

> Almighty God . . . you are the giver of preferments, the assigner of roles, the one who arranges official appointments. (*Deus . . . honorum dator, ordinem distributor officiorumque dispositor . . .*)[8]

The consecratory pryer continues, celebrating the existence of a three-fold ministry as one of the *mirabilia dei* for which God will be glorified.

The prayer of consecration of the presbyter affirms the same reason for praise of God:

> [you are] . . . the source of preferments, the one who assigns all ranks, the one through whom the whole world advances and everything is made secure . . . (. . . *honorum auctor et distributor omnium dignitatum, per quem proficiunt universa, per quem cuncta firmantur . . .*)[9]

God's gift of a structured order is further elaborated on this occasion, too:

> . . . when you appointed high priests to rule your people, you chose other men next to them in rank and dignity, to be with them and help them in their task . . . (. . . *ut cum Pontifices summos regendis populis praefecisses, ad eorum societatis et operis adiumentum sequentis ordinis viros et secundae dignitatis eligeres.*)[10]

In this particular prayer, the order is explicitly acknowledged to be both sacral and hierarchical. Not all the uses of elevation

---

8. *PR*: Deacon, 21. ICEL: "Almighty God . . . You are the source of all honor, you assign to each his rank, you give each his ministry."

9. *PR*: Presbyter, 22. ICEL: ". . . you are the source of every honor and dignity, of all progress and stability. . . ."

10. Ibid. ICEL translation given.

language cited up to this point have distinguished ranks among those who have been promoted. But here, the presbyter is "next . . . in rank" to the "high priests," that is, the bishops.

All of this is credited to divine action. Thus the rite of ordination of a bishop culminates in the proclamation:

> May God, who has brought you to share the high priesthood of Christ, pour out on you the oils of mystical anointing. May he nourish you with spiritual blessings. (*Deus, qui summi Christi sacerdotii participem te effecit, ipse te mysticae delibutionis liquore perfundat, et spiritualis benedictionis ubertate fecundet.*)[11]

As the consecratory prayer unfolds, the act of consecration is said to bring the ordinand to a spiritual summit. Divine election which began with Abraham, which continued in the choice of the rulers and priests of Israel, which culminated in the election of Jesus, and which was extended to apostles chosen personally by Jesus, has now been revealed again in this choice.[12]

The texts of the ordination rites deserve thorough examination for the total vision of Christian ministry they set out, and also for what they omit speaking of, namely the prior election of all the baptized. They are being investigated here only insofar as they exhibit a sustained understanding that ordination involves status elevation. That understanding is reflected in the verb choices that describe the nature of the transaction in which the ordinand is engaged; e.g., *sit provehendus* and *sint ascensuri*. The outcomes of the ritual actions are identified in terms of status—*honor, dignitas, officium, ordo,* and *gradus*—rather than in functional language, despite the admonition to the bishop. Furthermore, the texts express an understanding that those who participate in these rites are also distinguishable among themselves according to a scheme of ranking; e.g., *ad qualem in Ecclesia gradum; ad qualem ministeriis gradum; secundae dignitatis.* Finally, they convey a conviction that both the status elevation and the distinctions are the work of God; e.g., *Deus . . . auctor . . . et distributor; Deus . . . dator . . . distributor . . . dispositor.*

---

11. PR: Bishop, 28. ICEL: "God has brought you to share the high priesthood of Christ. May he pour out on you the oil of mystical anointing and enrich you with spiritual blessings."

12. Ibid., 26.

The history of this language deserves thorough examination. It is almost as old as the church; but it is not the language of the New Testament. The task of this essay is not to undertake a fully historical study of language traditions concerning ministry within the church. The focus will be rather on the human phenomenon of ranked or hierarchical ordering which is reflected in the language of the 1968 rites of ordination. While the language itself attributes the phenomenon it describes to divine wisdom and divine intervention, it is nevertheless human language and so invites reflection on the human community, which uses language in several ways: to name experience, to structure it, and to define it.

Human Community

Cultural anthropology characterizes human society as a process in which communities use ritual acts to express, among other things, the paradoxical twin truths of the *mythos* within which they live together: what unites them is prior to and is more fundamental than the distinctions among them, and yet the distinctions among them are essential to their continued existence as a people. The human community must live within the pull exerted by the truth of structure and the truth of prestructural realities which gives value to any ordered common life. Human communities are constituted and maintained through corporate symbolic acts which assert this vital tension as the basic condition of human social existence.[13]

Rites of ordination within the church are examples of this larger social phenomenon. The Christian community which gathers to ordain ministers for the community intends to affirm and to sanction distinctions among the members which are perceived to be essential to the very existence of the church. Ecclesial existence itself is valued because those who call themselves *ekklēsia* and ordain ministers for themselves believe themselves to be a holy people set apart from all other peoples for a mission. Accordingly, the factual phenomenon or ordering within the ecclesial community is not the matter under investigation here. What is under investigation is language which reflects the perceptions that some of those set apart for distinct ministries vital

13. Cf. Turner, 292–298. His terms for the polarity are structure and anti-structure.

to the well-being of the community have been divinely elevated, and that rank exists within the elevated group so that the relationships among the ordained are between superiors and inferiors. In the language of ecclesiastical documents, the church is not simply an ordered community, but one which is hierarchically ordered. Those not ordained into any of the ranks of the hierarchy are inferior to them all.

Language: Naming, Structuring and Defining Reality

The study of the many uses of a language has dominated recent Western philosophical inquiry. This essay cannot engage in a thorough exploration of such a major area of study. We must be content simply to point out and to summarize several considerations about the uses of language which are pertinent to our focus: status orientation in the public language of ministry in the Roman Catholic Church.

Original language is spoken language. In the kind of speaking which occurs within the situations of life, language provides the speaker the opportunity to take up a relationship with the experiences of corporate and personal life. Such speaking also allows the speaker the opportunity of structuring the experience in order to render it intelligible. Language used in the first way involves "naming." Language used for the second purpose involves "handling" experience.

Speakers use ordinary words, available language, for both the naming and the cognitive structuring of experience. In actual life situations, words inevitably function as metaphors. They are capable of partial discernments of truth, but the reality of unprecedented experience inevitably exceeds the structuring capabilities of available words. Thus, ordinary words have a wide range of approximate uses. In this lies their power and their weakness. Conceptual clarity can be achieved only if and when ordinary words are transformed into terms. Terminological language is a language of restricted meanings, of definition and precision.[14]

These considerations draw our attention to the fact that the original language of ministry in the formative stages of the church

14. F.J. van Beeck, *Christ Proclaimed: Christology as Rhetoric* (New York: Paulist, 1979) 64–104. This chapter contains a useful summary of pertinent issues in the functioning of language.

is a language of naming and structuring the unprecedented experience of ministry within the community. As the next section of the paper will show there is no single tradition of the original language of ministry. Only slowly does a consensus build about a common set of words to name the experience of ministry. Only slowly does a common set of ministerial experiences undergird the emerging common language. Even more slowly does the language of ministry receive precise definition which restricts its applicability in the speech of the community.

The related matter of the public use of a single set of words to name, handle, and define ecclesial experience is a particularly complex matter. The liturgical event as a moment of religious celebration of the saving mystery of Christ quite rightly uses language which is rich with metaphoric ambiguity. Language which is expansive in its applicability allows ritual participants to recognize through the words of their common life their own participation in the ministry of the church. At the same time the liturgical event of ordination, a rite of passage, is an occasion designed to introduce structural distinction and difference and limit into the community. It may thereby seem to demand language which defines, language which is technical and restricted in its applications. Words and ceremonial behavior joined together serve as language in this regard. Furthermore, the language proclaimed in the liturgical assembly inevitably carries with it a divine warrant. The community which speaks and listens and acts together in worship believes that what is said and done there reflects the intent of God for them and calls for faithful and obedient response.

How is the status-oriented language of ministry found in public rites to be understood? Is it allusive, descriptive, prescriptive, restrictive? A brief survey of the development of the original language of ministry is a necessary foundation for any reflection on the theological significance of the traditional language of ministry.

SACRALIZATION OF MINISTRY

Much New Testament research in the past decade has been directed to the matter of tracing the development of the Gospel ministry. However, less scholarly attention has been focused on the process whereby some of the NT language came to define a sacral order. That process will be the subject of the middle section of this essay.

Flux in Forms and Language: The NT Evidence

Scholarly consensus exists that the communities of the New Testament period were indeed organized or ordered. There is also agreement that several patterns of institutional order co-existed and evolved independently in the churches reflected in the New Testament. It is not the purpose of this section of the essay to weigh the merits of each of several possible interpretations offered to explain the data on which this exegetical consensus is based.[15] One position, that of André Lemaire, will be followed for convenience in the presentation of pertinent material. Lemaire proposes on the basis of his own extensive studies that the distinctive institutional patterns of ministry reflect not only different epochs in the life of the churches but also different ethno-cultural settings of the earliest communities. Whatever the case, different clusters of words name and interpret distinctive experiences of ministry within local communities. The language for speaking of ministry in the New Testament is neither technical nor precise. Thus, the ranking of fixed ministries hierarchically necessarily postdates the witness of the New Testament.[16]

What are the data that invite Lemaire to these judgments? A schematization of three time periods (30–45; 45–65; and 65–100) and three settings (Jerusalem, Antioch, and Asia Minor) provides him some insight into the development of public language for the gospel ministry.

The Jerusalem community in the years 30–45 A.D. comprised two ethno-cultural groups, the "Hebrews" (Palestinian Jews who spoke Aramaic) and the "Hellenists" (Greek-speaking Jews of

15. See, for example, R.E. Brown, "Episkopē and Episkopos—The New Testament Evidence," *Theological Studies* 41 (1980) 322–338; J. Delorme, *Le ministère et les ministères selon le Nouveau Testament* (Paris: Editions du Seuil, 1974); A. Lemaire, "The Ministries in the New Testament: Recent Research," *Biblical Theology Bulletin* 3 (1973) 138.

16. A. Lemaire, "L'Eglise apostolique et les ministères," *Revue de Droit Canonique* 23 (1973) 28.

the Diaspora). The original Jerusalem ministry of "the Twelve" spawned the parallel Jerusalem ministry of "the Seven" as a response to the internal ethno-cultural conflict attested to in Acts. Each group brought the good news of God's action in Jesus to the synagogues of its own people. Each developed its own treasury for the poor (Acts 6:1–11). And each provoked violent persecution from within the synagogues. The "Hebrews" Peter, James and John were arrested; the "Hellenist" Stephen was stoned.

Under these pressures the early order at Jerusalem gave way. When the Hellenists scattered, the institution of "the Seven" vanished, leaving its traces only in language. Language also preserved the memory of "the Twelve," an institution evidently rooted in the Galilean ministry of Jesus himself. Paul, for example, referred to "the Twelve" in the primitive credal formula of 1 Cor 15:3–5.[17] But when Paul actually dealt with the Jerusalem church, the leadership he knew in the decade of the '50s consisted of a council of elders.

A second period of ministerial development occurred in the period 45–65 A.D. Two centers, responding to local circumstances, had begun to speak in distinctive ways about the exercise of the Gospel ministry. The church in Antioch faced for the first time the task of incorporating non-Jews; its leading ministries were those of prophet and teacher. At Jerusalem, leadership among Jewish Christians developed through the innovtive appropriation and adaptation of the existing Jewish institution of the presbyterate or council of elders to meet new needs.

At Antioch, the prophet's task was to exhort, to console, and to build up the "Christian" community. The setting for this ministry was the Christian assembly. The forms the ministry took included the opening up of the scripture as the living word of God addressed to the gathered community and the proclamation of the great thanksgiving prayer, the *eucharistia*.[18] The teacher at Antioch was rather something of a technical specialist working in a non-liturgical setting. The teacher's exposition, *didachē*, provided formal knowledge of scripture according to Jewish methods of interpretation. Teaching was Paul's first ministry in the church at Antioch.

The prophet and teachers secured the community at Antioch.

17. Ibid. 20–21.
18. Ibid. 24.

The community so secured inaugurated the mission to the Diaspora and to the Greek-speaking world in general. The ministry of the apostle emerged to provide this missionary service. Barnabas and Paul were among those set apart for apostolic mission. Their first task was to announce the Gospel, then to form a community of those who accepted the good news; but they were to remain only until an organized community was esablished, and then move on, maintaining contact through letters and visits by co-workers. Paul's account to the Corinthian church of the basic ministerial structure may reflect the Antiochene scheme of values during this great missionary era: first are apostles, then teachers (I Cor 12:28).[19]

During the same era James and the elders ministered to the Jerusalem community as its presbyters. In Palestinian Judaism the presbyterate was a familiar institution, a college or assembly which exercised power within a political community. The elders of a village as well as the elders of the whole people exercised legislative power through interpretations of Torah in both civil and religious matters. They regularly exercised judicial power through excommunication.

In the *mythos* of late Judaism the "elders of the whole people," the Jewish Sanhedrin, were understood to have divine authority. The origins of the Sanhedrin, a literal "council of Seventy," were found in the express command of YHWH to Moses to share some of his Spirit (Num 11:16–30). These "elders of the whole people" were drawn from among both priestly and non-priestly families. Thus the presbyterate included laymen, regularly pharisees. The president of the Sanhedrin was the High Priest.[20] Elsewhere, the head of a local council was simply the chief *hēgoumenos*.

The emerging "presbyterate" of the Jerusalem church served the beleagured new community by guarding its teaching and practice so that these were faithful to and did not negate the scriptures, and also by taking care of the treasury and disbursements for the poor.[21] Ironically, to give dignity, meaning, and credibility to their efforts to build and to maintain a new com-

19. Ibid. 22–23; also "Recent Research" 144.
20. A. Lemaire, *Les Ministères aux origines de l'Eglise: Naissance de la triple hierarchie: évêques, presbytres, diacres*, Lectio Divina 68 (Paris, 1971) 21–27.
21. Lemaire, "L'Eglise apostolique" 24.

munity of faith in the holy city this marginal group of Jewish sectarians either boldly or naively had appropriated the identity of the Jerusalem council of elders. The name *presbyteroi* resonated with reference to the great Jewish religious-legal institution; the overtones were heard in later stages of development.

Still these two centers at Jerusalem and Antioch did not provide comprehensive ministerial models in this expansionist era of early Christianity. Thus, a third pattern of ministry took shape among the churches of the apostolic mission in which Paul was a principal actor; it left its linguistic traces in the New Testament phrase *episkopoi kai diakonoi* (Phil 1:1). The words were taken from the language of daily life. In ordinary speech, the generic word *episkopos* was available for designating anyone who exercised a function of supervision or inspection.[22] It had no particular or peculiar religious usage. *Diakonos* was a word of wide-ranging usefulness in ordinary Greek speech. While it might designate persons with social inferiority, e.g., employees and domestics, it was also used for merchants and for pagan priests whose work was service to the whole people. It was used indiscriminately to name male and female. When it was used in a religious context, sometimes but not always the Greek *diakonos* names one who was involved in the sacred meals of the cult.[23] Accordingly, in this middle era of ecclesial development, two ordinary Greek words, *episkopos* and *diakonis* were expanded in their reference. Christians employed them to name the new social and religious reality of the first century: the gospel ministry being exercised within the churches outside Jerusalem and Antioch, but united with these centers through the itinerant apostles.

Language remained fluid throughout the era, directed always to naming and handling evolving ministerial experiences. Evidence indicates that Paul and Barnabas, for example, organized the local ministers of the gospel into a quasi-presbyterate (Acts 14:23; cf. I Thess 5:12). Yet it is unlikely that councils of elders in the churches born from the apostolic mission could have imitated in every aspect the presbyteral ministry as it was exercised

22. Lemaire, "Recent Research" 145–146; cf. "Les Ministères aux origines" 27–30.

23. Lemaire, "Les Ministères aux origines" 31–34; cf. "Recent Research" 145–146.

at Jerusalem. On the contrary, differences in understanding about the requirements of the Gospel ministry are what precipitated the crisis of missionary expansion. The conflict was resolved through agreement that the one ministry of guiding the church must have flexibility in its exercise (Gal 2:1–8; cf. Acts 15).

In a third stage of ecclesial organization and development, 65–100 A.D., the presbyteral institution and the word "presbyter" spread from the Jewish-Christian center through the whole church.[24] It was a period of consolidation in matters of organization and ministry. What was at issue was assuring both the authenticity and the strength of the local churches after the deaths of the original Twelve and of the first apostles. Some in each local community were needed to direct the *ekklēsia* according to the norm of the Gospel message, which was still unfolding in its implications through their teaching. Presbyteral organization provided a needed structure.

The word "presbyter" had had a long history of technical use within Judaism to designate the institution of authority, dating from the word choice of the translators of the Septuagint. But the word had also survived in the ordinary language of the Greek-speaking world. The word itself is a comparative. The *presbyteros* is elder in comparison with the *presbys*, an old one. So it designated the senior among peers or colleagues or adults in a family. *Presbyteros* was also commonly used for another comparative purpose, namely to distinguish the failing and defecs of *neōteros*—the younger—from the experience, wisdom, and ability to guide which is characteristic of the *presbyteros*.

The word scarcely had a technical use in the Hellenistic world of the first century. When it was employed in the political sphere, in Asia Minor and Greece, it meant to designate maturity and wisdom. However, the word had gained some capacity for definition of social structures in Egypt. Evidence exists that members of a representative or administrative group within a community or an association were called *presbyteroi*.[25] So a social and linguistic context existed outside Judaism and the church of the "Hebrews" for using the word *presbyteros* to designate those responsible for Gospel ministry.

24. Lemaire, "L'Eglise apostolique" 20; "Recent Research" 153.
25. Lemaire, "Les Ministères aux origines" 17–21.

The need for an identifiable head or chief of the local presbyterate also intensified when the apostle to a church was no
longer living. The function of local headship had, of course,
begun to emerge earlier. Language is again a chief witness to
the development. Verbal substantives like *proistamenos, prōtoka-
thedritēs*, and *prokathēmenos* point to the emergence of someone
from within the assembly. Consensus about the naming of that
one apparently came more slowly. The use of *hēgoumenos* and
prohēgoumenos in Hebrews (17:7, 17, 24), in the first letter of
Clement (XXI, 6) and in the *Shepherd* of Hermas (II/2,6 and III/
9,7) support the hypothesis that *hēgemōn* was an early word
choice of the church at Rome, where that literature originated.[26]
In the church at Antioch, Ignatius was clear and decisive about
an alternative word choice: the one who is first or head is the
one called *episkopos*. Ignatius' preference eventually prevailed.
However, that development is reflected outside New Testament
texts, and so discussion of it must be deferred.

In summary, current research on New Testament texts related
to the original language of ministry yields the following data.
Clusters of words appear which designate various operative arrangements within the local churches for maintaining the Gospel
ministry. The Twelve and the Seven ministered at Jerusalem in
an early period, perhaps 30–45 A.D. The *episkopoi kai diakonoi*,
dependent on the apostles, were the contemporaries and counterparts of the prophets and teachers in the local churches established through the apostolic mission. In Jerusalem *presbyteroi*
administered the community. The extension of a local presbyteral order throughout the entire church occurred in the period
65–100 A.D. In the meeting of the two patterns of ministry, both
were transmuted. Slowly, with the deaths of the apostles, local
leadership established itself within the presbyteral structure. No
early consensus developed over the naming of this ministry of
local leadership. Thus, New Testament literature uses a range
of words like *episkopos, presbyteros, hēgoumenos, proistamenos*, to
designate local leadership without any technical precision or any
clear definition.

The phenomenon of community organization is everywhere

26. Lemaire, "Recent Research" 145–146; cf. "Les Ministères aux origines"
27–30, 169, 193.

evident. Some within the *ekklēsia* clearly have special responsibility for the Gospel ministry, precisely because the good news revealed in Jesus is what undergirds the community's existence. Along those in the *ekklēsia* with ministerial responsibility, there are further specifications of different ministries. But all forms of ministry, including the ministry of leadership, rise and recede according to what is needed for the different communities to be maintained in the Gospel hope.

The language of ministry does accord different relative values to the ministries—e.g., "first are apostles, then prophets, then teachers"—and it acknowledges the inevitability of a focus of leadership within a group. But the value placed on different ministries reflects the community's perception of how the Gospel is to be served. Among conceivable alternatives some form of ordering ministry had to shape the life of the local church at each given moment. But the language does not warrant conclusions about a single order, divinely mandated, or of any absolute ranking among those who serve the community.

Good Order: The Second and Third Centuries

If neither a stable language, a normative church order, nor a formal hierarchy among ministers is evident in the New Testament literature, all of these realities find expression in the literary witness of the next several Christian generations. These three developments will be considered in turn.

The seeds of stability in the language of ministry, normative church order, and hierarchy are all clearly planted in the letters of Ignatius of Antioch written at the turn of the second century. In his correspondence, Ignatius advocated a well-delineated ministerial structure for the local church. At the head is the one named *episkopos;* he is surrounded by the council of presbyters; he is assisted by deacons. The people for their part are to submit themselves (*hypotassomenon*) to this arrangement.[27]

Although Ignatius' choice of *episkopos* and *diakonos* might be explained in terms of the *koinē* usage evident in the New Testament, he clearly intended to expand the field of meaning for these words beyond secular to specific religious usage, indeed

---

27. Lemaire, "Les Ministères aux origines" 169–174, 199; cf. Ignatius of Antioch to Polycarp. VI, 1; to the Trallians, II. 1; Ephesians, II, 1.

even to venture sacralization. In his letter to the Trallians, for example, the *episkopos* is called "image of God," the *presbyteroi* are the "senate of God" and the "assembly of the apostles," and the deacons are to be "revered as Jesus Christ." His interpretative referents are not consistent, however. The Philadelphians are told that the bishop represents both God and Jesus Christ, the presbyteral senate is a tribunal of reconciliation for sinners, and the deacons are envoys.[28] Clearly his vocabulary choices were well-established. How words were to be understood with reference to the divine work in and through the ministry of the local church was not yet so clear.

Ignatius of Antioch, himself an *episkopos*, held an unquestionably high regard for the role. Contemporary correspondence revals that not all the local churches of his day shared either his administrative style or his estimate of its significance. When he wrote to the church at Smyrna, setting out his doctrine that the *episkopos* was the one through whom God attaches himself to the local church, he addresses it to Polycarp as *episkopos*. However, Polycarp's self-designation differed. When he wrote to the church of the Philippians, he wrote in his own name and in the name of those who were "presbyters with him," with no advertance to an *episkopos* functioning apart from or over them. In a fourth locale, Rome, the word *episkopos* was apparently not yet in use at the turn of the second century. In the extant writings from that church, leadership or headship was designated through the word *hēgoumenos*. Thus, only a retrospective reading of the early second-century witness can find an authoritative position in the teaching of Ignatius concerning a three-fold hierarchically ordered ministry. In his own era, he was one witness to the continuing evolution of language, structure, and function. Nevertheless, the position he advocated established the trajectory which extends to the church of Vatican II and the language of its rites of ordination. What circumstances fostered the developments?

Pierre Nautin proposes that it was the social realities pressing on the second and third century Christian communities which supported the consolidation of local church order under the

28. Lemaire, "Les Ministères aux origines" 167–171; cf. Ignatius of Antioch to the Trallians, III, 1; to the Philadelphians, IV; VII, 1; VIII, 1; X, 20.

headship of a monarchial *episkopos*. Alexandre Faivre maintains that it was growth in numbers and so in new ministerial needs that fostered development of "lesser ministries" in the same era, and created a correlative need for a scheme of distinction of status and definition of roles. A summary account of developments both "at the top" and "at the bottom" is in order.

Ignatius of Antioch had insisted that nothing was to be done by the presbyters and deacons of the churches without the approval of the bishop. Practically, this meant that the overseer or chief became the final arbiter in community disputes, approved choices of "marriage in the Lord" and made judgments about the distribution of alms to the poor and about wages for the presbyters and deacons from the treasury of the church. Because he had both patrons and clients, money and authority to make decisions, he acquired the social status of any powerful person. Civil authorities as well as church members dealt with him accordingly. The dynamic of episcopal ascendancy, says Nautin, was sociological in its origins. Yet a culturally grounded sacralizing tendency quickly gave episcopal ascendancy a foundation in divine wisdom.[29]

The Hellenistic cultural sense of divine order (*kosmos* or *taxis*) which is reflected in the hierarchical cosmologies of contemporary philosophical systems—Stoic, Neo-Platonic, and Hermetic—found its way into discussions of church order, too. Interest in such order is evident in the pastoral letters of the New Testament. However, this cultural assumption that the arrangement (*taxis*) of society was the work of God was a dominant motif in much Christian literature of the second and third centuries.[30] Early writers like Clement of Rome readily exploited the cultural horizon of divine cosmic arrangement to speak of the

29. P. Nautin, "L'evolution des ministères au IIe et au IIIe siècle," *Revue de Droit Canonique* 23 (1973) 48–50, 54–56; cf. Ignatius to Polycarp, V, 2.

30. The role of the household codes in the development of church order is discussed in C. Osiek, "Relation of Charism to Rights and Duties in the New Testament Church," in *The Jurist* 41:2 (1981). See also Nautin, "L'evolution"; also R. Roques, *L'Univers Dionysien: Structure hiérarique du monde selon le Pseudo-Denys* (Paris: Aubier, 1954) 36; P. van Beneden, *Aux Origines d'une terminologie sacrementelle ordo, ordinare, ordinatio dans la littérature chrétienne avant 313* (Louvain: Spicilegium Sacrum, 1974) 14–15. Cf. Clement to the Corinthians 20.2; 40.1; 48, 1.

Christian realities of creation and redemption. Initially this use of *taxis* in Christian writing was non-technical, even exploratory, as authors sought to determine its usefulness for understanding the theological significance of the already operative three-fold ministry of bishop, presbyters, and deacons within the church.

Latin writers of this era like Tertullian translated *taxis* through the common Latin *ordo*. In doing so they refocused the meaning field of *taxis* but also reinterpreted the word *ordo*. Previously, the Latin *ordo*, unlike the Greek *taxis*, had little cosmological valence. It specified a social group or an organized class, or some part of that group or class which had responsibility for its direction, or a social hierarchy.[31]

Thus, the common Latin *ordo* fitted the sociological phenomenon of ecclesial ministry on several scores. The bishops, presbyters and deacons together exercised a ministerial function in the local church. As a part within the whole they were immediately distinguishable from those who had no such public responsibility. They were equivalently an *ordo*. Furthermore, they were differentiated themselves, "arranged" according to roles and functions. Such arrangements were open to interpretation as a divinely constituted hierarchy when *taxis* and *ordo* were played against each other in discussions of the significance of the *klēroi*.[32]

The first systematic presentation of Christian ministry as a manifestation of the hierarchical divine economy would come from the pen of the fifth century Pseudo-Dionysius, and would be taken up by successive generations of medieval thinkers. Between the second and the fifth centuries, socially induced developments in church order occurred which later seemed to warrant such a comprehensive interpretation. The *Apostolic Tradition* of Hippolytus, product of Roman church life in the late second and early third centuries, contains traces of what was happening. Faivre's interpretation of the document in the context of its derivatives offers a plausible account of the significance of those developments for the birth and eventual maturation of the institution of an ecclesiastical hierarchy.

What data from the *Apostolic Tradition* shed light on the matter?

31. van Beneden 2–4, 13–14.
32. Ibid. 14–15; cf. p. 44, n. 99.

First, Hippolytus wrote of a church some of whose members were already clergy. He knew where the distinguishing line was to be drawn. *Klēroi* are those who take part in the offering. They were publicly recognized as a distinct group because the *episkopos* had laid hands on them in the assembly. Others whose service in the community was public but unrelated to the offering are not *klēroi*: widows, readers, virgins, sub-deacons, and healers.[33] According to Hippolytus, virgins had claimed their place in the community by their own choice; healers, by the evident truth of their service. Widows, readers, and sub-deacons were to be installed by the *episkopos* to render service. But he deliberately declined to lay his hands upon them.

Several developments are notable in Hippolytus' presentation of what he considers the proper arrangement of things. First, differences and limits were an acknowledged part of ecclesial life. Second, value judgments continued to be made about the services performed by community members, although the values were different from those established at Antioch in the first century, where "first were apostles, then prophets, then teachers." Now the focus of service is not the Gospel but "the offering."[34]

In a third development, public demarcation of ecclesial status was being established through the use of a gesture or its absence. By it, the community had been differentiated into a top and a bottom. Even at the top, rank among the *klēroi* was further refined through this same gesture. While all had hands laid on them, only one rank had authority to extend the gesture. This assertion of episcopal prerogative implies a fourth development. The prerogative rests on a claim to divine power, which the bishop may confer and delegate as he sees fit for the good order of the community.[35]

If the claim to power calls for some explanation, Hippolytus provided it in his prayer for the ordination of the bishop. That explanation has more than antiquarian significance, since the ordination rite of 1968 draws deeply from the third century text

33. I. de la Potterie, "L'origine et le sense primitif du mot 'laïc'", *Nouvelle Revue Théologique* 80 (1958) 847–53. He notes the original identity of *laikos* as that part of the *laos* not consecrated for the service of cult.

34. A. Faivre, *Naissance d'Une Hiérarchie: les Premières Etapes du Cursus Clérical* (Paris: Beauchesne, 1977) 58–61.

35. Ibid. 54–56.

as an expression of the faith of the church even in the twentieth century. Hippolytus' prayer celebrated God's compassion preceding and establishing the order to all things, including the order of his church.[36] In his compassion and for his glory God selected a people and then chose rulers of the people and priests for the sanctuary. These were to receive a share of his Spirit. The original world Hippolytus called upon for the language of his prayer is clearly that of the High Priest presiding over the Sanhedrin of late Judaism and officiating at the temple cult. His prayer also incorporated the self-understanding of the Sanhedrin, namely that they were descendant from the patriarchs and prophets. What Hippolytus might have, but did not evoke, is equally significant. He does not celebrate the divine disorder of Pentecost. For whatever reasons, his prayer celebrates an *ekklēsia* more orderly than the *ekklēsia* of the new age in which all the *laos* of God unexpectedly have received some share of the Spirit of God.[37]

Hippolytus' interpretative frame for the preferred order of the church at Rome at the turn of the new century is neither self-explanatory nor original. It represents one emphasis among available alternatives, evidently a culturally favored one. He is witness to the contemporary reinterpretation of the early "institutions" for the Gospel ministry. The original patterns of apostles, prophets, and teachers, *episkopoi kai diakonoi,* and local presbyterates leading an odd sort of priestly people have been overlaid by the sacerdotal and sacralized images of late Judaism. Ranks of levites, priests, and a high priest presenting the offering had caught the imaginations of Hellenistic churches in the second century; it would capture them by the end of the fifth. This occurred even as Judaism was abandoning the horizon of a sacralized sacerdotal locus of spiritual power—albeit against its will—and risking the very possibility it had rejected in the original preaching of the Gospel.

Whatever the irony, the Hellenistic church had to take shape and find language to express its self-understanding, and it did so. The image world of a sacralized social order, that found in

36. B. Botte, ed. *La Tradition Apostolique de Saint Hippolyte,* LQF 39 (Munster Westfalen: Aschendorffsche Verlagsbuchhandlung, 1963) 3. Cf. *PR:* Bishop, 26.
37. de la Potterie 841–842.

the ancient scriptures and in defunct institutions, provided a conceptual buffer against cultural disorientation. But it also blocked memory of the radical newness of the original experience of resurrection faith with its unexpected breakthroughs of the Spirit of God. Hippolytus' church was still familiar with the possible disruptive choice of God's Spirit manifesting itself in the confessor of the faith. He himself did not try to suppress the phenomenon by presuming to lay hands on one whom God had chosen independently of the *episkopos*. However, he did insert the confessor within the local presbyterate, finding him a place within the established order. Genuine spiritual power had to be subordinated to the bishop, locus of all legitimate spiritual authority in the world of orthodox Hellenistic Christianity.

A World to Live In: Fourth to Sixth Centuries

In 313 A.D. the free exercise of religion was authorized in the empire; in 381 the emperor imposed the religion of the apostle Peter on all the peoples of the empire. These political developments challenged the church structurally, pressing it to organize itself for its new public role. In addition to adjustments related to sheer numerical growth, key organizational developments contributed further to status orientation within church order and in the public language of ministry. First was the establishment of an expanded clerical *ordo* as a public institution. Accompanying it was the process of juridical, liturgical, and theological legitimization of a hierarchy within that new *ordo*. A summary of these developments is appropriate.

The exploratory and clearly metaphorical use of the word *ordo* among Christian writers of earlier generations—Tertullian tried *ordo episcoporum, ordo ecclesiae, ordo sacerdotalis, ordo ecclesiasticus, ordo viduarum,* and *ordo Melchisedec*—became precise technical language to identify a public institution in the late fourth and early fifth centuries.[38] An order of clerics gradually took its place alongside the old Roman *ordines* of senators and knights in the decaying empire. Clerics eventually formed a distinct social group, ranked internally, for the performance of distinct public service. The process of constituting the new *ordo* as a public

38. J. Gaudemet, "De la liberté constantinienne à une Eglise d'Etat," *Revue de Droit Canonique* 23 (1973) 60–61; cf. van Beneden 15.

institution was effected by both civil and ecclesiastical legislation. Law did not merely reflect life, but performed a creative function in this matter. Thus, the Theodosian Code (438), reflecting civil developments through the fourth century, specified: ". . . *qui divino cultu ministeria impendunt, id est hi qui clerici appelantur"* (16.2).[39]

Extant church orders document the development of the public *ordo* through their listings of who was to be named in the litanies, in what sequence members of the assembly were to receive communion, and how and by whom persons were to be ordained or installed in the various positions; church councils and synods legislated who were suitable candidates. In Gaudemet's judgment, the first ecclesiastical legislation in this formative era of "Christendom" may have served primarily for the emulation of imperial style itself, organizing, distinguishing and defining, and legislating. In any case, the practical impact of early rounds of legislation about clerics was not strong. Exceptions were common; regional differences flourished; new rounds followed on earlier decisions, repeating them and modifying them.[40]

But some ground was gained. An earlier understanding of *klēroi* as those who serve the offering was extended and then redefined through a series of distinctions. Early on, the group called *klēroi* had been coextensive with the ordained, those on whom hands had been laid by the bishop. But the *Apostolic Constitutions* (Book VIII 2.12), dating from the end of the fourth century, witnesses to an expanded clerical group whose special standing in the community was publicly recognized in the arrangement for the distribution of the *eulogia* remaining after the celebration of the mysteries: the bishop received four portions, presbyters three, deacons two, and others one: sub-deacon, lector, psalmist, and deaconess. The distribution scheme, it was claimed, showed honor expressive of the dingity of each in a church which is not a school of disorder (*ataxias*) but of *eutaxias*, felicitous arrangement. Notably, even as the group of *klēroi* had expanded, it too had been sorted into a top and bottom. Nevertheless, despite the protestations of the text, the bottom was not

39. Faivre 279–292.
40. Ibid. 64.

yet as clearly ordered as the top. That matter would occupy several more generations.[41]

One of the points of uncertainty in the fourth and fifth centuries was the matter of women's place in a well-ordered imperial church. If the Syrian *Apostolic Constitutions* (VIII 19.2) had room for laying hands on women, situating them among the *klēroi*, albeit at the bottom, the Canons of Hippolytus (ca. 340), while ostensibly maintaining an old distinction, had actually introduced a new one. In that Egyptian schema for a well-ordered church, while the chosen (*klēroi*) included many groups, only bishops, priests, and deacons are ordained through the laying on of hands. However, the Canons also pronounce unequivocally that ordination is only for men.[42]

Gaudemet and others have noted that the process of excluding women altogether in the emerging scheme of things was not without its difficulties. Local monophysite and nestorian churches of Syria and priscillianist and montanist churches in the west certainly continued including women among their deacons and presbyters during this era. Moreover, repeated civil and ecclesiastical legislation through the fourth and fifth centuries, including explicit condemnations of clerics who allowed women ministerial functions reserved to men, suggests that the exclusion of women from the clerical *ordo* was disruptive of actual ministerial practice in many places in the empire.[43]

Uncertainty about good order was also evident in efforts to determine the relative significance of the various services among the lesser ministries "at the bottom" of the emerging clerical *ordo*. These were forming a pool from which the higher orders might draw as needed to maintain their numbers. Sub-deacon

41. Faivre 81. Cf. F.X. Funk, ed., *Didascalia et Constitutiones Apostolorum* (Paderborn, 1895; reprint, Torino: Bottega d'Erasmo, 1959) Book VIII, 31,2.

42. Faivre 71–73; cf. J.M. Hanssens, *La Liturgie D'Hippolyte*, Orientalia Christiana Anelecta 155 (Roma: pont. Institutum Orientalium Studiorum, 1959) 73–75.

43. Gaudemet, p. 63; cf. R. Gryson, *The Ministry of Women in the Early Church* (Collegeville: Liturgical Press, 1976); also E. Schüssler-Fiorenza, "Wood, Spirit, and Power: Women in Early Christian Communities," in R. Ruether and E. McLaughlin, ed., *Women of Spirit* (New York: Simon and Schuster, 1979) 30–70.

and reader vied for status, each gaining ascendancy or losing it in different local churches during the fourth century. The matter was apparently settled in favor of the sub-deacon according to a cultic scale of values in which the handling of sacred vessels for the offering had greater significance than the presentation of the sacred text.[44]

Consolidating the *cursus* for clerics occupied bishops of the fifth and early sixth centuries. At Rome, with no women under consideration to disturb the metaphor, Sosimus, Celestine, and Leo cast the matter in military terms in which good performance and good conduct at entry ranks were rewarded with promotion and perhaps eventually admission to the highest.[45] At the close of the period, the bureaucratic notion of an orderly *cursus* through which men could advance by grades was firmly in possession. The notion was supported by a range of decretals and other legal texts (many falsified for the sake of advocacy, according to the custom of the day) and effected through liturgical rites marking each step of advancement.[46]

What has not yet been addressed directly is the specific role of concepts of hierarchy in the process of sacralization of the Gospel ministries. This sacralization process was concurrent with but not identical to the development of the clerical *ordo* as a public institution. Since the idea of sacred hierarchy is captured linguistically throughout the texts of the 1968 Roman Catholic ordination rites cited earlier, it needs to be accounted for. It is no more self-explanatory, from a twentieth century perspective, than Hippolytus' presentation of Gospel ministry in the super-imposed sacerdotal images borrowed from an obsolescent Jewish institution or the fifth century presentation of Christian ministry as a graded public *ordo*, a form of civil service system in which males who meet specific qualifications ascend by degrees.

In reflecting on the phenomenon of ranked ministries, Faivre asserts that it is a fact of the ancient world that groups were composed of unequal members who were inevitably orderd hierarchically. L. Dumont, citing the sociologist Talcott Parsons for support, argues that social stratification necessarily occurs in all

44. Faivre 96.
45. Ibid. 330.
46. Ibid. 327–352.

epochs.[47] What distinguishes the "ancients" from Parsons is the interpretation given to the phenomenon of internal ranking in a group. Contemporary sociological theory explains stratification within a group in functional terms. Every group distinguished from others by some self-understanding and some goals makes practical judgments about what has relative significance for promoting its good and its goals. Groups necessarily organize to survive. Contemporary anthropological theory explains that social groups are always in process, maintaining themselves precisely to the degree that they attend not only to group structure but also to the prior reality which gives them identity as a group for which the internal order exists and because of which it may change.

Hellenistic cosmological theories provided a different account of the significance of ranked ministries. They were earthly manifestations of heavenly hierarchies. Although Dionysius, pseudonymous author of the extant fifth century treaties on this topic, has been credited with having introduced the *mythos* of neoplatonic hierarchy as a useful construct for interpreting the ecclesiastical developments of his day,[48] he did not create a new field of experience. Rather, he provided culturally congenial language to name and to handle theologically the organizational and aspirational realities of the late Hellenistic *ekklēsia*. Through the appropriation of the language of hierarchies, subtle but significant shifts occurred in the understanding of the purpose of ranked ministries.

Consensus exists among scholars that the mystical neo-platonic ideas which had gained authority in the East in this period reflected broad cultural concerns about nearness to God.[49] Accordingly, in the grand design of Ps-Dionysius' text, the purpose of the earthly ecclesiastical hierarchies was to assure progressive

47. Ibid. 57; cf. L. Dumont, *Homo Hierarchicus* (University of Chicago Press, 1970) 19–20.

48. Ibid. 172.

49. G. Tellenbach, *Church, State and Christian Society in the Time of the Investiture Contest* (Oxford: B. Blackwell, 1948) 8; cf. Y. Congar, "The Sacralization of Western Society in the Middle Ages," *Concilium* 47 (New York: Paulist, 1969) 67; also Congar, "Les Ministères d'Eglise dans le monde féodal jusqu'à la reforme gregorienne," *Revue de Droit Canonique* 23 (1973) 82.

divinization: assimilation to, participation in, and union with God.[50]

The triadic form of neo-platonic schemata had to be trimmed to the empirical phenomenon of the church. So Ps-Dionysius posited a double, not a triple, triadic form for the ecclesiastical hierarchy. An active triad, the bishop, priests, and deacons, worked on the passive triad of monks, laity, and the catechumens along with their penitential counterparts, in proportion to the powers each had received. In the active triad, the episcopal hierarch was said to possess a triple spiritual power to purify, to illuminate, and to unify. He conferred two shares of that power on the next in rank but only one share on the deacon. They in turn used these powers on those in the inferior receptive hierarchy.[51]

Orthodox theologian John Meyendorff has called Ps-Dionysius' hierarch a Gnostic because his spiritual power was not a function of the inner structure of his ecclesial community but his personal possession. Meyendorff goes further, attributing the "magical clericalism" of the West to the later influence of Ps-Dionysius on medieval speculations about the progressive powers of the ecclesiastical hierarchy. He suggests that further research is needed in order to establish the measure of considered and of unreflective Ps-Dionysian influence on the development of Western ecclesiology in both the scholastic and post-scholastic periods.[52] Certainly, his scheme of progressive hierarchical power is not unfamiliar in Western theology. Nor is his localized interpretation of ministerial mediation as residing squarely in the person of the hierarch. The episcopal ordinand who is told through the text of the 1968 Roman Pontifical that it is his responsibility to act for people in matters pertaining to God is a linear descendant of Dionysius' hierarch.

As noted earlier, the range of concerns involved in Christian appropriation of neo-platonic schemes of hierarchy was broader

50. Roques, *L'Univers Dionysien* 92–100.

51. Faivre 174; cf. Roques 99–100.

52. J. Meyendorff, *Christ in Eastern Christian Thought* (Washington: Corpus, 1969) 79–82; cf. G. Thery, "L'entrée du Ps.-Denys en Occident," *Melanges Madonnet*, II. Bibl. Thomiste XIV (Paris, 1930) 23–30.

than longstanding interest in orderly ministry in the *ekklēsia*. Nearness to God was an emerging preoccupation. Within the horizon of hierarchical interpretations of ministries, Ps-Dionysius was able to address this distinctive cultural interest. Nothing in the hierarchical world was accidental or optional; every arrangement was *taxis hiera*, holy disposition coming from God and so *thesmos*, norm or command. People and things had their place by divine choice. But the manifest ecclesiastical arrangement and the situation of each individual soul reflected the harmony of the heavenly realm. Rebellion against the given order was both futile and sinful. Ps-Dionysius even specified that burial sites were to be located according to this arrangement, so that at the moment of regeneration the deceased would be "in the right place." Hierarchical organization was, for him, both constitutive and expressive of intrinsic moral perfection.[53]

With this new interpretative overlay of divine-human intimacy and ultimacy superimposed onto the matter of ecclesiastical status, a cultural dynamism was confirmed. Paradoxically, that dynamic was *stāsis:* a divinely willed arrangement cannot change. If it seemed that the earlier generations of God's holy people had lived by other arrangements, more careful reflection would disclose the hidden presence of earthly hierarchies foreshadowing and anticipating the fullness of ecclesiastical hierarchy. Not only was church order holy gift; it is eternal, sacred, and inviolable harmony.

The sacralizing impulse was already noted in the episcopal ordination prayers and directives of Hippolytus, as it was in the second century letters of Ignatius of Antioch and in the fourth century *Apostolic Constitutions* (Book III). If neo-platonic churchmen like Ps-Dionysius gave it its first systematic form and comprehensive elaboration, the highly ceremonialized rites of ordination had been communicating the *mythos* of divine hierarchy for some time.

The *Apostolic Tradition* of Hippolytus had already presented an overt ceremonial distinction between those who had episcopal

53. Faivre 174. To this day, it is customary at the funeral of clergy to place the head of the deceased closest to the altar; a deceased layperson's head is away from the altar.

hands laid on them for the purpose of establishing a share in the Holy Spirit and those who did not.[54] The texts explained the ceremonial protocol in terms of distinctions between the bishop's authority to act in this matter and the presbyter's more limited authority either to receive the Holy Spirit through the bishop's act, or to confirm the bishop's act on behalf of other presbyters. Hippolytus' schema for establishing ecclesial order also provided for a ceremonial handing over of the paraphernalia of lesser ministries. Thus, the bishop was to give the reader the book.

The ceremonial impulse flourished as a way of effectively communicating differences, distinctions, and ranks in the ecclesial *ordo*. In the fifth century Western document *Statuta Antiqua Ecclesiae* the ceremonial aspects of rites of ordering have been systematized and refined.[55] Many episcopal hands and the book of the gospels superimposed appropriately signify the empowerment of the new episcopal ordinand. The hands of one bishop and many presbyters are fitting for the empowerment of a new presbyter; for a deacon, the hands of one bishop only. The subdeacon received no such spiritual empowerment from episcopal hands. Instead, the bishop and the archdeacon hand over to his care cup and plate and oil and water cruets for the offering. The bishop instructs an acolyte but hands nothing over; the archdeacon hands him lamp and oil. The bishop only hands the exorcist the manual of exorcism; but he gives him authority to lay his own hands upon the possessed. The bishop hands the lector the book; he hands the doorkeeper the keys to the church building. A presbyter empowers the psalmist with a word of command to bring song and life into harmony.

Whether or not the third century *Apostolic Tradition*, the fifth century *Statuta Antiqua Ecclesiae* or Ps-Dionysius' *Ecclesiastical Hierarchies* were actually reflective of contemporary practices or were advocacy documents, they had vast influence on subsequent generations.[56] The tenth century Romano-Germanic pontifical incorporated ceremonies handed down from the *Statuta*

---

54. Botte, *Tradition Apostolique* 2, 7–9; cf. 9–14.

55. C. Munier, ed., *Statuta Ecclesiae Antiqua* (Paris: Presses Universitaires de France, 1960) nos. 90–98.

56. Ibid.

Antiqua Ecclesiae. Provisions for distinguishing and ranking lesser ministers and superior ones either through direct episcopal agency or through the indirect agency of the archdeacon or presbyter are firmly embedded within even more elaborate ceremonies.[57] Each of these ritual exchanges publicly confirmed ecclesial relations; and all of them together established a well-ordered *ecclēsia* in which the bishop's authority in the empowerment of ministers was indisputable.

Congar maintains that the Roman Church, even the whole Western church, officially resisted the overlay of mystical hierarchical interpretations of ministries as personal spiritual powers until the twelfth century.[58] That calls for some distinctions. Power became an acute political issue in the eleventh and twelfth centuries in the wake of investiture controversies involving lords spiritual and lords temporal. In the fray, Pope Gregory VII asserted his claim to supreme power. His claim could be and was supported by appeal to the mystical cosmological scheme of earlier writers like Ps-Dionysius, whose works had been circulating for some time in scholastic circles. However, the medieval liturgical ceremonies long-established in the west effectively dramatized the *mythos* of degrees of power, controlled access to it, and personal appropriation of it. The churches East and West had long known, unsystematically even prethematically, but none the less cognitively, about the locus of spiritual power in the bishop, its conferral on others by degrees, and inexorable divine choice in the hierarchical scheme of things. The churches knew these things from the ceremonial language of the liturgy. The early medieval canonists and schoolmen did not create a new ecclesiastical order; they explicated the *mythos* of the hierarchical order in which they were already dwelling in a effort to control untimely harbingers of its collapse. Through an ironic final twist in the differentiation process, those members of the *ekklēsia* who had been excluded from the handlayings and the handings-over characteristic of the clerical holy *ordo* were judged

57. C. Vogel et R. Elze, ed., *Le Pontifical Romano-Germanique du Dixième Siècle* I. Studi e Testi 226 (Città del Vaticano: Bibl. Apostolica Vaticana, 1963), XV; cf. XVI. Also, Munier, *Statuta Ecclesiae Antiqua* nos. 90–98.

58. Y. Congar, "My Pathfindings in the Theology of Laity and Ministries," *The Jurist* 32 (1972) 180.

spiritually impotent by the medieval churchmen.[59] At the high point of the medieval conflict over power, spiritual and temporal, Ps-Dionysius' imaginary hierarch took flesh in the West in the person of the Roman Pontiff.[60]

LANGUAGE OF MINISTRY TODAY

In order to evaluate the course of developments in the matter of language for speaking about ministry, it is necessary to recall premises stated earlier in the paper about the several uses of language and about the intentionality of all structuring within groups. Language serves to name, to handle, and to define experience. The handling of experience linguistically will mean interpreting that experience through available heuristic frames. One of the goals of the interpretative process will be establishing significance; another will be the shaping and controlling of world. The process of development of public language always has a touchstone. The reference point for authenticity will be the intentionality of the group which uses the language.

The preceding survey indicated that only a limited number of the words which accumulated in the original naming of the experience of Christian ministry have persisted as actual names of ministries: bishop, presbyter, and deacon. It also indicated that at least three interpretative overlays used in the first six centuries are firmly deposited in the texts of the 1968 rites for the ordination of bishop, presbyter, and deacon. The first draws upon the sacerdotal theocratic world of late Judaism; the second, the sacral and hierarchical schemes of platonism and neo-platonism; the third, the organizational wisdom of the public institutions of the Roman empire.

The church's ordination prayers and rites have been the depository for the most cogent interpretative insights from this formative era about the larger significance of the ones who are called bishop, presbyter, and deacon. First, these ministers main-

59. C. Lefebvre, "Les Ministères de direction dans l'Eglise à l'âge classique," *Revue de Droit Canonique* 23 (1973) 99–112; cf. Congar, "Les Ministères" 80–88; Tellenbach, Church, *State and Society* 38; cf. 6–8.
60. H. Mühlen, *Entsakralisierung* Paderborn: Schöningh, 1970) 393–394.

tain the theocratic order intended for those chosen to be God's own people; among them can be found high priest, councillors, and cultic functionaries who together both rule the people and attend to the offering. Second, the triad are visible manifestations of invisible realities; together they act as earthly representatives of the Father, of Christ risen and glorified, of the apostles. In their very triadic form they attested to the ascending order of divine triads which serve as intermediaries between the heavenly summit and the earthly realm. In the person of the bishop these realms meet; divine power enters in to the world and is disseminated through his activity. Third, this hierarchical triad which had essential public services to perform took on the organizational shape of known public service institutions, the Roman *ordines*. Positions were graded; personnel were classified. Candidates aspiring to the triad entered at lower levels according to qualifications, and were promoted on the basis of length of service, suitable performance and divine choice disclosed in the bishop's act.

Those who crafted the prayers of consecration for bishops, presbyters, and deacons, throughout this era gave selective emphasis to one or more of these themes of significance.[61] In Hippolytus' prayer texts the first image world, that of sacerdotal theocracy, dominates. However, his comprehensive church order reveals an operational mode for the bishop which also draws upon the platonic and neo-platonic preserve. His bishop tends to be a hierarch through whom power flows. So his ceremonial protocol for episcopal hand-layings and handings-over suggests. But the tendency is still checked by his consciousness of the charisms of confessor and healer in relation to which he had no *auctoritas*. He is at ease with the fact that such gifts, evident in the lives of some of the community, are the result of the direct action of God. As bishop, he is to acknowledge them and welcome them.

Hippolytus is an early witness to the interpretative process. However, the 1968 use of his prayer for the ordination of bishops is situated in another context which interprets the bishop's hierarchical role in a way which sets aside that early Roman's

61. See, for example, *Apostolic Constitutions*, Book VIII, 3; also, 46; cf. Book II, 25, 26, 30.

restraint. The official "homily" to be addressed to the assembly and the subsequent address to the ordinand assert publicly that the bishop is the one through whom spiritual power will pass and who will mediate between heaven and earth.[62] Furthermore, apparently minor modifications of the original text of Hippolytus also serve to bring his prayer into line with the later, more fully elaborated, heuristic developments. For example, the extant Latin version of Hippolytus' prayer designates the episcopal ordinand *primatum sacerdotium;* the 1968 text substitutes a neo-platonic *summum sacerdotium.*[63] Similarly, Hippolytus' prayer designates among the bishop's tasks *dare sortes secundum praeceptum tuum,* the assigning of lots in the church, that is, the neo-platonic responsibility for constituting church order as a manifestation of divine law. The 1968 text has introduced canonical language aquired from the world of the imperial *ordo* to designate the neo-platonic task. The bishop *distribuat munera secundum praeceptum tuum.*

If such is the trajectory of Western church interpretation of the significance of those called bishop, presbyter, and deacon, what of the authenticity of that process? Is truth served by maintaining it? The answers to those questions are basically ecclesiological. Any interpretative frame both discloses and conceals. This one is no different. Three issues must be addressed briefly to determine the implications for the church of maintaining it. These are the church as a group in process; sacralization and pseudo-sacralization; and the liturgical assembly as locus of power.

The Church as Group in Process

The Church necessarily functions as any human group. Its self-definition incorporates what distinguishes it from other groups; its structures protect and promote values which are judged essential for the life of the group. The received tradition of interpreting ministries in the church has been directed to the latter function. However, that process is necessarily based on a prior perception of the distinctive characteristic of the group. Yet most of what has been written about the church between the early apologists and *Gaudium et Spes* misplaces the initial distinction. The original church leaders knew that the important dividing line was between those who were chosen as the *ekklēsia tou theou*

62. *PR:* Bishop, 18.
63. Botte 3; *PR:* Bishop, 26.

and those outside to whom they were to act as ambassadors of reconciliation and bearers of good news. Hippolytus is witness to the early emergence of a second dividing line between those chosen for "the service of the offering" and the rest of the church. It matters which of those two frontiers is identified as decisive, for that judgment shapes the whole rest of the organizational and interpretative process. Ecclesiastical literature tends erroneously to treat the second distinction as primordial. As Heribert Mühlen notes, the difference between clerics and laity has been treated as though it were as significant as the distinction between the baptized and the unbaptized.[64]

Overcoming the error demands beginning at the right starting point. When the church/not-church frontier was clear, as it was for the first Christian generations, there was room for organizational flexibility and imaginative response to new development. Ministerial forms shifted often in response to the dual needs of fulfilling the group vocation and serving group needs: so the Twelve and the Seven; so also, apostles, then prophets, then teachers; so also the presbyterium and *hēgoumenoi;* so even deacons and sub-deacons. The clarity of that Church/not-church frontier exists again at the end of the twentieth century at least for the so-called new churches in Asia and Africa. It seems to have produced the same need for local development of new ministerial structures, some to serve the well-being of the church itself and others to serve the proclamation of the Gospel directly.[65]

The right starting point theologically for establishing the church/not-church frontier is pneumatology informing eschatology. The underdevelopment of these themes in the theology of Vatican II testifies to the malformation of the self-understanding of the church and so its structuring and interpretation of ministries over many centuries.

Sacralization and Pseudo-Sacralization

Preoccupation with divine choice of an hierarchical *ordo* overshadows the significance of the divine choice of a Spirit-filled church. The result has been what Mühlen calls pseudo-sacrali-

64. Mühlen, *Entsakralizierung* 377.

65. Federation of Asian Bishops Conferences, "Ministries: Heralding A New Era," Asian Colloquium on Ministries, Feb. 27–Mar. 6, 1977, *Origins* 8/9 (August 3, 1978) 129, 131–143.

zation.[66] That disorder has had many witnesses through the centuries. Little official evidence yet exists that it is being eschewed.

In 1906 Pius X asserted, "In the hierarchy alone reside the power and authority necessary to move and direct all the members of the society to its end. As for the many, they have no other right than to let themselves be guided and so follow their pastors in docility."[67] The 1918 Code of Canon Law made the point with less rhetorical flourish: *Ordo ex Christi institutione clericos a laicis in Ecclesia distinguet ad fidelium regimen et cultus divini ministerium* (Can 948). The revised Code has abandoned that directness but not the point:

> *Sacramento Ordinis ex Christi institutione inter christifideles quidam, charactere indelebili quo signantur, constituuntur sacri ministri, qui nempe eodem consecrantur et deputantur ut, pro suo quisque gradu, in persona Christi Capitis munera adimplentes Evangelium annuntiandi, christifideles regendi et divinum cultum celebrandi, Dei populum pascant.*[68]

The assertion that the ordained function *"in persona Christi"* resonates with the early sacralizing tendencies of an Ignatius of Antioch. Why is it pseudosacralization? Is there any authentic sacralization?

Mühlen's study of the sacralization phenomenon has led him to the judgment that humans inevitably tend toward sacralizing.[69] The tendency is good, for it is rooted in the relationship of creation and the Creator. Insofar as the Creator is called holy, whatever is created is alongside but outside, that is, profane. That very profanity is a manifestation of God's holiness, for in Mühlen's reading of the New Testament revelation, God's holiness means that God is not turned inward but outward. The genuine sacredness of the world lies in its corresponding ordination to the holiness of God.

Within this horizon the church is necessarily profane, but the

66. H. Mühlen, "Sakralität und Amt zu Beginn einer neuen Epoche," *Catholica* (1973) 77–78; cf. *Entsakralizierung* 385–396.

67. Pius X, "*Vehementer Nos,*" Feb. 11, 1906: ASS 39 (1906) 8–9; cited in Congar, "Pathfindings" 171.

68. Pont. Commissio Codici Iuris Canonici Recognoscendo, *Schema Codicis Iuris Canonici* (Vatican City: Libreria Editrice Vaticana, 1980), can. 1008.

69. Mühlen, "Sakralität" 72–75; cf. *Entsakralizierung* 106–140.

church's vocation to holiness contains the imperative to announce to the whole world the self-giving holiness of God. Only when the church is diaphanous, says Mühlen, is it sacred. By contrast, all theocratic claims of church authorities to possess the authority of God and to act in God's place, as vicar, as representative, "*in persona Christi*," negate the difference between the holiness of God and the divinely willed profanity of every created thing.[70] The result is pseudosacralization. Mühlen proposes Mark 12:28–34 as a key Gospel pericope for the pursuit of this aspect of the good news. In the dialogue between Jesus and the lawyer, Jesus confirms the anti-sacralizing lawyer's insight: "You are right in saying God is one and beside him there is no other." Because of this truth, Jesus necessarily confronted the temple and sabbath ideologies of his own day. He redirected the aspirations of the pious to a radical truth: to revere God above all else is to love your neighbor.

This is a hard saying, because pseudo-sacralization serves some basic human needs.[71] First, what is chaotic is menacing. Whatever gives order and structure, whatever provides a world to live in is fascinating, worthy of admiration, even worship. It is saving; it seems divine. Secondly, as historians of religion note, ritual functions to master the chaotic and to disclose good order. Accordingly, cultic priesthood in every religion serves a stabilizing function for the community. Certain persons and places are inevitably set apart for priestly service. In their work, priests tend to look backward to "the beginning of the world" and inward to their own agency and responsibility for the maintenance of the divinely given order.

It is in this context that the "priesthood" of the new covenant is genuinely new. Those who gather to give thanks with bread and wine for *anamnēsis* of Jesus find themselves confronted with the unexpected disclosure that life poured out for others is only apparently menacing and chaotic. It is the source of the world's salvation, a manifestation of the holiness of God. The genuinely sacred character of the church will be discernible if this disclosure is believed and responded to. Therefore the distinction between the holiness of God and the profanity of everything else, in-

---

70. Mühlen, *Entsakralizierung* 393–395; cf. "Sakralität" 74–80.
71. Mühlen, "Sakralität" 70–71.

cluding the church, must be preserved. So must be the distinction between the genuinely sacred revealed in Jesus and the pseudosacralizing self-protective schemes evident in human religiosity.

But the fact is that a pseudosacral horizon constrains the church and finds expression in the public language, public worship, and public behavior in the matter of ministry. The distortion has consequences. The ecclesial community's well-being, perhaps even its being, is at stake. Social psychologist and communication theorist Gregory Bateson observes that potential for internal rupture exists whenever a community which starts with a shared ideology undergoes progressive and cumulative complementary differentiation. The process, which he calls complementary schismogenesis, is played out as the two subgroups take up opposing or contrasting behaviors and goals and these effectively isolate the two groups. He notes: "Unless it is restrained, [it] leads to progressive unilateral distortion of the personalities of both groups, which results in mutual hostility between them and must end in the breakdown of the system."[72] The Roman Catholic Church has such a cumulative program for rupture in language about ministry which continues to draw the sacred/secular line between *klēroi* and *laikoi* and which continues to assert *"Sacram ordinationem valide recepit solus vir baptizatus,"* thereby isolating men from women in the service of the Gospel.[73]

Restraints and redressive action can reestablish equilibrium, Bateson notes. The isolated groups may actively introduce more symmetrical behavior to balance themselves and stabilize the situation. Or they may merely wait to respond to the "negative feedback" that moves through the group. Both these courses of action can be undertaken to repair and maintain the old system. But groups can also pursue them in ways that will eventually design a whole new organizational system. It is evident that the post-conciliar church has explored a growing range of pastoral responses in order to span the lay/clerical chasm, and more recently even to close the male/female breach. It is equally clear

72. G. Bateson, *Steps Toward an Ecology of Mind* (New York: Ballentine Books, 1972) 68.
73. *Schema Codicis Iuris Canonici*, can. 977.

that both rationales—repairing the old or forming the new—are motivating factors in all groups.

The Liturgical Assembly as Locus of Power

Finally, however, the judgment about what is appropriate motivation for any action at all must be theological, just as the judgment about which are the radical frontiers for the church's self-understanding and mission is theological. Nevertheless, because of the central role of liturgical rites in disclosing within a community the important delineations and for presenting the mysterious holiness of God, the liturgical assembly will continue to be, as it has been for centuries, decisive for the church's self-understanding. It is in assembly that what the church knows to be true can and must be celebrated, and the very physical shape this public praise of the holy God takes will contribute to the slower work of theological reflection.

The regular eucharistic assembly of the local church is already the place where those named bishop, presbyters, deacons, and the many other named and unnamed ministers of the gospel may meet each other and call each other to be a people filled with the Spirit of Jesus. Wherever that meeting takes place with openness and trust in God's holiness and their own vocation to be a holy people, the language of the current ordination rites will become progressively less intelligible. But the church as a holy people will also know better by then how it must pray together—in an age preoccupied with national security, the nuclear arms race, and economic imperialism—for those it will designate specially for leadership in service of the Gospel.

10

The Baptismal Roots of the
Preaching Ministry

IT IS THE COMMON OPINION OF THEOLOGIANS AND THE GENERAL
understanding of Roman Catholic clergy and laity that the sacrament of orders provides the basis for the preaching done in
the church. Correspondingly, it is commonly believed that the
baptized members of the church lack the radical capacity necessary for the full ministry of the word. One investigator, R.T.
Hanley, looking at the ordinary magisterium of the popes right
up to the Second Vatican Council, says that the witness has
remained constant: "Although it cannot be ascertained from the
writings of the modern popes [Pius X to John XXIII] just what
might be the precise nature of the existing relationship between
the sacerdotal character and the preaching of the word, nev-
erthless such a ralationship is readily inferred from their statements."[1]

That same writer, investigating the common teaching of twentieth-century theologians, noted a similar consistency among
them. But he makes a significant judgment: ". . . it must be
admitted that the nature of the existing bond between preaching
and sacred Orders is in too embryonic a state of theological
development to allow for a definite satisfactory solution at the
moment."[2]

1. R.T. Hanley, "The Theology of Preaching in Modern Papal Teaching,"
Catholic University of America Dissertation Series 2, no. 155 (1964) 52.
2. Ibid. 57.

Hanley completed his work in 1964. Today, the notion of the bond between orders and preaching is still in force, as it has been since the eleventh or twelfth century, and it continues to be more the subject of assertion than of investigation since the Council of Trent anathematized anyone who would say that all Christians have the power for the ministry of the word.[3] Nevertheless, the consequences of the assertion serve the church poorly at the end of the twentieth century. This fact alone should make it a subject for serious critical scrutiny.

Some theological refinements in the assertion of a bond between ordination and preaching have indeed been made, but the practice of lay preaching is still regularly attended to in sacramental theology as an exception to the basic position that those in holy orders are the ones equipped for the full ministry of the word in all its forms: evangelization, catechesis, exhortation, and the liturgical homily. Exceptions are popularly explained on the basis of what may be familiar as Catholic action theology, which asserts that the hierarchy may, on its initiative, delegate extraordinary powers to selected laity to participate in the ministry of the word—at least to evangelize, catechize, and exhort. Deputing the non-ordained to preach in the liturgical assembly has been more problematic within this Catholic action scheme. Some say that such delegation is impossible in the nature of the case, since action in a sacramental setting requires sacramental power. Others point to cases where the non-ordained have done liturgical preaching and done it effectively, and conclude that it must, in the nature of the case, be possible.

Eusebius is the mentor of all those who take an empirical approach to the matter. In his *History of the Church* (6:19), written in the first half of the fourth century, he notes that a bishop of Alexandria had claimed that "it was an unheard-of, unprecedented thing that where bishops were present laymen should preach." The bishops of Jerusalem and Caesarea called their Alexandrian brother's statement "glaringly untrue," pointing to at least three cases where holy bishops had called on laity to

---

3. Session, VII, On the Sacraments, canon 10; see H. Denzinger-A. Schönmetzer, *Enchiridion symbolorum definitionum et declarationum de rebus fidei et morum*, 36th ed. (Rome: Herder, 1976) 1610.

preach, and then concluding, "Probably there are other places too where this happens unknown to us."[4]

Operating in our twentieth-century discussion, if apparently not at issue with Eusebius and the bishops whose controversy he reports on, is a mystique of spiritual sacerdotal power. Hanley, cited earlier on the common teaching and common opinion of the bond between orders and preaching, noted a recurrent language pattern in the discussion, namely, references to a "sacred fitness" and also to a "special power of the Holy Spirit" available to the ordained through an "indelible character making him, as it were, a living image of the Savior."[5] A special power, a sacred fitness, an indelible character, a living image of the Savior—this language sustains a mystique within the Roman Catholic Church to the measure that it is posited, repeated, and internalized, but not examined. It provides a framework for a worldview that diminishes the identity of those who enjoy the grace of holy baptism, while enhancing and exalting those Christians who enjoy the grace of holy orders. What does the language mean, and in what context is it intelligible?

In this short presentation, I will pursue only the matter of the theological language of a sacred fitness and of the special power of the Holy Spirit that confers the living image of the Savior. I will show that this technical language of the theological and magisterial traditions is originally liturgical language and that, as such, it is incomprehensible when, as technical language, it becomes cut off from its original liturgical matrix, the assembly of the believing community celebrating Christian baptism. The use of the language "sacred fitness," "power of the Holy Spirit," and "living image of the Savior" to refer to the ordained is secondary and derivative in the prayer life of the church. When it is used by either the magisterium or the theological community to assert exclusive claims for the ordained at the expense of the Christian identity of the laity, it may also be ideological.

This line of investigation will bring us to the point where we can and must question the assertion that the sacrament of holy

4. Eusebius, *History of the Church*, trans. C.A. Williamson (Baltimore: Penguin Books, 1965) 260 [6:19].

5. Hanley, "Theology of Preaching" 49–52.

orders is the adequate foundation for the ministry of the word, and acknowledge, rather, that it is in holy baptism that the church can recognize the radical capacity and the fundamental imperative for the preaching ministry. The preaching of the nonordained may be problematic for the church at the end of the twentieth century; but it is not accurate to say that the root of the problem is in some radical spiritual incapacity of the baptized. The unbroken tradition of the praying church knows differently.

Theology and the Liturgical Tradition

The liturgical tradition of the church, that is, the church's actual way of celebrating its living faith in its identity and mission, can be called the church's sacramental praxis, in the language of contemporary theology. The church's liturgy is at one and the same time symbolic behavior that enfleshes doctrine, and symbolic vision that judges ecclesial life and institutions. This sacramental praxis of the liturgical assembly ought properly to provide the empirical data for systematic sacramental theology. It is *theologic prima*, primary source for *theologia secunda*, or systematic theology. Unfortunately, much of the work of systematic sacramental theology has failed to take account of the public prayer of the church. It has overlooked it as irrelevant or dismissed it as non-data because aspects of the living tradition of worship have simply not fit into favored conceptual schemes. Such selectivity in dealing with the data of the tradition of public prayer has contributed to the present theological impasse in the matter of whether the authentic sacramental foundation for the ministry of preaching is ordination. The church's faith is fuller and deeper than what has been given systematic form since the twelfth century.

The church's liturgical tradition shows that the original insight into notions of sacred fitness, empowerment by the Holy Spirit, and transformation into the living image of the Savior arose in the context of celebrations of Christian baptism. The original insights were embodied in ritual language, which is not abstract and discursive but allusive and expressive.

The language of liturgical rites may lack the precision of the analytic language of systematic theology, but it does not lack cognitive context. On the contrary, the meaning of the language used in the celebration of baptism was so forceful in the first millennium that Alcuin, advisor to the Emperor Charlemagne in the eighth century, was troubled by the gap he saw growing between the faith the church expressed in the rites of Christian initiation and the actual conditions of ecclesial life in the Frankish realm. His solution was not to bring the liturgy into conformity with the "real world" of ecclesial life, but to ask Charlemagne to back a pastoral program that would give substance to the faith of the church regarding the identity and mission of the Christian.[6] He did not get what he asked for; the forces of history were against him. But the liturgy of baptism has remained a constant, if eccentric, witness to what is possible, normal, and indeed normative for the laity in ecclesial life.

Selected Witness from Two Centuries

Two moments will be considered here from the unbroken witness that it is God's deed at baptism which confers a sacred fitness, makes believers into images of the saving Lord Jesus, and empowers them to proclaim the Gospel. The first testimony, that of the baptismal liturgy of the Frankish realm of the eighth century, Charlemagne's world, shows a high doctrine of baptism in a highly elaborated liturgical language that is at no small distance from the actual facts of ecclesial life. It is a witness from a church faithfully handing on the mystery it has received despite the tension between liturgical celebration and ecclesial life. The second witness, St. Cyril's reflection on the baptismal praxis of fourth-century Jerusalem, speaks of a moment when there is a notable correspondence between the faith celebrated and the ecclesial life lived.

Before we look directly at this *theologia prima*, one further note is in order concerning the nature of these sources and the necessarily selective use of them here. In this discussion, reference to the baptismal liturgy extends not to the water bath only, or even to the water bath, chrismation, and first eucharist—the so-called Easter sacraments—but also to all the liturgical celebrations that surround them—those of Holy Week, which anticipate them, and those of the Easter season, which consolidate, refine, elaborate, and confirm their meanings. The parts of a liturgical

6. Alcuin to Charlemagne, *Monumenta Germaniae Historica: Epistolae Carolini Aevi,* ed. E. Dümmler, Series 18 tome IV, letter 110.

rite have their fullest intelligibility only in the context of the whole. This liturgical whole has its greatest intelligibly only in the context of the ecclesial community whose life of faith is being celebrated. That, too, will enter into our consideration.

My method of approach to the witnesses was to question them on their references to the church's belief in "sacred fitness," "empowerment by the Holy Spirit," and "transformation into the image of Christ." The language was made the subject of scrutiny because it is part of the language subsequently taken up by systematic theology to make claims about the special identity of the ordained and to explicate the special connection between orders and the preaching ministry.

Charlemagne's Realm. In the Frankish baptismal liturgies of the eighth century, we see the church entertaining an already traditional metaphor of "garment" as a way of getting hold of the meaning of baptism in humanly comprehensible terms. The wordplay in the English language on *suit*ability and *fit*tingness is similar to the wordplay in Latin. Someone or something that was *habilitatus* was clothed, or equipped, or suited, or outfitted for a role or function. The Latin word *habilitatus* yields the English-language concept of ability, suggesting correspondence between one's *out*fits and one's *inner* habits. But such abstraction is not the mode of ritual language, which prefers to allude to meaning. In the Frankish baptismal liturgy, the garment metaphor alludes to the mysterious act of God on behalf of the newly baptized.[7]

The Gallican baptismal liturgies proclaim the church's faith that baptism habilitates, or better, rehabilitates, because of the Spirit's work. If the baptized are divested of the garment of corruptibility and mortality, what is more important is that a garment of incorruptibility is put on. What is of interest for our concern in understanding this witness to the identity and mission of the baptized is that the Frankish church did not tie the

7. A. Chavasse, "La bénédiction du chrême en Gaule avant l'adoption intégrale de la liturgie romaine," *Revue du moyen-âge latin* 1 (1945) 111–113. See, for example, *Missale Gothicum,* Henry Bradshaw Society 52, ed. H. M. Bannister (London, 1917). For a discussion, see J. Levesque, "The Theology of the Post-baptismal Rites in the Gallican Liturgical Sources of the Seventh and Eighth Centuries," Catholic University of American Dissertation Series 2, no. 266 (1977).

meaning to a dramatic clothing switch, as had earlier generations. Its focus was on the unction or chrismation as the significant act of vesting, for the garment being put on at baptism is
nothing less than Christ and Christ's Holy Spirit.

Accompanying this ritual clothing with holy chrism was a
verbal elaboration of what occurring: this chrism put on as a
garment was identified as the sevenfold gift of the Spirit, once
proclaimed by the prophet Isaiah as the garment of the messianic
king.[8] Yet even this allusion to Isaiah's messianic oracle was
packed with a greater density of meaning than appears at first
notice. Because ritual language is allusive, whoever wants to
understand it must follow the many directions in which it points.
The Gallican liturgies wove webs of meaning for this baptismal
outfit of chrism on a loom stretched between Isaiah and Luke-
Acts. The meaning is available, not through a strategy of human
logic, but through the strategy that created it: openness to the
Paraclete teaching the church the way of salvation.

According to all the Gospels, when Jesus came up out of the
water bath of the Jordan, the Holy Spirit enveloped or covered
him (Luke 3:21–22). According the Luke's Gospel, when Jesus
subsequently presented himself to his own people as the one
with a God-given mission, he did so by citing the messianic
oracle of Deutero-Isaiah: "The Spirit of the Lord is upon me . . . . "
(61:1). That oracle concludes with lines not cited by Luke, but
familiar in the church: "Let me rejoice in the Lord with all my
heart . . . for he has robed me in salvation as a garment and
clothed me in integrity as a cloak" (61:10). Isaiah's garment of
salvation is the Spirit of the Lord upon the one chosen.

But this is not the end. In this Gallican baptismal tradition,
the web of meaning requires a shuttling from Luke to Isaiah and
back to Luke, then on to Acts, and back to the prophet Joel.
Luke's Gospel closes with a foreshadowing of what is to come
in Acts, on Pentecost. The risen Lord Jesus tells his disciples
that they are to wait in the city until they themselves are, like

8. *The Gregorian Sacramentary*, Henry Bradshaw Society 49, ed. H.A. Wilson
(London, 1915): Oratio and infantes consignandos, 57–58; also *Liber sacramen-
torum Romae Aeclesiae Ordinis anni circuli* [Gelasian Sacramentary], Sacramen-
torum Cod. Vat. Reg. Lat. 316 ed. C. Mohlberg (Rome: Herder 1968) no. 451.
Parallels also in the sacramentaries of Gellone (no. 711) and Angoulême (no.
761).

him, clothed (*endysesthe*) with power from on high (24:49). Then, in reporting on the events of Pentecost, Luke borrows from the oracle of the prophet Joel to account for what has happened. God says that in the last days, "Yes, I will cover over even my slaves, both men and women, with a portion of my spirit" (Acts 2:18).[9]

This great web of meaning is gathered up into the ritual transaction of the chrismation of the tribal folk of the Frankish kingdom, the Huns and their newborn infants. The church extravagantly identifies their baptismal chrismation with the messianic garment of immortality.[10] By the Holy Spirit given to them in the anointing, God is regenerating, rehabilitating, fitting them to take up new life with all its consequences. But for what did the church believe they were being suited? The prayer continues to provide the testimony.

As we suggested earlier, the density of ritual meaning is such that everything that needs to be played out cannot be celebrated in a single moment. So we must expand the focus of the inquiry into this *theologia prima*, the imaginative expression of baptismal faith. We will look backward to the Holy Thursday rite for the consecration of the chrism itself, and forward to the Sunday after Easter, when the great baptismal celebration was reaching its denouement.

Among the texts provided for Holy Thursday in one of the Gallican liturgical books is the prayer for the consecration of chrism, used also in the Roman Church to this day. It proclaims that the chrism is to be used so that "they also may be made thy Christs."[11] The prayer conceives of the chrism as a garment of power, to be worn as a visible sacrament of the royal, priestly, and prophetic honor that accrues to the baptized as bearers of the name Christ. The formula actually establishes a ritual frame

9. "Legenda in Sancto Pentecosten," *Le lectionnaire de Luxeuil*, Collectanea Biblica Latina 7, ed. P. Salmon (Rome, 1944–53) 1:173–175.

10. Levesque, "Theology of the Postbaptismal Rites" 43–49. See *Missale Gothicum*, no. 261; there are echoes also in the Holy Thursday chrism preface of the Gelasian Sacramentary.

11. *Missale Gallicanum Vetus*, Chrism Mass, "Contestatio," no. 82. Translation from L. Mitchell in *Baptismal Anointing*, Alcuin Club Collections 48 (London: SPCK, 1966) 118. For a discussion of this, see Levesque, "Theology of the Postbaptismal Rites" 95ff.

of meaning for identifying the newly baptized. It is repeated in a prayer said on Easter day, after the baptisms have occurred. Having sketched Christ's messianic role as that of priest, prophet, and king, it notes that the baptized were incorporated into his life in order to share in his functions.[12]

When, on the Sunday after Easter, the *Clausum Paschae*, the newly baptized removed the material white garment of their baptism, they did so at the end of a liturgical rite that had once again proclaimed the text of Isaiah 61, "The Spirit of the Lord is upon me . . . ," a text that had reverberated in overtones and undertones during all the baptismal events.[13] The newly baptized were confronted with a saving paradox: even though the church directed them to set aside the outward white robe, they had all received an abiding garment of splendor—their anointing with the Spirit.

The church of Charlemagne did not moderate its convictions about the power and the purpose of baptism. Alcuin, advisor to Charlemagne, clearly believed that the baptized had been strengthened by the Holy Spirit for the purpose of preaching to others (*ad praedicandum aliis*) the faith they had received at baptism.[14] He saw in the unlikely *rudes*, to whom the church was capable of giving only the most rudimentary presentation of the gospel, people who were by the design of God radically fit for a messianic mission. This was a church whose poverty of resources was great. Its people were an illiterate and semi-literate folk, and their ordained leaders were much like them. It was a

12. See Levesque, "Theology of the Postbaptismal Rites" 96–101, 107–108; also *Missale Gallicanum Vetus*, no. 195

13. "Legenda clausum Paschae," *Le lectionnaire de Luxeuil*, 1:133.

14. Alcuin to Oduin, *Monumenta Germaniae Historica: Epistolae Carolini Aevi*, ed. E. Dümmler, Series 18, tome IV, letter 134. See also Levesque, "Theology of the Postbaptismal Rites" 175. The meaning of *praedicandum* in medieval Latin has been disputed. C. Mohrmann shows that in the course of the fourth century the verb *praedicare*, used in earlier generations to designate the preaching of the Lord and the apostles, came to mean preaching done in the church. Even when ecclesial circumstances curtailed that "preaching" to reading texts, the language was not entirely cut off from its original matrix. "Praedicare, Tractare, Sermo: Essai sur la terminologie de la prédication paleochrétienne," *La Maison-Dieu* 39 (1954) 101ff. For an illustration of the medieval equation of "preaching" with reading of texts, see Peter Lombard, *IV Sentences*, dist. 24, cap.l vi, on the office reader.

church cut off from its Jewish and Hellenistic past and, as a result, incapable of offering its members a full formation in the Gospel as a source of meaning. Yet the church's liturgy continued to entertain the truth and keep alive the faith that all the baptized are, by God's deed, chosen and outfitted for the preaching of the Gospel.

If we ask why this era maintained such a high doctrine of holy baptism when it was not in any way able to equip all the baptized for an actual exercise of a full Christian vocation, we must fall back on the essentially conservative character of the baptismal liturgy. It is a reliable witness to sound traditional faith, despite social conditions that obstructed its enfleshment.

Underneath the ritual entertainment of the root metaphor of messianic vesting lies the basis for the more abstract notion that the church's sacramental activity *fits* the church for its mission. If the magisterial and theological traditions from that high Middle Ages tie preaching to ordination on the grounds that the ordained have "a certain sacred fitness" for the task, it is necessary to critique whatever absolute claims are implicit in this argument. The unbroken witness of the baptismal liturgy, maintained even in one of its least favored epochs, asserts that the sacred fitness for joining in the messianic mission, and so in the preaching ministry that is part of it, is a gift given at baptism.

Cyril's Jerusalem. To appreciate the baptismal faith that the church of Charlemagne was professing liturgically but was unable to conserve operationally, we can compare its witness with the doctrine and practice of Cyril and the Christian community within which he presided in the fourth century at Jerusalem. Cyril's episcopacy also occurred in an expansionist era. Christianity had been made legal and was about to be made obligatory for the citizens of the Roman Empire. But two witnesses to Cyril's milieu show an ecclesial life that was circumstantially different from the world about which Alcuin wrote to Charlemagne. Both the Jewish and Hellenistic cultures on which the Mediterranean churches were built enjoyed longstanding and highly developed traditions of literacy and rhetorical skill able to be directed to the service of preaching the Gospel.

The Spanish noblewoman-nun Egeria, traveling to Jerusalem in the midst of the excitement of its boom years, kept a journal that gives us an outsider's observations about the Eastern Mediterranean church in operation in the fourth century. She reported that preaching was an important part of Jerusalem church life, and so many were so eager to preach that the bishop allowed several presbyters to preach in turn in assemblies at which he presided.[15]

Eusebius, bishop of Caesarea by vocation and church historian by avocation, reported an even fuller range of preaching practice in the generations before Cyril. He cites a letter to the emperor from two bishops (one of them a predecessor of Cyril) saying that they know of several situations in which the bishop has invited a lay person to preach and that they presume the practice is common. Eusebius the bishop-historian then notes that the practice of lay preaching is in no way forbidden but is in fact the way the famous Origen got his start as preacher "though not yet ordained to the presbyterate."[16]

What equipped the laity for this work? At a human level, perhaps human skills of interpretation and rhetoric. But Cyril was himself quite eloquent about the way in which baptism radically fitted the baptized for full participation in the messianic mission. Cyril wrote in his mystagogical catechesis "On the Holy Chrism": "[the anointing] shall teach you all things."[17] He specified that what the neophytes would learn from their anointing was that they were figures of Christ.[18] His approach to the transformation of the neophytes through the rites of initiation has been called mimesis theology.[19] It is a rich manifestation of *theologia prima*, the expressive and allusive testimony to living faith that precedes and exceeds its systematic thematization.

Cyril started with a text from 1 John (2:20–28) aimed to assure the baptized of the importance of their anointing: it is "real and no illusion." Then he elaborated: What happened to Jesus happens to the disciple. When Jesus came up out of the waters of the Jordan, the Spirit covered him, anointing him for his messianic mission. Such is the case with the neophyte.

15. *Egeria's Travels*, trans. J. Wilkinson (London: SPCK, 1971) 125 (25:1).
16. Eusebius, *History of the Church*, 260 [6:19].
17. *St. Cyril of Jerusalem's Lectures on the Christian Sacraments*, ed. F. L. Cross (London: SPCK, 1951): "On the Holy Chrism," 3:7, 66.
18. Ibid. 3:1, 64.
19. H. Riley, *Christian Initiation*, Studies in Christian Antiquity 17, ed. J. Quasten (Washington: University Press of America) 365–367.

But what is the messianic mission? Cyril recalled the Old Testament accounts of the anointing of priests and kings, but unlike the Frankish interpreters, not for the sake of comparison but for contrast.[20] Great as were the priests and kings, they shared neither in the gift of the Spirit of Jesus nor in his mission. Cyril looked elsewhere for the meaning. He cited the Letter to the Ephesians (6:11–20), where they were exhorted to put on all the protective armor that God provides: the belt of truth, the coat of integrity, the shoes of the gospel of peace. Here his mimesis theology draws upon the clothing metaphor, which seems a constant in the tradition. For Cyril, the Ephesians text echoes the Isaiah test (11:5) that sings of the messianic heir who will be wearing around his waist the belt of justice and on his body the mail of good faith. The one so clothed can be recognized as the one on whom the Spirit of the Lord has come to rest, the spirit of wisdom and understanding, counsel and power, of knowledge and fear of the Lord (11:2).

Cyril gathers these texts to point to the meaning: Just as Jesus' anointing was for the mission of the Gospel of peace, so is the anointing that accompanies the water bath a messianic commissioning by the power of the Holy Spirit. For Cyril, these ideas are neither abstract theories, nor religious gnosis, nor mystical or vaguely futuristic in their reference. They are also operational. The neophyte is actually empowered to cooperate in the messianic work: "He hath anointed me to preach glad tidings to the poor."[21]

To underscore this point of the messianic transformation, Cyril continues to focus on the anointing, even as he engages another metaphor, defying the conventions of logic. The anointing on the forehead is not only an outfitting for the messianic mission; it is also an unveiling.[22] Cyril recalls Paul's teaching that the baptized "with uncovered faces . . . reflect as in a mirror the glory of God" (2 Cor 3:18). The shining splendor of the oiled countenance was for Paul a manifestation of the restoration of

20. Ibid. 368.
21. *St. Cyril of Jerusalem's Lectures,* 3:1, 64. For an extended theological reflection on Cyril's teaching, see Riley, *Christian Initiation* 365–379.
22. *St. Cyril of Jerusalem's Lectures,* 3:4, 65. See also Riley, *Christian Initiation* 372–373.

humankind to God's image, a work of the Holy Spirit of Jesus. By association, he baptized and anointed neophytes mirror forth the glory of God with their shining foreheads. The mimetic significance is then underscored. "You are Christs," he says unqualifiedly to his assembly.[23] Just as Christ, the anointed, the perfect image of the Father, was the One sent as a messenger, so the annointed Christian, in his image, is also a messenger of the good news.

A full plumbing not only of Cyril but of the whole liturgical tradition of the early centuries would yield a vast list of citations woven together into fabrics of meaning, some intricate, some elaborate, some homespun. Why cite them at all? They serve to put into perspective the theological tradition that uses the language of empowerment by the Holy Spirit, a certain sacred fitness, and the sacramental imaging of Christ as technical language that has the ordained clergy as its primary referent.[24] That tradition has the whole thing backward. If the witness of the *theologia prima* is given credence, if the norm for believing is in some authentic way tied to the norm of the church's public prayer, then things commonly claimed for the ordained as the basis for preaching are already attributable to every person growing into the fullness of the one baptismal gift of the Spirit with its many charismatic manifestations.

Systematizing and Narrowing the Tradition

The church celebrated the same faith in its eighth-century poverty as in its fourth-century abundance. Nevertheless, the witness of the baptismal liturgy was set aside by the twelfth century for many reasons. One important one was the rise of a novel conceptual scheme among practitioners of *theologia secunda*, the systematic theology of the schools. As a result of this develop-

23. *St. Cyril of Jerusalem's Lectures*, 3:1, 64.
24. See, for example, the appropriation of this baptismal witness to serve purposes of clerical self-definition in Peter Lombard, *IV Sentences*, dist. 24, cap. iii: "Tales enim decet esse ministros Christi qui septiformi gratia Spiritus sancti sint decori . . . . In sacramento ergo septiformis Spiritus septem sunt gradus ecclesiastici . . . ." Also, in cap iv: "Unde ministri Ecclesiae reges esse debent, ut se et alios regant; quibus Petrus ait [1 Pet 2:9]: Vos estis genus electum, regale sacerdotium," found in the context of interpreting of clerical tonsure.

ment, ordination underwent a pseudo-sacralization and baptism was profaned.[25] The circumstances of the second Christian millennium encouraged these developments.

The preaching of the Gospel had deteriorated during the early medieval period, as Alcuin testified. Although the church grew numerically, it no longer had access to the knowledge nor possessed the skill necessary to preach in the rabbinic tradition of a Paul, nor did it have many trained in the classical rhetorical tradition familiar to an Origen or Augustine. Councils enjoined bishops to see to it that pastors formed those they had baptized with the living word of the Gospel. But bishops often settled for compromise, encouraging of use of Latin sermon texts from earlier generations to be read, where possible, by the pastors to the people.[26] That strategy filled the breach. But the mystery of the baptized Christian as a living image of Christ outfitted for the messianic mission was celebrated during the eighth through the twelfth centuries primarily in faithfulness to the received tradition rather than as a lively truth.

Monastic scriptoria prepared for the eventual rise of the theological schools of the high Middle Ages; the schools stimulated new interest in organizing and interpreting the faith of the church. Reform movements invigorated ecclesial life. By the twelfth century, interest in preaching the Gospel and the requisite literacy, grammatical competence, and rhetorical skills had revived. As a result, for several generations preaching was "out of control" in a church unprepared to order the resurgence of the charism of preaching. Lay preaching had erupted, had been sanctioned, subject to episcopal or papal approval, and had been suppressed in the wake of clerical objections. The acts of synods and councils document the problem.[27]

25. M. Collins, "The Public Language of Ministry," *The Jurist* 41 (December, 1981) 261–294; also this volume, Chapter 9.

26. For an account of these developments, see H. Dressler, "Preaching (History of)," *New Catholic Encyclopedia* (New York: McGraw-Hill, 1967); also E.C. Dargan, *A History of Preaching* (New York: Armstrong, 1905) 132–137 and passim.

27. For an account of the Waldensians and the Humiliati, see L. Christiani, "Vaudois," *Dictionnaire de théologie catholique*, 15/2; also F. Vernet, "Humiliés," *Dictionnaire de théologie catholique* 7/1.

Thomas Aquinas, writing in the thirteenth century, reflects the tensions that several generations of new experiences of preaching has spawned.[28] Is preaching properly limited only to those priest-pastors to whom the bishop has given the care of souls? Is it fitting to have a religious order of preachers? Is it fitting that preachers should live on the alms of people? Can monks preach to the world if they have died to the world? Thomas's writings also reflect a significant theological development that would effectively weaken the witness of the baptismal liturgy, even though that liturgy continued to celebrate the unbroken faith in the fitness of the baptized for an active role in the messianic mission. For via the Abbey of St. Victor in the eleventh century, the theologians of the medieval schools had become familiar with the conceptual scheme of a pseudonymous sixth-century work from Asia Minor, *The Ecclesiastical Hierarchies*.

This work, authored by one calling himself Dionysius—by inference, the companion of Paul the Apostle—provided systematicians with an influential logical schema derived from Hellenistic philosopohy, namely, a distinction between active powers and passive powers.[29] Using this distinction, it was possible to affirm simultaneously and without apparent contradiction the notions that both the baptized and the ordained had a share in the gift of the Holy Spirit, but that the shares were qualitatively different. The laity's share was passive, the ordained's active. With their passive share, the laity could recieve the other sacraments, hear the word of God, receive the goods of salvation. With their active share, the ordained could confect sacraments,

28. *Summa theologiae*, II–II, 183–189; see *The Pastoral and Religious Lives*, Summa Theologiae Series 47 (New York: McGraw-Hill, 1964).

29. For these ideas in Aquinas, see *Summa theologiae*, III, 62–72, and especially 63, 6, in *Baptism and Confirmation*, Summa Theologiae Series 57 (New York: McGraw Hill, 1964): "Sed ad agentes in sacramentis pertinet sacramentum ordinis . . . ad recipientes pertinet sacramentum baptismi." Interestingly, however, Aquinas cities a text from Rabanus Maurus, itself a citation of his mentor Alcuin (see note 14 above), as an objection to the details of this logical schema, and responds that God is not bound by the sacraments(!): "vitus divina non est alligate sacramentis" (III, 72, 6). See also G. Thery, "L'éntrée du PsDenys en Occident," *Mélanges Mandonnet*, Bibliothèque thomiste 14 (Paris: J. Vrin, 1930) 2:23–30; *Dionysius the Pseudo-Areopagite: The Ecclesiastical Hierarchies*, ed. T. Campbell (Washington: University Press of America, 1981).

especially the eucharist, and preach the Gospel. The ordained were agents of the apostolic mission; the baptized were the recipients of the active work of the clergy. Systematic sacramental theology and ecclesiology and magisterial teaching have been frozen within his construct to this day.

In the revised rites of Vatican II, which are for the most part authentic witnesses to the ancient faith, we have a striking example of the power of this twelfth-century theological opinion to continue to assert itself and so to influence church life, church order, and consequently the theological reflection on the preaching ministry. What is ironic is that the encroachment of this construct on the baptismal liturgy has occurred so belatedly, and during this time of church renewal.

The Chrism Mass of Holy Thursday has been, since the fifth century, a constant witness to the baptismal faith of the Roman Catholic Church. The consecratory prayer from the Galasian Sacramentary exalts the chrism as solemnly if not as lavishly as the *Exsultet* of a later era praises the Easter candle during the Paschal Vigil. The prayer sings of the joy that the oil of the olive has brought to the world from the time that the dove brought the olive branch as a token of reconciliation and peace to Noah and his family. The prayer credits David the prophet with dubbing the chrism "oil of gladness" because God faithfully showed saving power through the anointing of priests, prophets, and kings.[30]

In its liturgical telling at the Chrism Mass, the story of the oil culminates in the account of the baptism of Jesus, on whom also the Spirit descended as a dove, a messenger to him of his messianic mission of peace. Then it focuses on the present: May those who will share the same anointing through the oil receive its power and so cooperate with Christ's messianic work. At the time of the origins of the great song of the chrism, the references were unambiguously baptismal, for the chrism was used exclusively for the baptized in the Roman liturgy. In fact, several centuries elapsed before Roman ordination rites incorporated

---

30. *The Rites of the Catholic Church* (New York: Pueblo Publishing Co., 1980) 1:303. For a full discussion of the origins and history of this text, see H. Schmidt, *Hebdomada Sancta*, 3 vols. (Rome: Herder, 1957).

actual ritual anointings of presbyters (and then their hands, not their heads) and before the hierarchy took up anointing kings and emperors.[31] These developments were secondary and derivative, and betrayed a reductionist reading of ancient baptismal texts, assuming them to refer to the actual social and ecclesiastical order, which by that time had no small number of priests and kings.

This ancient consecratory hymn is kept in the 1970 revised order of the Chrism Mass. Its ancient baptismal meaning echoes in the readings from Isaiah and Luke assigned for the celebration: "The Spirit has anointed me . . . to bring good news to the poor . . . " But the baptismal intent is upstaged by an unprecedented development that makes this celebration of baptismal identity a minor theme in the revised Chrism Mass. The Roman Pontifical of 1970, breaking with the tradition, presents as a major motif of the Chrism Mass the celebration of the cultic priesthood shared by the ordained, bishops and their presbyters.[32]

However unwitting, the development is a bit of liturgical piracy—raiding the ship's hold for valuable cargo. On the basis of an examination of a new combination of texts, it can be shown that this liturgy intends to guarantee agency to the active and to encourage the laity to assent that their baptism is a deputation to dependence. The vocables "priest" and "priesthood" cannot ever entirely lose their rich baptismal meaning. But the 1970 rite fairly effectively narrows the reference in the Chrism Mass to the company of the ordained.[33] In this whole development from the twelfth to the twentieth centuries, the most high-handed act of encroachment of an ideology of ordained priesthood on the baptismal liturgy may be the composition, in this era, of a special preface of ordained priesthood to replace the ancient preface for

31. D. Power, *Ministers of Christ and His Church* (London: G. Chapman, 1969) 89–93 and 193, on the appropriate of both the anointing and the vesting metaphors.

32. "Ordo benedicendi oleum catechumenorum et infirmorum et conficiendi chrisma," *Pontificale Romanum* (Vatican City: Typis Polyglottis Vaticanis, 1971) Praenotanda 1.

33. F. Henderson, "The Chrism Mass of Holy Thursday," *Worship* 51 (1977) 149–158.

this day, which has proclaimed the royal, priestly, and prophetic identity of the baptized.[34]

Where the Burden of Theological Argument Lies

The intent of this examination of the liturgical tradition of baptism has been to establish that first theology (*theologia prima*) knows more about the identity and ministerial vocation of the baptized than is reflected in the tradition of systematic theology (*theologia secunda*) since the Middle Ages. Church discipline more accurately reflects what the liturgy of baptism celebrates than systematic theology does. Church discipline has regularly provided for episcopal authorization of lay people as ministers of the word in a wide range of situations. The discipline has at times strained the minds, hearts and theological imaginations of those who have considered as divine law the Scholastic distinction between active and passive shares in the gift of the Holy Spirit. Given those foundations, theologians were forced to speculate on how the bishops effectively empowered the radically unsuited before commissioning them to preach.

At the present time the church has good reason to rejoice in the living tradition that the non-ordained are fitted by baptism to be collaborators in the ministry of the word as evangelists and catechists, as teachers and preachers. The 1973 indult to the West German bishops from the Congregation for the Clergy asserted that the non-ordained are even suited to give the liturgical homily upon proper episcopal authorization—an authorization a bishop also gives to presbyters.[35] Despite that document, a line of resistence persists in the theological community and in the magisterium which wishes to argue on theological grounds that the liturgical homily must be reserved to the ordained, or at least that this is the case with the eucharistic homily. One of the most

34. For the priesthood preface, see the 1970 Roman Missal; for the earlier preface, which is found in Pius XII's restored order of Holy Week, see *Ordo Hebdomadae Sanctae instauratur* (Vatican City; Typis Polyglottis Vaticanis, 1956) or Schmidt, *Hebdomada Sancta* 1:65.

35. Letter of John Cardinal Wright, prefect of the Sacred Congregation for the Clergy, to Julius Cardinal Doepfner, president of the Episcopal Conference of West Germany (November 20, 1973) 4; also, Decree on Lay preaching, Roman Catholic Synod of West Germany, 2:32–2:34, see *Canon Law Digest* 8 (1973–77) 941–944.

cogent presentations of that position is found in a 1965 essay by the eminent French liturgist Joseph Gelineau.[36]

Gelineau's reasoniong deserves scrutiny, since his is a representative presentation of the most cogent rationale for what is commonly thought and taught to be the church's official position, the 1973 letter of the Congregation of the Clergy to the contrary notwithstanding. According to Gelineau, it is ordination that fits the ordained minister for the public celebration of the mystery of the word of God. The homily is, by definition, that form of public commentary on Scripture suited to bishop, presbyter, and deacon because of the hierarchical status conferred by their ordination.[37] (Gelineau's phrase "apanage de l'évêque" means literally that the bishop has the bread, metaphorically, that he is equipped for exercising his role in life. Note: we are back to a variation on the clothing metaphor.) But at this point the argument is circular. Furthermore, it reflects dual assumptions: 1) that the merely baptized are unsuited for the public ministry of the word because the Holy Spirit is a passive presence within them, and 2) that the Holy Spirit is activated by ordination.

The theological argument for reserving the liturgical homily to the ordained seems to be suspended over an abyss created by the unexamined Scholastic distinction between active and passive endowments of the Spirit of Christ. Nevertheless, Gelineau's concern for the finality of the liturgical homily is on more solid ground. He conceives of the homilist as exercising a ministry of mediation, as guiding the assembly of believers into communion with the mystery of salvation-present that is being celebrated. Mediation is by definition a priestly function. But it remains unclear on what legitimate grounds it can be maintained that the priestly, royal, and prophetic identity and mission of the baptized leave them radically unsuited for this mediatorial task. To assert as much is to profane Christian baptism, a condition toward which the tradition of systematic sacramental theology has been contributing wittingly and unwittingly for too many centuries.

36. J. Gelineau, "L'homélie, Forme pléniere de la prédication," *La Maison-Dieu* 82 (1965) 29–42.
37. Ibid. 34.

In all of this, there is no intention to negate the necessity of an orderly church nor to deny episcopal responsiblity for ordering the exercise of the ministry of the word, whether the preachers have received holy baptism or both holy baptism and holy orders. But the hard fact is that the church does not have a systematic sacramental theology adequate to the data of ecclesial life past or present. Least of all does the Roman Catholic Church have an adequate systematic theology of baptism, perhaps because of a hypertrophic interest in ordination.[38] Baptismal theology has been preoccupied with the notion of the removal of original sin, on the one hand, and with the effort, on the other, to advance the odd position that Christians whom God has chosen to empower for the messianic mission nevertheless remain pneumatic cripples in the church.

The question of the tie between word and sacrament, especially but not exclusively in the eucharist, remains. But theologians must seek a theological model for understanding someplace other than in past theories of sacramentality that too quickly identify the ordained with the image of Christ in such a way that he is exclusively *in persona Christi* for the rest of the church. The baptismal liturgy, confirmed by postconciliar ecclesial experience, suggests that sacramentality is a quality of the whole *ecclesia*, the community of those who are being transformed slowly, by God's power, into living images of the saving Christ. It is the whole church together that makes eucharist, says the new experience, although the church struggles with the residual question of whether the one who prays the prayer and says the words of institution is not the one who really counts after all.

But if the eucharist is the act of the whole church, and if the ordained is someone who presides within, not over, the community of believers, then it seems both possible and necessary to seek new models for understanding sacramentality in relationship to liturgical presidency. Ecclesial experience confirms that it is possible for the one who presides within the liturgical assembly by office to engage another believer to lead them all

38. Even the excellent introduction to liturgy, *L'Église en prière*, ed. A.G. Martimort, 3rd ed. (Paris: Desclée, 1965) gives a logical and theological priority to ordination over baptism. See also Martimort, *The Signs of the New Covenant* (Collegeville, Minn.: The Liturgical Press, 1963).

together into deeper communion with the mystery of Christ by the power of the word, and that this collaborative ordering does not fracture the sacrament of unity. Perhaps the question is whether the presidency of the ordained minister in the liturgical assembly inevitably involves prelacy or may just as authentically manifest collaboration within the one Body.

Unless and until the theology of baptism and the theology of ordination are examined together within the theological community for their christological and pneumatological foundations and for their adequacy to contemporary Christian experience, those who want to find solid ground for developing lay collaboration in the full preaching ministry, including liturgical preaching, will be kept on the defensive. But the witness of the baptismal liturgy shows convincingly that the burden of proof should rest rather with those who want to disquality the laity as a class from preaching in any or all of its forms.

11

Inclusive Language: A Cultural and Theological Question

THE CHURCH IS BEING CALLED TO EXAMINE THE LANGUAGE IT USES in public prayer as this language includes or excludes women as referents. The matter has theological implications, but it arises as a cultural question, and the cultural context needs to be acknowledged and addressed prior to any theological reflection. One aspect of the cultural context is the changing role of women in society; another is the development of the English language under the influence of social change.

Language in Church and Society
Popes from John XXIII to John Paul II and the Council itself have taken repeated note of the changing social role of women worldwide as one of the "signs of the times." *Gaudium and Spes* had observed: "Where they have not yet won it, women claim for themselves an equity with men before the law and in fact."[1] Earlier, John XXIII had recognized this aspiration of women as part of a universal movement of human aspiration. He wrote first of women: "Since women are becoming ever more conscious of their human dignity, they will not tolerate being treated as inanimate objects or mere instruments, but claim, both in do-

1. *Gaudium et Spes.* (9) W.M. Abbott, ed. *The Documents of Vatican II.* New York, N.Y., 1966. The Latin text reads *paritatem . . . cum viris.* The decision to translate the phrase into English as "a certain equity . . . with men" raises the issue of androcentris bias. The word is certainly open to translation as "equality."

197

mestic and in public life, the rights and duties that befit a human person." Then in a summary statement, he concluded, ". . . in our day, in very many human beings the inferiority complex which endured for hundreds and thousands of years is disappearing, while in others there is an attenuation and gradual fading of the corresponding superiority complex which had its roots in socio-economic privileges, sex or political standing."[2] Such citations from *Pacem in Terris* establish clearly enough not only the fact of change but its meaning for the future. In Pope John's judgment, women should not be expected to remain satisfied with anything that diminishes their status as human persons.

In the past two decades, the field of women's studies has developed rapidly as part of the larger women's movement in the U.S. When scholars engaged in women's studies reflect on the various aspects of societies and cultures in order to expose and critique whatever structural biases operate against women as full human persons, they are working from a critical feminist perspective. Feminist scholarship has named the generally pervasive, socio-cultural bias against women "androcentrism."[3] The term points to the cultural tendency to make male experience normative human experience, with the effect of marginalizing women's experience, making it secondary and making women themselves a subspecies of human being. Androcentrism has found expression in a wide range of forms; social and political structures which promote male dominance and female subordination are commonly identified as patriarchal.

Feminist scholarship in the United States has recently put the English language under scrutiny, asking how it functions in expressing and shaping a world of social relations and cultural values. Such questioning has exposed the androcentric character of the language to view and to criticism. New knowledge, disseminated rapidly in a mass media culture, has made the general public aware of the recently identified, named, and vigorously

2. Pope John XXIII, *Pacem in Terris* (New York: America Press, 1963) nos. 41, 43. In no. 44 the pope talks about the obligation of those who become aware of their rights to claim them.

3. Rita M. Gross, "Androcentrism and Androgyny in the Methodology of History of Religions," in R. Gross, ed. *Beyond Androcentrism* (Missoula, Montana: Scholars Press, 1977) 9. Also, Valerie Saiving, "Androcentrism in Religious Studies," *Journal of Religion*, 56 (April 1976) 177–97.

challenged bias against women in ordinary English usage. As a result of both popular and scholarly awareness, accelerated changes are occurring in English language usage. The movement is toward usage which is inclusive of women as referents and away from usage which is ambiguous or exclusive. It is in this context that Catholics have become concerned about inclusive language in the usage of the church's public prayer.

Some brief reflections on the historicity of language itself are in order, with particular reference to the English language to contextualize the question about English usage in the liturgy. Historians of English note that both religious and social circumstances had discernible influences on the development of modern English. English Bible translation stimulated free development of the language in the sixteenth century. Subsequently a movement for a prescriptive grammar introduced conventions and control over English usage in the seventeenth and eighteenth centuries.

William Tyndale, a contemporary of Martin Luther, published an English New Testament in 1526, and in subsequent years sections of the Old Testament.[4] In his translations, he adopted a popular English style, using the idiom of his period. Where the idiom was deficient, he coined new English words and phrases, many of which have become a permanent possession of the English language, like "passover," "peacemaker," and "scapegoat." His use of English was creative and effective; and it set a norm for subsequent sixteenth century translations, including Miles Coverdale's first complete English Bible published in 1535, and the first efforts at English translations of the liturgy. Archbishop Thomas Cranmer, like Tyndale, used the English language in its common form, but with an uncommon grace. Both were freed for this approach to the language by their own cultural circumstances; the sixteenth century continued to enjoy a delight in a "new," malleable language, a delight manifested in the earlier creativity of a Chaucer and the contemporary freshness of a William Shakespeare.[5]

In the seventeenth century, some English speakers, nervous

4. Daniel B. Stevick, *Language in Worship* (New York, NY: The Seabury Press, 1970) 20–21.

5. Albert Baugh, *A History of the English Language*, 2nd edit. (New York, NY: Appleton–Century–Crofts, Inc., 1957).

about the fact that the English language was not yet clearly governed by rules as were Latin and French (thanks to the efforts of the French Academy in the latter case), began to push for a normative English grammar.[6] Perhaps the English tradition of common law provided the context for an extended debate on whether usage or rule should provide the norm, and also for the subsequent failure of various efforts to establish such an English Academy. In any case, self-appointed arbiters took control of the situation, most of them men without any special qualification for the work.[7] It is the judgments of these aggressive grammarians and those of their successors which feminist scholars have exposed as fundamentally androcentric.[8] Two such judgments are particularly pertinent to the current debate about inclusive language. The first relates to the development of false generics and the second to the rules governing pronoun usage.

"Man" as a generic term is a case in point in grasping the issue of false generic terms. True generics are equally applicable both to a class or a group and to the individual members of that class or group. False generics are terms used of a class or group that are not applicable to all members of that group.[9] By these criteria, "man" is a false generic; so also is "brother" in such a phrase as "the brotherhood of man." In contemporary English usage, adult females singly or in groups are not referred to as "men"; nor are they appropriately identified as "brothers."

The historians can trace the development of the word "man" from the time in Old English when it was a true generic, equivalent to the Latin *homo, hominis,* referring to all adult persons, through an intermediate period when it sometime served as the equivalent to *homo* and sometimes referred only to *vir,* to the contemporary period, where ordinary usage recognizes "man" as referring to adult males in distinction to "woman" which

6. Sterling A. Leonard, *The Doctrine of Correctness in English Usage 1700–1800* (Madison: University of Wisconsin, 1929).

7. Baugh, *History* 331.

8. Ann Bodine, "Androcentrism and Prescriptive Grammar: Singular 'They', Sex-Indefinite 'He', and 'He or She', " *Language in Society* 4:2 (August 1975) 129–45; Julia P. Stanley, "Sexist Grammar," *College English* 39:7 (March 1978) 800–11.

9. Casey Miller and Kate Swift, *The Handbook of Non-Sexist Writing* (New York: Lippincott and Crowell, 1980) 9ff.

designates adult females.[10] The insistence that "man" is a generic term by appeals to earlier usage reflects an ahistoric approach to the language. Language, too, has a history. The appeal to earlier conventions tries to make the prescriptive grammar of "authoritative" grammarians (heretofore always adult males) an absolute arbiter over usage.

Feminist scholars have also traced the history of the rules governing the use of "he" as the pronoun of reference in statements where the gender of the antecedent is unclear, in such constructions as "If anyone . . . he . . . ."[11] Throughout and beyond the seventeenth and eighteenth centuries, common usage regularly handled that situation through the use of the English plural pronoun, "If anyone . . . they . . . ." Debate over rules of concord exercised grammarians attempting to apply their own operating principle that the pronoun should agree in gender, number, and person with the antecedent. The consensus of historians of English who have examined the issue is that the decision that "he" would be the correct singular pronoun of reference in uncertain cases was apparently prescribed as "correct," without explanation, for the first time in 1795.[12] Implicit in such a judgment and all concurrence with it is the unconscious androcentric bias of the grammarians that "he" adequately designated the species. When pressed to argue the case, more than one grammarian was able to appeal to a "common sense" recognition that the male is superior to the female and is therefore the appropriate choice unless there were clear "female markers" in the statement. In a seventeenth century grammar we read one such common sense rationale for the assigning of gender to make English more latinate, "The Masculine is more worthy than the Feminine, and the Feminine is more worthy than the Neuter."[13]

That "common sense" appeal also undergirded the decision of the seventeenth- and eighteenth-century English grammarians to use the pronoun "he" to refer to God. One version of the position is worth quoting: "The Supreme Being (God . . .)

10. Ibid.
11. Stanley, "Sexist Grammar" 802.
12. Ibid. 801.
13. Cited in Miller and Swift, Handbook 63.

is, in all languages, masculine; in as much as the masculine sex
is the superior and more excellent . . . ."[14] That usage is clearly
recognizable as androcentric.

At the end of the twentieth century, once the history and the
issues involved have been exposed to light, decisions have to be
made. Should this new knowledge about the story of English be
suppressed as serving the self-interest of "elites"? (The impli-
cation of such a question is that women as a group constitute a
self-serving elite.) Or must the knowledge be taken into account
in both popular and professional decisions about contemporary
usage? Whether or not English-speakers want to face the questions about false generics, sexist rules of concord, and all other
manifestations of androcentrism in the English language, these
matters have been brought forward into the public forum. It is
evident from the history of the language, starting with Old English through Tyndale, Coverdale, Cranmer, Chaucer and Shakespeare, that the language has the capacity to be crafted creatively
to meet new social realities if there are gifted users and crafters
of language at hand. Women's claim to the recognition and inclusion of their full human personhood in all social and cultural
institutions, including language, is one such distinctive late
twentieth century social reality.

Presently trade and textbooks publishers, journalists, television commentators, and feminist grammarians, are acting as pace-
setters for the development of the language.[15] At these levels,
the false generic has generally been discredited; lapses into such
usage are perceived and treated as lapses. Various approaches
to alternatives to grammatical and lexical androcentrism are being
tried. If none of them are yet wholly congenial to the ear, nevertheless, large numbers of English speakers and writers have
committed themselves to exploring and expanding the limits of

14. Gould Brown. *Grammar of English Grammars*, (1851), cited in Stanley,
"Sexist Grammar" 804.

15. Scott, Foresman and Company and McGraw-Hill, major textbook publishers, had produced guidelines to non-sexist writing for editors and authors
by 1975. The most recent edition of *The New York Times* stylebook provides
norms for its editors. Other organizations of all kinds who deal in written texts
and spoken languages have found themselves falling in line, whether out of
conviction or necessity.

the English language. In this regard, English is at a new stage of its continuing development. It is in this context that episcopal conferences vested with responsibility for authorizing suitable language for public prayer must reflect on the implications of this socio-cultural development for the continuing cultural adaptation of the liturgy. As with so many other matters, not to decide is to decide. The English of the liturgy will be inclusive, or it will be exclusive, androcentric, and sexist.

Liturgical English: Theological Foundations

Not only are society and the English language in a time of transition with regard to their inclusion of women; so also is the church itself struggling with the matter of the inclusion of women in its public life. In order to determine an appropriate way of responding to the challenge of inclusive language in the liturgy, the matter must be considered in its fuller ecclesial setting.

Four foundational considerations warrant attention if the church is to find its way forward in the matter of inclusive language. First, the work of translation of liturgical texts, whether from Hebrew, Greek, the Vulgate, or ecclesiastical Latin, is inevitably an hermeneutical process. The translator interprets in order to mediate between the worlds of the two languages being negotiated and also to establish correspondence between doctrine and ecclesial praxis. Second, the Catholic tradition understands that the Scripture and the liturgical books are books of the church, sacred records of revelation yet documents written by a human church and interpreted by an historical church. Third, the norm for their interpretation is faith in the risen Christ present in his Holy Spirit and presiding over our human concerns. Fourth, Vatican II, as a council of the church, has provided some clear ecclesiological principles to guide the universal church in its self-understanding as it ventures every contemporary interpretation of its faith. These four foundational elements will be commented on briefly.

1. The Hermeneutics of Faith. Theologicans guided by linguists have become increasingly sensitive to the fact that religious language—whether that of the Scripture or the liturgy—becomes meaningless to its users if the language does not contain some recognizable reference to the actual social and ecclesial

experience of those users.[16] That same point is reflected in the 1969 Roman document on liturgical translation which asserts: "The prayer of the church is always the prayer of some actual community assembled here and now . . . . The formula translated must become the genuine prayer of the congregation and in it each of its members should be able to find and express himself or herself."[17] Accordingly, the language proposed by the church as the language of faith needs to be scrutinized not only to determine fidelity to past experiences of faith but also to discern ways in which it corresponds to the experience of the contemporary church, including ways in which it either embodies or provokes alienation. Where formulas are incongruous with evangelical faith, they cause ecclesial as well as social deformation.

2. The Tradition and the Church's Books. All decisions about the language proposed for public prayer must be guided by a sound interpretation of the whole formative Christian tradition, including the scriptures, non-canonical witnesses to Christian antiquity, and the liturgy as a celebration of ecclesial existence. Put simply, the contemporary church must inquire how and why women were included within and excluded from ecclesial experience from the beginning if it is to have an evangelical standpoint from which to respond to the challenge of inclusive language. Repetition of time-honored cliches about women's place drawn from church fathers cannot substitute for critical scholarly investigation into the place of women in "the Jesus movement" and in early Christianity.[18] Neither can a living tradition be shepherded adequately in an age of historical consciousness by falling back on Vincent of Lerins' dictum (*quod semper, quod ubique, quod ab omnibus*) that the authentic tradition embraces what was taught everywhere and at all times by all the pastors of the faithful.

16. See, for example, E. Schillebeeckx, "The Crisis in the Language of Faith as a Hermenutical Problem," J.B. Metz and J-P. Jossua, ed., *The Crisis of Religious Language*, [Concilium 85] (New York: Herder and Herder, 1973) 31–45.

17. Consilium. Instruction on the Translation of Liturgical Texts for Celebrations with a Congregation. Jan. 25, 1969. *Documents on the Liturgy 1969–79: Conciliar, Papal, and Curial Texts* (Collegeville, Minn.: The Liturgical Press, 1982) no. 123.

18. See, for example, Elizabeth Schussler Fiorenza, *In Memory of Her* (Crossroads Books, 1983).

Society and culture have, from the beginning, played an influential, perhaps even decisive role, in the shape given to Christian institutions. Not all possibilities of the inculturation of Christianity in human society have been exhausted, even in its Graeco-Roman-European trajectory. The church's books—its Scriptures and its liturgical texts—its ecclesial order, and its public worship, are human responses to divine grace. Grace will continue to invite fuller human response.

3. The Gift of the Paraclete. The criteria for discernment concerning inclusive English in the liturgy are the same criteria according to which the church must make judgments about its inclusion of women in its mission and ministry. One such criterion is the question: what are the fruits of inclusion or exclusion? Discernment of spirits is understood as a spiritual art grounded in a life of prayer, for pastors of the church no less than for its religious and laity. Much has been written about the art of personal discernment and that form of institutional discernment proper to the magisterium. Further, the church in every generation but especially in periods of renewal has been blessed with guides to authentic discernment. Yet it seems that simple holiness, humility, and the wisdom of love are the church's final protection against ideological distortion of the Christian faith from any quarter. Christian insight into the inclusive language question and the integration of women within the church will overcome ideology only in a church universal capable of obedient listening to what the Spirit is saying through the local churches.

4. The Council as Point of Departure. The immediate fruits of the Vatican II council suggest that the council was an event of grace sustained for several years through the holiness, humility and wisdom of love alive in its chief pastor John XXIII and called to life in his co-pastors. Vatican II ecclesiology provided the foundations for responding to the inclusion of women in the language of prayer and in the public life of the church. It did so by constructing an ecclesiology of "the people of God" whose Christian identity and mission were grounded in baptism.[19] A full theology of baptism is yet to be developed. Nevertheless, post-conciliar decrees for the implementation of the council immediately opened up new, even if limited, possibilities for women's par-

19. *Lumen Gentium*, Ch. 2.

ticipation in the church's ministry, in administrative, pastoral, and liturgical roles. Where the ecclesial experience of women has been expanded for two decades, the incongruities and discrepancies of sexist language in the church's public prayer has grown beyond being a simple irritant to being an occasion for alienation and anger within the community. Yet insofar as women's experience of themselves as non-persons in the church persists, some Roman Catholics may perceive the official introduction of inclusive language into public prayer as hypocritical. Post-conciliar praxis—what the church does—is basic to clear judgments about the appropriate language of public prayer— what the church says at prayer.

The rapidity with which translators of liturgical texts worked in the late 1960s and the general absence at that time of any cultural concern about women may reasonably account for the uncritical androcentric translator's bias on the one hand, and for the widespread use of false generics like "man," "brother," "son" and the purported sex-indefinite "he." In fact, the 1969 Roman document on translation anticipated difficulties caused by haste in the preparation of vernacular texts. Yet neither translators nor church officials foresaw the rapid cultural shift which has given rise to the inclusive language issues of the 1980s. Nevertheless, the new situation must be faced. The Roman translation instruction itself provides a warrant for a thorough review of the ecclesial implications of the androcentric bias of currently authorized English translations of liturgical texts. "Above all," it says, "after sufficient experiment and passage of time, all translations will need review."[20]

Establishing the Scope of the Issue

In the church's recent discussion of the matter of inclusive language, it has become a commonplace convention to distinguish the "horizontal" and the "vertical" realms.[21] Such a dis-

20. The International Commission on English in the Liturgy, a mixed commission of episcopal conferences which use English as a principal liturgical language, has begun the work of revision of the texts of the Roman Missal. The projected completion date is the early 1990s.

21. See, for example, *Newsletter* of the Bishops' Committee on the Liturgy, April, 1985, "The Revised Grail Psalter: Statement of Archbishop Pilarczyk" 13–14.

tinction intends to differentiate between the way the church uses language to refer to itself as an historical community made up of male and female members and the way it uses language to refer to the living God.

1. "Horizontal" Language. Even when we limit the discussion to the way the church refers to itself in the language of its public prayer, we are faced with a diverse range of issues. At a first level are those items in the church's lexicon already identified as false generics, like "man," "son," and "brother." Since both the liturgical rites and the lectionary use these false generics routinely in translations, the magisterium has to come to terms with its own authority over its ritual books, including the liturgical lectionary, both in the original languages and also in official English translations.

Where a Latin *homo* has been rendered "man," one kind of judgment is called for, namely, whether "man" adequately expresses *homo* in today's English. But when a Greek *adelphoi* appears in the Scripture, a *fratres* in the Vulgate, and a "brothers" in English bibles, another kind of judgment is called for about the presentation of such a text in the liturgical lectionary. Here two kinds of critical historical judgments are called for. First, did the ancient languages, too, deal in androcentric terms which concealed their intended inclusion of women as well as men? Were these words true or false generics in the classical languages? Second, did "the Jesus movement" which used *adelphoi* to name the community of believers nevertheless include women in the life setting of the text? If women were intended in the male reference, the question is once again simply about an adequate translation of such terms in today's English.

At a third level for judgment are those liturgical texts in which women's inclusion in some aspect of ecclesial life is itself at issue. Priests, bishops, and deacons are males, and ordination prayers may thus seem to be ruled out as irrelevant to the discussion of inclusive language. What about the texts for the Installation of Readers and Acolytes in a U.S. church in which women regularly exercise those ministries? Must resolution of the antecedent androcentric bias about ecclesial behavior come before resolution of suitable ways to translate the church's prayers into contemporary English?

A fourth area of judgment concerns both lectionary and sacramentary texts which involve androcentric projections about human persons and androcentric personifications of people and things. For example, opening prayers for feasts of missionaries assume that pastoral leaders in the missions are male. Also, women martyrs constitute a subspecies of martyr in the sacramentary, and their commemoration still evokes references to weakness and to sex.[22]

Israel sinful or unfaithful, a type of the new people of God, is personified as woman—adultress, whore, defiled like a menstruous woman—in the lectionary for the Liturgy of the Hours.[23] David, biblically certified adulterer, lecher, and murderer is a liturgical type for the obedient and faithful believer. Here the resolution of stereotyping problems will not come from translations into inclusive language in a narrow sense, since the distortions have been created by an established androcentric tradition of juxtaposing types. It is worth noting in this regard that the Roman liturgy prior to the promulgation of the 1969 lectionary did not regularly read from the Old Testament in the eucharistic assembly. Thus the patristic tradition of sexist stereotypes has been kept alive primarily through the (predominantly) male clerical and monastic praying of the Liturgy of the Hours. This fact suggests that further lectionary reform for the readings of the Hours may already be in order if the church, in the light of new knowledge, is to go beyond simple concern for inclusive language to face other manifestations of androcentric bias in the liturgy.[24]

2. "Vertical" Language. When attention is turned to the language the church uses in its public prayer to name or to address the triune God, complex questions emerge, some linguistic, some theological.

At the linguistic level, it is useful to recall the eighteenth-century grammarians' motives for making "he" and the reflexive

22. Roman Sacramentary, 1969. Common of Pastors, 10, 11, 12. Common of Martyrs.

23. Liturgy of the Hours. Readings from Ezekiel and Hosea. Eighteenth and twenty-fourth weeks of Ordinary Time, with their responses. See also lectionary for Mass, year 2, nineteenth week of Ordinary Time, Friday.

24. Marjorie Proctor-Smith, "Women in the Lectionary," in Women: Invisible in Church and Theology. Ed. Mary Collins and Elizabeth Schussler Fiorenza. [Concilium: 182] (Edinburgh: T & T Clark, 1985) 51–62.

"himself" the "correct" pronoun of reference for God ("the masculine sex is the superior and more excellent"). It is evident that
there was no intent to assert that this usage was intended as a
"sex-indefinite he." Quite the contrary. Nor was anything said
about a poverty of the English language with regard to a generic
pronoun that would leave gender underdetermined in the face
of mystery.[25] The androcentrism of an eighteenth century patriarchal church and social system found the maleness of God
fully intelligible. Is it possible to judge simply that the prescriptive grammarians' argument was weak, but that they were expressing, nevertheless, some transcendent wisdom about the
mystery of God? At that point, the theological question is raised.

Certainly the weight on an unexamined biblical and ecclesial
tradition seems to support the position that the God of Israel
("He had no female consort") and the God of Jesus ("Abba")
was male. Within this perspective, the occasional use of female
images by biblical writers is explained as poetic interlude, as
metaphorical use of language, an interesting departure from the
normative (male) language which pointed to God's essential
mystery.

Recent critical re-examination of the biblical tradition by scholars is raising doubts about the "normative" revelatory character
of male imagery even in a corpus of Scripture produced in a
patriarchal culture. The church is remembering that the author
of Genesis proposed that male and female together imaged God.
Scholars point out that the word choice "Elohim" rather than
the singular "El" as a designation for the one true God expressed
an experience of ineffable plurality within the divine essence.
The most high God, *El Shaddai*, bore a name which had cultural
reference to the many-breasted nurturing deity revered in the
ancient near East.[26] The name revealed to Moses, *YHWH*, was
a designedly ambiguous utterance which blocked all human effort to present God's mystery in the image of anything whatever
in the heavens and on the earth. The decalogue carried an explicit

25. Gail Ramshaw Schmidt. "De Divinis Nominibus: The Gender of God,"
Worship 56 (1982) 117–131.

26. David Biale, "The God with Breasts: El Shaddai in the Bible," *History of
Religions* 21 (1982) 24–56; F.M. Cross, "Yahweh and the God of the Patriarchs,"
in *Canaanite Myths and Hebrew Epic* (Cambridge: Harvard University Press, 1973)
52–60.

prohibition of images, which more or less effectively controlled the production of carved female idols. It was less successful in controlling verbal images. When the continuing revelation of a saving God had to be expressed in words, so scholars propose, the androcentric bias of a patriarchal society inevitably dominated the religious tradition.

In any case, a religious tradition which seems to worship its words rather than the ineffable reality which the words mean to evoke has not escaped idolatry.[27] Verbal literalism is characteristic of every fundamentalism. The significance of the Sinai revelation of the one true God as YHWH might well be the center of the church's re-examination of its current commitment to exclusive use of male images for God in public prayer.[28]

Similarly, the recent reduction of Jesus's experience of God to an *"Abba"* experience, with the implied judgment that "Father" is therefore the preferred and even normative Christian liturgical title for God, is questionable in the light of recent re-examination of the New Testament corpus. Such an approach to liturgical naming is ironically novel, not in any way traditional. The Roman liturgy itself exercised great reserve in its use of gender-specific forms of address like "Father" to name the divine mystery. The classical Latin collect, for example, preferred *Deus qui . . .* , *Deus cujus . . .* , and *Clementissime Deus* as appropriate liturgical address.[29]

This last point does not thereby rule out consideration of the question whether the Christian people in this culture might not need overt reference to the triune God's "feminine" attributes in an era when the unqualified adulation of "male" values like dominance, control, and rationality need to be corrected by celebration of nurturance, reverence for all created reality, and intuition as sacraments of divine mystery. In the words of the U.S. Bishops, "We are the first generation since Genesis with the power to virtually destroy God's creation."[30] Insofar as the image of God presented to the people in public prayer seems to endorse

27. M.B. Dick. "Prophetic Poiesis and the Verbal Icon," *Catholic Biblical Quarterly* 42 (1984) 246.

28. Mary Collins, "Naming God in Public Prayer," *Worship* 59:4 (July, 1985), 299; also this volume, Chapter 12.

29. Ibid. 300–04.

30. USCC. "The Challenge of Peace: God's Promise and Our Response," May, 1983, in *Origins* 13:1 (May 19, 1983) 30.

androcentric symbols of the divine rather than to celebrate an integrated experience of human reality and divine mystery, the church's "vertical" language is not simply neutral.

The meaning of the Incarnation, too, is liable to linguistic distortion, depending on whether the church's liturgy presents the humanity of Jesus Christ or his maleness as the center of soteriological significance. The translation of the Latin *et Verbum caro factum est* as "he became man" introduces into the liturgical creed the unnecessary use of a false generic, if indeed the problem is only on that level. Catholic people were once quite familiar with the *Angelus* formula, "and the Word became flesh." Thus, any suggestion that the use of "man" is an expression of orthodoxy guarding against the recurrence of classical adoptionist heresies lacks pastoral credibility.

On the other hand the assertion that maleness itself is the "natural symbol" for which the English "man" (meaning an adult male) is the appropriate creedal statement raises another range of theological questions.[31] The ambiguity of meaning is inevitably interpreted by ecclesial praxis. The church's restriction of women's participation in the mission and ministry of Christ seems to point to the meaning that Christianity believes "maleness" itself has intrinsic soteriological significance.

All these are serious language issues for the church's presentation of its faith in public prayer. Once a new horizon has opened up within the church concerning the androcentric character of Christian religious language, whether "horizontal" or "vertical," those who reflect on such questions in good faith are likely to perceive as ideological, a manifestation of bad faith, magisterial efforts to set certain critical questions off limits.

Ecclesial Readiness and Episcopal Responsibility

No doubt androcentrism remains the "common sense bias" of the faith community, bishops, priests, and laity alike.[32] But a new horizon is opening up among women and men who are

31. "Declaration on the Question of the Admission of Women to the Ministerial Priesthood," *Congregation for the Doctrine of the Faith*, Oct 15, 1976, nos. 27–30. Cf. "the Incarnation of the Word took place according to the male sex . . . and . . . this fact . . . cannot be dissociated from the economy of salvation."

32. Bernard Lonergan, *Insight* (New York: Harper and Row, 1978) on dramatic bias, 191–99.

questioning the received tradition because they find incredible
a Christian revelation that excludes women; among theologians
who have begun to reflect systematically on the presence and
identity of women in a sacramental church; and among those
pastors of the church who are attuned to such voices. U.S. Bishops so attuned are faced with a complex challenge to their role
as teachers and as guardians of the tradition. Some observations
about the challenge are in order.

First, bishops cannot do the work proper to the theological
community. Neither can they do without it. Accordingly, they
can expect and even demand serious scholarship from theologians in response to hard questions. Furthermore, they can refuse easy answers both from those who would dismiss the new
questions outright and from those who would reject the tradition
as irrelevant for the present situation. Maintaining a climate of
academic freedom within which the theological community can
work is one essential element in the exercise of episcopal responsibility in regard to the theological questions raised by the
inclusive language issue.

Second, the episcopal conferences can proceed without further
delay to deal with particular questions that are open to resolution
without any theological difficulty—e.g., the widespread use of
false generics in liturgical texts in sacramentary and lectionary.

Third, episcopal conferences can encourage their own commissions, the International Commission on English in the Liturgy (ICEL) in its recently undertaken revision of the Roman
missal and in all future revision projects, to look again at the
naming of God in its translation of the traditional Latin collects
and to avoid androcentrism in any texts to be newly composed
during the revisions.

Fourth, insofar as the call for inclusive language arises in the
context of tension about ecclesial praxis, conferences of bishops
can continue to promote the integration of women within the
public life of the local church, securing for women those roles
and rights already recognized in universal law. Further, the U.S.
conference can take the initiative to collaborate with other conferences within the universal church to extend official recognition to women's actual exercise of pastoral office and ministerial
roles in local churches.

Fifth, bishops in their own dioceses can establish and maintain
a pastoral relationship with those who, in gatherings for para-

liturgical and devotional prayer, are attempting to extend in creative ways the limits of both the "horizontal" and "vertical" prayer language, so that what is learned in such experience of prayer is not lost to the rest of the church in an era of renewal and cutural adaptation. It is axiomatic within the field of liturgical scholarship that what is prayed must be believed and conversely that what is believed must be prayed (*lex orandi, lex credendi*).[33] New experiences of God's presence, God's absence, God's hiddenness must be allowed to come to expression.[34]

Sixth, the bishops of the church, in the exercise of their teaching office must consider whether aspects of the tradition of religious images that served the church's public prayer in other eras might best be allowed to lie fallow, if not formally suppressed, for a time. Here the concern goes beyond inclusive language narrowly understood to a wider concern for the imagery of the Christian tradition. Does the androcentric and misogynist homiletic tradition of the early church fathers promote Christian faith, hope, love, wisdom and holiness, today? If not, is there either theological or pastoral reason to present such patristic images in readings for the Liturgy of the Hours or to suggest them in lectionary arrangements? Can the contemporary revival of the homily form be trusted to yield new gain over a period of time, generating a biblical-liturgical spirituality responsive to the human concerns of this era? Here the underlying question is about pastoral commitment to a life of prayer grounded in the reading of Scripture.

Further, does a tradition of the messianic reading of the psalms have absolute authority and take precedence over any other considerations in psalter translation and interpretation? Or is liturgical presentation of the psalter also subject to pastoral judgment about how some psalms might best be prayed in a new pastoral situation different from the one which first gave birth to the tradition?[35]

33. Geoffrey Wainwright, *Doxology* (New York: Oxford University Press, 1980) 218ff.

34. See my discussion of this process in "Devotions and Renewal Movements: Spiritual Cousins of the Liturgy," in *Called To Prayer* (Collegeville: The Liturgical Press, 1986) 47–68.

35. Balthasar Fischer, "Christ in the Psalms," *Theology Digest* 1 (Winter, 1953) 53–57; Pierre Salmon, *The Breviary Through the Centuries* (Collegeville, Minn: The Liturgical Press) 42–50.

Just as a liturgical lectionary is a selection of Scriptures to be presented to the church at prayer, a "canon within the canon," so also, comparably, every liturgical reform involves a selection of elements from a living tradition of public prayer. Judgments are always being made about the liturgical presentation of the church's faith. The cultural concern about the inclusion of women has introduced an additional, indispensable, criterion for the decision-making.

12

Naming God in Public Prayer

IT IS A COMMON ERROR THAT THE QUESTION "HOW SHALL WE ADDRESS God in public prayer" is an outcropping from an amorphous, socially marginal mass called "the women's movement." I do not think "how shall we address God in prayer?" is a tangential "woman's issue" but a radical theological and ecclesial question, although I am aware that my calling this matter a theological and ecclesial question and bringing it to the attention of liturgiologists will not protect it from the vagaries of human perception. Nevertheless, with all its potential for provoking misperception and even refusal of the question, I presume to bring it.

Critical thinkers in the field of liturgical studies may each have a distinctive specialization, a preferred method of inquiry, a peculiar pastoral competence. The new question—"how shall we address God in prayer?"—can only receive a thoroughly critical and authentically traditional answer if the whole field of inquiry which is liturgical studies receives the question. One of the best gifts for the critical mind and for a living tradition is the gift of a new question. The proximate source of this new question is the culture within which the U.S. and Canadian churches live. This is not the place to trace cultural history. But a context for the question can be sketched with a few bold strokes.

Cultural historians tell us that a Kennedy-era commission headed by Eleanor Roosevelt focused the cultural issue of women's rights in the United States by identifying a range of economic, legal, and educational injustices and inequities in society's dealings with women. The solution to such inequities was believed to be in preventive and corrective legislation to promote women's rights. That women's rights movement coincided, so the cultural historians also tell us, with the emergence of the related but distinct women's liberation movement. The women's liberation movement got its momentum not in Eleanor Roosevelt's high-level commission meetings but in the grassroots strategy sessions of the black civil rights movement of the 1960s. There women learned firsthand the sober truth that even in the intentionally egalitarian struggle to overcome the discrimination of racism there was a persistent assumption of female inferiority. Sexism was experienced and named by those women working in the struggle against racism who were limited to doing women's work—the cooking, the typing, the backup chores—so that male leaders could lead.

Women and men who began in that era to examine the cultural question "what about women?" discovered quickly that androcentrism was the common sense bias of the culture. Almost as quickly they recognized that androcentrism—the assumption that the male is the normative human being—gets its weightiest warrant from an unexamined religious cosmos. So it is not surprising two decades later that the questioning has spread: "what about God?" thoughtful people now want to know.

If we lived in a more orderly world, the question "what about God?" might be put off until systematic theologians have had time to give it their considered attention. One of my Catholic University colleagues, Elizabeth Johnson, set out a weighty research agenda for systematicians in a 1984 article on "The Incomprehensibility of God."[1] But our world is not orderly; and each week, while academicians and other church professionals struggle to meet deadlines on old commitments before taking up emerging agendas, liturgical assemblies assemble and begin to pray. The unknowability of God is not the premise of the liturgical assembly. The premise of the liturgy is that God's self-disclosure is occasion for celebration, for praise and thanks and intercession. Rightly or wrongly people who assemble for liturgy assume the divine presence and anticipate communion with the

1. "The Incomprehensibility of God and the Image of God Male and Female," *Theological Studies* 45 (1984) 441–65.

living God who continues to speak a word of invitation. But who among us knows with confidence how best to name this God of Jesus Christ today? "Our Father?" "Our Mother?" "Loving Parent?"

Some thinkers who presume this is not at all a difficult question start from the premise, finding support from Edward Schillebeeckx's *Jesus*, that the church should gratefully receive the revelation of Jesus' privileged experience of God.[2] Extended to the liturgy, the position carries the corollary that the gratitude of disciples should find expression in our willingness to name God "Father" as Jesus did. My own unease with the simplicity and clarity of such a starting point is as great as is my discomfort with the equally simple approach to the liturgical naming of God as "Mother–Father," or "Loving Parent." The remainder of this paper will identify three cognate areas of research which need to be taken into account as having some bearing on this vexing question for the church, "how shall we name God at prayer?" The first area is recent biblical research concerning the names *YHWH* and *Abba* as privileged names for the God of Jesus. That information is basic to all further discussion. The second and third areas are treated together more briefly: the Roman liturgy with its distinctive tradition of addressing God, and research being done in the field of medieval spirituality, specifically in the use of feminine metaphors for God.

One further preliminary observation is in order in contextualizing the question. It would be easy to assume that the naming of God is a problem for a relatively few liturgical assemblies, namely, those made up either of educated elites or of the alienated. Were that the case, such assemblies could be left to their own devices, to cope or to fade into oblivion in due time as marginal groups finally do. But what if the assemblies where neither presider nor preacher nor congregation are troubled by androcentric address to God are unwitting or willing participants in idolatry?[3] Then the stakes for the church of Jesus Christ are high indeed.

2. (New York: Seabury 1979) 256–59.

3. The question of idolatry has been raised by more than one feminist theologian; it has not been engaged but ignored in magisterial and theological arenas. See, for example, R. Ruether, *Sexism and God-Talk* (Boston: Beacon 1983) 22–27.

The refusal of the question in church and academy is no solution. It is no solution because it assumes that truth about God
is already in possession. At best the refusal signals an abdication
of critical thinking in favor of the common sense bias of androcentrism; at its worst it may signal the arrogance of the powerful
or the indolence of the complacent. At the deepest level, the
refusal may reflect a profound inability or unwillingness to trust
in the very mystery of God.

Monica Furlong, writing in *Contemplating Now*, speaks indi-
rectly to that last circumstance. She observes that the common
assumption is that the church means to put people in touch with
the living God. But she notes that few people attend to the
church's other role, namely, filtering out an experience of transcendence which might be overwhelming.[4] She notes that liturgy
particularly serves that purpose, putting an assembly in touch
with the mystery they wish to approach without their experiencing that reality too immediately. Liturgy's buffer role is not
without a potential for distortion.

Theological talk about mediated immediacy is familiar to liturgical theologians. But the symbols of mediation must be kept
supple, tensive, if they are to be useful to the church not only
as buffers but also as paths bringing access to the living God.
We have good reason to ask whether "Our Father," "Our
Mother," or "Our loving Parent" are normative liturgical symbols whether they are exclusively effective paths to God in this
culture at this time.

The ancient norm is to pray to God with, in and through
Christ. But how do we name the Living One, the Holy One,
who is ineffable? Monica Furlong is certain that God seekers can
afford randomness in their naming of God since "God (and religion) are metaphors for something for which we have no words
and which we cannot adequately describe."[5] But can the church's
official liturgy risk greater randomness in the naming of God,
and so risk abandoning androcentrism, anthropomorphism, and
even all personalizing metaphors? If randomness is possible, are
there any limits to it? If randomness is not permissible, why not?
What norms must be honored?

4. 2nd ed. (1971; rpt Cambridge, Massachusetts: Cowley 1983) 36.
5. Furlong 38.

Are There Normative New Testament Names of God?

The research of Joachim Jeremias has given rise to what has become conventional wisdom about the normative character of the Aramaic "*Abba*" for naming the God of Jesus Christ. Jeremias' work lies behind the now commonplace assertion that Jesus' use of *Abba* is an unprecedented expression of intimacy, behind which lies his unique experience of the Holy One of Israel.[6] That position has led to further speculation, and recently significant correlative positions have been advanced in popular and semi-popular discussions of the liturgical naming of God on Jeremias' authority. These have had implications for the public prayer of the church. One such proposition is that *Abba*-Father cannot be considered one metaphor among many others, that it is no metaphor at all but in fact the self–revelatory new name. A second increasingly popular proposition is that *Abba*-Father is normative address for Christians gathered in public prayer.

Because of the authoritative nature of Jeremias' work, and because of its widespread dissemination and reception at the scholarly and even popular levels—no doubt in part because of its attractiveness and cogency for Christian self-understanding in a time of confusion and in part because of its unwitting reinforcement by early ICEL decisions related to the English translation of Latin liturgical texts—few liturgical and systematic theologians have been attending to dissenting voices elsewhere in the scholarly world. But dissenters there are, and a critical approach to the church's public prayer requires that not only Jeremias but his critics be heard on this question of the centrality of *Abba* as the distinctive New Testament revelation of God's name.

One early counterposition was advanced by G. F. Moore, whose classic study of rabbinic literature led him to the judgment that there is little distinctive or unprecedented in Jesus' use of *Abba*. According to Moore, "our father in heaven" was neither unique nor original language, but religious idiom characteristic of "the type of piety in which Jesus and his immediate disciples were brought up."[7]

---

6. *The Prayers of Jesus* (Naperville, Illinois: Allenson 1967) 53ff. See also *The Central Message of the New Testament* (London: SCM 1965).

7. *Judaism*, 2 (Cambridge, Massachusetts: Harvard 1950) 211.

More recently Joseph Fitzmyer of Catholic University, among others, has taken exception on philological and textual grounds to the now widely repeated position of Jeremias that *Abba* is intentionally informal and intimate, in contrast to the more formal and distant Aramaic *"Ab."* Fitzmyer finds no clear evidence to substantiate the assertion; his judgment has endorsement from his peers in the field.[8]

A third scholar, Madeleine Boucher of Fordham University, has undertaken research examining once again the same Old Testament and New Testament textual data which lies behind Jeremias' interpretations and conclusions. A preliminary report on her research, given to the Catholic Biblical Association in August 1984, records her finding that Jeremias has seriously overestimated the number of Synoptic texts which are pertinent to the discussion about *Abba* as central either to Jesus' understanding of God or his prayer.[9] Boucher's critical reconsideration of the Synoptic texts brought her to the judgment that four texts at best might be considered authentic sayings of Jesus, and of these only one is an address in prayer. That is the text in which Jesus teaches his disciples, "Pray, then, like this: 'Our Father in heaven. . .'" (Mt 6:9, Lk 11:2). Boucher's own concluding remarks in her preliminary report are worth citing: "While it does not overturn the thesis that Jesus called God 'father' and used the Aramaic word *abba,* it does suggest, I think, that the view that *abba* represents the central statement of Jesus' mission must be reassessed. It casts serious doubt on Jeremias's thesis concerning the centrality of the father-image for God for Jesus' theology."[10]

Boucher's research is pertinent to what is happening in liturgical assemblies, because it challenges positions now being advanced by systematic theologians who are opinion makers, like Edward Schillebeeckx. Boucher notes, for example, the way in which Jeremias' work has recently gained new authority

8. *A Wandering Aramaean* (Missoula, Montana: Scholars 179) 134–35. See also, for example, K. Stendahl, *Meanings* (Philadelphia: Fortress 1984) 156; also 161, n. 13.

9. "The Image of God in the Gospels: Towards a Reassessment" (unpublished address to the Catholic Biblical Association, August 1984).

10. Ibid.

through Schillebeeckx's master work *Jesus*. Schillebeeckx's work draws heavily on Jeremias' exegetical authority; that authority is at the basis of his discussion of Jesus' Abba experience. Yet with a circular force, Schillebeeckx's own systematic development of the Abba experience now lends new authority to those who now argue or simply assume it is proven that "'Abba' is God's Christian name."

What if, as Boucher proposes, Abba is not so central as has been claimed to Jesus' own experience of God and hence not normative for ours? What if the widespread use of Abba in the Synoptics, in John, in the rest of the New Testament corpus, is derivative of the early church's experience of Jesus as Son of God? Does New Testament usage block off all further development of and critical reflection on the church's naming of God in prayer? Or does God remain ineffable, even in the face of the new revelation made in Jesus Christ as recorded by the evangelists? Does the church have the only one true name Abba, or are we left with more or less adequate metaphors for our naming?

Raymond Brown's Fourth Gospel research opens the question further.[11] John's Gospel designates God as *pater* 109 times, but Brown does not draw from the frequency of usage any conclusion about the normative character of "Father" for naming the God of Jesus in the Fourth Gospel. Rather, he finds the key to Johannine understanding of Jesus' own experience of the ineffable God in the *ego eimi* strata of that Gospel.

In reflecting on the matter of the divine name in the Fourth Gospel Brown notes the use made in late Judaism of I AM as a divine name. He proposes that such usage in the religious milieu of the early community may explain the central use of I AM in John. It is that name I AM which claims Jesus, which he reveals to his disciples, and which he must glorify. Suggests Brown, "it is quite possible that John thinks of *ego eimi* as the divine name given to Jesus."[12] C. H. Dodd, earlier, had read the evidence of John 17:6 and 26 as leading to a conclusion similar to Brown's. In his 1958 book, *The Interpretation of the Fourth Gospel*, Dodd had

11. *The Gospel According to John I–XII* (Garden City, New York: Doubleday 1966) 533–38.
12. Brown 537.

concluded, "the mission of Christ in the world was to make known the Name of the Tetragrammaton."[13]

Brown's disinterested study of the Johannine tradition within the larger New Testament tradition of the naming of God draws him to point out the diversity within that formative tradition concerning Jesus' own receiving of, bearing, and revealing the name of God. Brown makes no claim for a single privileged name of God central to the identity and mission of Jesus, as Jeremias does for Abba, for example. Rather, Brown underscores the fact of diversity, drawing attention also to the point that for Acts and Paul the name given to Jesus at which every knee should bow is Kyrios (Ph 2:9).[14]

"Abba?" "Kyrios?" "Ego eimi?" The twentieth century church cannot draw closer to Jesus' own experience and naming of God than the evangelists allow us to come. The variety and plurality in the gospel tradition is a positive asset at this moment in church history. More particularly, the rediscovery of the centrality of the ineffable I AM in the Johannine presentation of the God of Jesus opens up greater possibility than we currently allow ourselves either in liturgical or devotional prayer for what Monica Furlong calls "randomness" in addressing God. That opening up is critically important for the church of Jesus Christ caught up in a culture which is caught up in the idolatry of androcentrism.

Religious imagination and mature faith cannot be separated. Accordingly, literalism and confusion about the nature of religious language are serious barriers to mature faith when the church gathers for public prayer. Academic liturgists and church professionals are not powerful enough to control what occurs in the imaginations of Christian assemblies. But we can influence decisions about what images are set out before believers if we are willing to do the hard work of research and critical reflection.

In this regard, it would be well for liturgists to consider a recent study on the question of verbal icons and verbal idols as a problem already operating within the Old Testament tradi-

13. C.H. Dodd, *The Interpretation of the Fourth Gospel* (Cambridge: CUP 1958) 96.

14. Brown 537.

tion.[15] The biblical prohibition against making images (Dt 4:15ff) was carefully detailed and subsequently interpreted as a prohibition against fashioning idols in plastic form. But the text itself concludes with the warning: "Take heed, therefore, lest forgetting the convenant which the Lord, your God, has made with you, you fashion for yourselves an idol *in any form whatsoever*" (emphasis added). The study shows that the prophets as writers of great power, crafters with words, became increasingly vulnerable to their own strictures against human crafting of divine images. A self-critical church might well ask whether it has ever been guilty of worshiping its own words, e.g., Abba-Pater-Father, or Kyrios.

It is my premise that the primordial revelation of the ineffable God, the name given to Moses which has come down to us as the enigmatic YHWH is the sole normative biblical revelation of the divine name. God remains mystery, even after Jesus Christ. All other language, including the pronouns, is metaphor, or verbal icon, if you will, pointing us to the experience of God, drawing us into the mystery, participating in a measure in its reality, but never comprehending it.

The metaphorical status of pronouns is worth singling out because their power of interpretation is all out of proportion to their virtual concealment in our ordinary nonconscious use of language. Although gender-specific third person pronouns do not figure directly in the address of public prayer, in their subsequent occurrence in prayer texts, they function to interpret our naming and so to control our imaginative freedom.

Gail Ramshaw Schmidt has already discussed the problem of the pronouns in the context of her 1982 *Worship* article on the gender of God, concluding with the judgment, "It is incumbent upon us to eliminate altogether in American English the expository use of pronouns referring to God."[16] In place of detailed

15. M.B. Dick, "Prophetic Poïēsis and the Verbal Icon," *Catholic Biblical Quarterly* 42 (1984) 246.

16. "De Divinis Nominibus: The Gender of God," *Worship* 56 (1982) 129. For further discussion of this and related issues of gender in liturgical language see Ramshaw-Schmidt's *Christ in Sacred Speech* (Philadelphia: Fortress Press, 1986).

recounting of the problem, let me cite only a single sentence to illustrate the interpretative power of the pronoun in every reference to God, theological or doxological. Speaking about Raymond Brown's and C. H. Dodd's discovery of the centrality of the I AM as the decisive name of God in the Fourth Gospel, a sympathetic commentator wrote an ironic summary of the argument: "Revealing the Name means revealing the very reality of YHWH *himself*."[17] The primordial revelation of the ineffability of God must be proclaimed again in our churches and must be believed. Our readiness to believe will be tested by our freedom from or bondage to gender-specific pronouns or to an uncritical, univocal, androcentric, liturgical "Father."[18]

Feminine Metaphors for God and the Liturgical Tradition
What about feminine metaphors and so also feminine pronouns when we address the ineffable God of Moses and Jesus? Recent scholarship has uncovered sound evidence that language expressive of the motherhood of God has a firm place in the Christian religious imagination.[19] The language appears often enough in the writings of mystics and in devotional prayer texts; there is no evidence that it ever broke through into the liturgical assembly. Why? Some preliminary observations are in order.

Liturgical prayer is trinitarian, and the development of trinitarian language was inevitably caught up in the androcentric undertow of human language. Theologians like Gregory of Nazianzus made valiant efforts to hold the line against confusing the realms of rational discourse, religious imagination, and verbal literalism. In the course of his fifth theological oration Gregory took note of traps in trinitarian language: "maybe you would consider our God to be male . . . because he is called God and Father . . . and that deity is feminine because of the gender of the word and Spirit neuter, because it has nothing to do with

17. Emphasis mine. G.H. Parke-Davis, *Yahweh. The Divine Name in the Bible* (Waterloo, Ontario: Wilfred Laurer University 1975) 78.
18. *Women and the Word. The Gender of God in the New Testament and the Spirituality of Women* (Mahwah, N.J.: Paulist Press, 1986).
19. C.W. Bynum, *Jesus as Mother. Studies in the Spirituality of the High Middle Ages* (Berkeley: UCP 1982) 110–11. Notes 1–3 provide extensive bibliographic data.

generation."[20] Yet Gregory himself asserts, with full confidence in the power of his own rationality to recognize the technical use of language in theological discourse, "if I saw the necessity of distinction, I should have acknowledged the facts without fear of the names."[21] But what are the facts about appropriate ways of praying to God *per Christum Dominum nostrum?* And should Gregory and the whole church have had more fear of the names and their power to remake God in their image?

It is a matter of record that the classical Roman liturgical tradition was most circumspect in its naming of God in the collects and the whole repertoire of orations. The celebrated sobriety of the Roman liturgy expressed itself at least in some places in religious language which resisted the ordinary androcentric undertow of human language. Where the classical Roman collects were able to avoid overt androcentrism in their address, it was for the most part because they first avoided the more explicit forms of anthropomorphism.

However, it was their very abstract quality that has made them unattractive to many who gather in our churches to pray in English in this late twentieth century. In our mass, depersonalized culture, Christian people have seemed to need to speak to a God capable of providing acceptance, consolation, nurture, and love.[22] Accordingly, the classic Roman patterns of invocation—"Almighty and merciful God" or "Almighty and eternal God" or simply "God who . . ."—have recently yielded more and more to "Father." The distance from "Our Father" to "Our Mother" to "Loving Parent" is not great in this culture. Having begun this movement in our assemblies, we have good reason to continue to be self-critical about how we are naming God in liturgical prayer.

There is an unspoken assumption in much of this development that naming God "Mother" in public prayer means celebrating divine compassion and mercy rather than God's justice and redemptive power, and that this of itself is a great gain for women,

20. Gregory of Nazianzus, "The Fifth Theological Oration: On the Spirit," in *Christology of the Later Fathers*, 7, tr. C.G. Browne and S.E. Swallow, ed. E.R. Hardy (Philadelphia: Westminster 1954) 198.
21. Ibid.
22. For a discussion of this cultural issue and its impact on liturgy, see U.T. Holmes, "Ritual and Social Drama," *Worship* 51 (1977) 197–215.

who presumably embody the former but not the latter attributes of God. I would like to examine that assumption out of a genuine concern for and commitment to the full stature of women as whole human beings, as disciples of Jesus, as images of God, and as members of the Christian churches. Before we embrace narrowly construed feminine images and feminine pronouns just as uncritically as we have embraced androcentrism, it is useful to be attentive, however briefly, to critical study of the tradition of feminine imagery in prayer and mystical writing.

Carolyn Walker Bynum's study *Jesus as Mother*[23] looks carefully at textual evidence of the use of female imagery for God in the Cistercian writings of the twelfth to the fourteenth centuries and in the works of the nuns of Helfta toward the end of that period. Her findings are pertinent to this discussion.

First, she establishes that what she calls the feminization of religious language takes place primarily among male writers. Gertrude of Helfta, for example, has less interest than Bernard of Clairvaux in dwelling on the way in which God is Mother for those who draw near. Second, she finds the key to the difference between the Cistercians and the Helfta nuns in the content and the context of the writings themselves. Feminine images appear regularly in devotional discussions of the abbot as image of God.[24] Third, she observes that the issue at stake in these discourses about the motherhood of God is male ambivalence over suitable exercise of their authority. In her reading of the texts, female images of God gave the Cistercian abbot authorization to nurture as well as to judge, to comfort as well as to discipline.[25]

By contrast, Bynum notes, women writers of Helfta like Gertrude and Mechtilde express a high measure of comfort with and confidence in themselves as images of a God who, simply as God, judges and also shows compassion, disciplines and also comforts, acts justly and fairly and also forgives. Bynum's judgment is that the spirituality of these women writers reveals a solid sense of themselves as whole human persons who are images of a whole-making God.[26] The evidence suggests it is the

23. See note 19 above.
24. Bynum 113–25, 158.
25. Bynum 112ff, 154.
26. Bynum 225–27, 255; on the *imago Dei* theme see 17, 101f, 134.

Cistercian men who define themselves first as stereotypical males and then have to negotiate stereotypically feminine qualities for themselves.

Bynum underscores two patterns that emerge from the data. The first is that the male writer's use of feminine images of God is consistently stereotypical throughout the twelfth to the fourteenth centuries.[27] The convention of stereotyping is much less prominent among the women mystics of the era, though not all women writers avoid it.

The second pattern has to do with what we would today call projection. According to Bynum, it seems to be the case that the feminization of religious language, the use of feminine images of God in this era, had very little, if anything, to do with real women's identity as human persons and as images of God.[28] Male writers employed feminine metaphors for their own purposes, without doing any damage to the common sense androcentric bias of the religious culture. Rather, their efforts served to protect and to bolster men's sense of themselves as normative images of God.

Why is this data on the medieval feminization of religious language pertinent here? In my experience, much if not most of what is currently happening in our liturgical assemblies, ostensibly to try to overcome androcentrism in God language still operates within that same androcentric horizon. It still has little to do with real women as full human beings capable of manifesting the whole range of human gifts and defects, as capable as men of imaging the God who is creator and redeemer of the world. The pronouns continue to give us away, exposing our androcentric mentality. When a presider, in leading the community at prayer, ventures a pronominal "she" or "her" to refer to the God of Jesus Christ, it is virtually certain that the prior metaphorical referent has been maternal. The persistent assumption, that what characterizes women's personhood is motherhood, is solidly androcentric.

Certainly the metaphor of God's motherhood can enrich the religious imagination and the language of public prayer, and some adventure in this area will bring gain to the church's re-

27. Bynum 131ff, 147, 166.
28. Bynum 146–50.

ligious imagination. This is not an argument to suppress the maternal metaphor, but an argument to contextualize it. Women are mothers; but as the Helfta nuns knew, women as women are also agents of justice and judgment; women act with fairness; women courageously use their power to challenge the mighty on behalf of the poor. In fact, in this present era we are increasingly aware of women all over the world who have been leading the way in confronting structures of violence and calling nations and men to justice and reconciliation. Are these not the characteristics of the one ineffable God YHWH in biblical tradition?

An uncritical cherishing of androcentric images of God in public prayer at the end of the twentieth century is self-indulgent, whether men or women do the cherishing. Still, if we are willing to take up a self-critical stance about the naming of God in public prayer, we are in danger of being left speechless in our liturgical assemblies—stumbling over our words as Jeremiah and many mystics have done: "Ah . . . I do not know how to speak" (Jer 1:6). The meeting house of the Society of Friends where the North American Academy of Liturgy gathered in 1985 was a good place for liturgical professionals and academicians to acknowledge the poverty of our language and the inadequacy of our imaginative resources when we wish to call upon or speak of the ineffable God made known to us in Jesus. We believe, with the Quakers, in an inner light which will enlighten those who sincerely seek God. Meanwhile, we must wait prayerfully and expectantly for the coming of the Holy Spirit of Jesus to teach us again how to pray in our own day.

Nevertheless, while we are waiting to be taught through more profound prayer as a church, while we are struggling to be open to the experience of God among us, while we begin to reflect critically on that experience and on our linguistic resources, our liturgical assemblies continue to gather. How shall we pray? Certainly in the name of the Father and of the Son and of the Holy Spirit. But that is not the whole of the tradition.

If we set aside the androcentric inflection of the Latin God language, the address of the classical Roman collect—*Deus qui, Deus cujus, Omnipotens sempiterne Deus, Clementissime Deus*—may be more of a resource and guide for addressing God in public prayer than we have yet realized. Carefully crafted descriptive adjectives and clauses used to name a contemporary Christian

experience of God offer immediate relief for breaking our stereotypically androcentric language patterns. Such linguistic re-
sourcefulness also offers promise for long-term development of
an English language tradition for addressing God in public
prayer. Members of the North American Academy of Liturgy
have an opportunity to lead the church in critical reflection on
an issue which matters to all of us personally and which matters
also to our churches, whether or not they or we want the question. Hard questions are what an academy thrives on.

THE PRACTICE OF
WORSHIP

Introduction

In the early days of the liturgical movement in this century, its most articulate proponents knew that there was an intimate connection between worship and the life of the church. Studies of the efforts of Lambert Beauduin in Western Europe and Virgil Michel in the Midwestern U.S. leave no doubt that these men expected that the renewal of church and society would come through the renewal of the liturgy. If they were short on theory about how it would occur, they were deep in their conviction.

In the post-conciliar period, it became commonplace for Roman Catholics to isolate the commitment to liturgical renewal from concern for a just social order. It was as though one could "choose a constitution"—*Sacrosanctum Concilium*, on the liturgy, or *Gaudium et Spes*, on the church in the modern world—and promote its agendas in some exclusive way. Social activists castigated liturgical enthusiasts for their religiosity, while devotees of liturgical reform could find magisterial foundation for their cause in the assurance that the liturgy was in some inscrutable way the "source and summit" of Christian life (SC, 10).

The work of cultural anthropologists who speak of religion as a cultural system which expresses and challenges itself most authoritatively in its public rituals now provides a human language with which to talk about what the best forerunners of the conciliar reform knew in faith, whether experientially or intuitively. The reform of worship is not an end in itself; it is not a self-contained system of mystery disconnected from ordinary life. Nor is it an aesthetic undertaking with validity apart from its capacity to draw the church more deeply into the paschal mystery of the death and resurrection of the whole Christ, head and members

Liturgical renewal will thrive on imaginative ritual redundancy, the expression again and again of the paschal mystery that abundant life is God's gift to those capable of loving their own lives and yet giving them for others. Where there is little or no insight into the paschal mystery as the way of salvation, cultural distortions continue to creep into and even take over the liturgical event. Cultural Catholicism will never be a thing of the past; it is always a present possibility. Elsewhere, because of lack of religious insight, traditionalism calcifies every familiar form from the recent past, confusing the familiar with living faith. The church everywhere is vulnerable to these distortions. None of us really wants to die to ourselves for the life of the world. Yet the authentic renewal of worship may yet empower the Christian people to commit themselves to the renewal of the social order. Faith and social theory both support that possibility.

13

Obstacles to Liturgical Creativity

ANY ASSERTION THAT CREATIVITY IS A CENTRAL VALUE FOR THE Roman liturgy requires us to go beyond the terms on which the Roman Catholic Church currently understands its own liturgical tradition. The text of the Constitution on the Sacred Liturgy provides little overt support for the element of novelty which is at the heart of the theoretical analyses of creativity in the twentieth century. The conciliar document indeed authorised a series of transforming interventions relative to the liturgy: renewing, restoring, reinstating, returning, correcting, emending, altering, adapting, doing away with, setting aside, suppressing, even introducing and producing. But the very authorising of such interventions confirmed not simply the fact of a well-established tradition of public worship but also the responsibility of institutional authority to guard it. Not surprisingly, the official pronouncement on novelty was caution against it: there must be no innovations unless the good of the church genuinely and certainly requires them. Even when the good of the church is at stake, any new form which might be adopted is expected to meet the criterion of growing organically from forms already existing (SC 23).[1]

Despite the magisterium's firm preference for the given rather than the novel, liturgiologists can point to many moments when

1. *Sacrosanctum Concilium* 23. Subsequent references will be noted only in the text.

bursts of liturgical creativity resulted in the displacing of the familiar by the unprecedented and in the gratuitous praise of God in novel but culturally congenial forms. The phenomenon of the continuing unselfconscious creativity of early generations of Christians, rediscovered in this century, has led one interpreter of the traditions to judge that the church of the first eight centuries welcomed everything good and noble into the liturgy.[2]

The purpose of this essay is not to debate that matter, although it is debatable whether the church consistently gained through its selective nurturing and suppressing of the unprecedented. The Chinese rites controversy is the most celebrated case, but it is not an isolated instance, nor necessarily the most important one, many women would argue. However, the essay is concerned with another matter. It aims first to establish a context for understanding present-day concern with liturgical creativity; next, to look at the creative process and the individual in the community as the agent of creativity; thirdly, to consider the social process by which the individual creative act enters the public tradition, and finally on the basis of these foundations to talk about the most serious obstacles to liturgical creativity in the Roman Catholic Church in this post-conciliar period.

Creativity as Cultural Value: Two Views

The notion that creativity is good and that a dearth of creativity is bad is relatively recent even in Western culture. Talk of human creativity first appeared relative to the individual artist as late as the nineteenth century and was extended to other human enterprise like economics, city planning, and liturgical worship only in the twentieth. Prior to this, God alone was called creator, since the concept creation meant fashioning something from nothing. In the nineteenth century, however, creation came also to mean making something new, and those able to generate the novel were called creative. The esteem for human creativity has grown steadily in Western culture, leading one philosopher to note that an indifferent or negative attitude towards creativity is virtually incomprehensible to contemporary people. It is in this cultural context that efforts to promote or inhibit liturgical

---

2. K. Seasoltz, *New Liturgy, New Law* (Collegeville 1980) 184.

creativity are taking place. Not surprisingly, the "ideology of creativity" has itself come under critical scrutiny recently.[3]

Some say Western preoccupation with human creativity simply mirrors the consumer culture and its taste for the novel, or the technological mentality for which the manufacture of a new product is good in itself. It is also said that the willingness to cherish individual self-expression as the supreme value of life is a natural outcome of this exaltation of creativity. The "punk" decadence of Western European youth is thought to be intelligible within this perspective. Such themes provide the basis for most negative judgments on the late twentieth century Western preoccupation with creativity.

But another more benign interpretation is possible. Creativity may be a "category of difficult life" according to an observer who notes that the fascination with human creativity and individual self-expression has paralleled the rise of the totalitarian state and the post-industrial mass society.[4] People who promote "creativity" are doing so, in this view, because of the conditions of their social existence, namely, life lived under institutions which diminish or curtail the human spirit. Exaltation of creativity in such situations might best be heard as the longing of peoples for transcendence and for the transformation of dehumanising social forms. Considered on these terms, it is possible to look positively on the recent Western preoccupation with creativity.

This philosophical discussion bears on efforts to understand developments relative to the Roman liturgy since Vatican II. In one form or another, each of these themes has appeared during the last fifteen years in the pages of *Notitiae*, the official publication of the Congregation for Divine Worship. The negative motif has been sounded recurrently to curb the perceived taste for novelty on the part of the clergy. Warnings seem to rise from and to be directed primarily to established churches in the North Atlantic countries, the cultural homeland of individualism. On the other hand, *Notitiae* has also published in its pages the li-

3. Pertinent papers delivered at an international conference on Creativity and Social Life held at Jablonna, Poland in August 1978, are published in *Dialectics and Humanism* 4 (1977) and 5 (1978).

4. B. Suchodolski, "Creativity-Reality: Hopes and Doubts," *Dialectics and Humanism* 5 (1978) 29ff.

turgical programme of the bishops heading the churches of the poor in Latin America. These churchmen assert that their peoples must have new forms for public worship precisely because so many lives are intolerably miserable. In order for these poor to be empowered to collaborate with Christian hope to overcome the political, economic, and social forces that oppress them, their bishops say that the worshiping assembly must itself be open to the liturgically unprecedented. Here the positive judgment prevails: creativity is a "category of difficult life."

Notitiae also reflects a positive Roman attitude towards the introduction of the unprecedented in the liturgical forms of the young churches of Africa and the minority churches of Asia. The welcome of the novel into the liturgical assemblies clearly aims to affirm the human spirit manifested in the cultural ethos of these non-Western peoples. Yet the very ambivalence of official Roman response to the post-conciliar impetus towards liturgical creativity invites further reflection.[5] Is novelty tolerable, permissible, desirable? For some but not all churches in the Roman rite? What are adequate criteria for making a positive or negative judgment on the creative impulses of local churches? Where is individualism at work? Where the effort to overcome human diminishment through celebration of the reign of God?

When philosophers evaluate the public significance of new art works and new social arrangements they focus on a central point: what is the impact of this novelty on the human community? Will the novel element generated by someone's unprecedented response to life help to build up the common tradition? Does it consolidate group identity and loyalty in changing times? Does it enable people to move forward together in a new situation? Does it break the power of repressive forces that constrict human hearts? Or does the novelty fragment the community? Does it increase alienation and group instability by encouraging individualism? Any of these outcomes is possible with the introduction of novelty into the public world of meaning. Underlying all the questions are a pair of clear criteria: is the new element intelligible to the community? and is it valuable for its life?[6]

5. See volumes 5, 7, 13, 18 of *Concilium* for examples of positive response to innovation; see volumes 8, 13, 14, 15 for typical warnings.

6. C. Hausman, "Criteria of Creativity," *Philosophy and Phenomenological Research* 40 (1979) 237–249.

Creativity: The Personal Act Within a Community

The novel element initially appears in the world of private imagination because someone searching for meaning perceives it as both intelligible and valuable. Imaginative individuals within a social group are the original locus of any form of creativity, whether artistic, social, or liturgical. In imaginative women and men the common tradition of public meanings meets the expansive human spirit aspiring to be and to understand more, and a creative interchange occurs.

Inculturation theory suggests that religious and so liturgical creativity is likely to occur as a local community with a generally coherent cultural system of public meanings, symbols, and behaviours seeks to appropriate to itself in culturally congenial forms the living tradition of Gospel faith which is already embodied in the cultural forms of earlier generations of believers.[7] Two currents converge to create a new one. But the creativity leading to that convergence begins inevitably in the private realm, and the agents of genuine creativity are seldom those who exercise authority over either operative tradition or conscious public meanings, ecclesial or civil. The genuinely creative form rises from the unconscious, and most predictably from persons searching for new possibilities of meaning not yet available in either tradition. Inculturation theory presupposes sparks of creative imagination already glowing in a community.

But imaginative persons venture more than their less imaginative sisters and brothers. They entertain images whose integration is possible only at the cost of the destabilisation or even the disruption of the known symbolic world. If the entertainment of unfamiliar images from private visions should yield new intelligibility, imaginative persons are often willing and at times even compelled to express publicly what they see. They will rearrange and even recreate the symbolic world for the sake of personal integration of their own further insight. Imaginative persons become creative, producing the unprecedented as they work at the psychic integration which generates insight and augments meaning for them personally.

Still, more than personal integration may be achieved. Once the novel has become known in the cultural community, it may

7. A. Roest Crollius, "What Is So New About Inculturation?: A Concept and Its Implications" *Gregorianum* 59 (1978) 735.

eventually be welcomed into the common public tradition. Inculturation theory becomes pertinent here. So does other research into processes of social endorsement.[8] Development within the public tradition depends on the community's readiness, leaders and members alike, to affirm that the new symbol or form is both intelligible and valuable. The community of faith is the sole arbiter of what religious creativity it will receive from its own members and employ publicly in its common life.

The dynamic of what is now being called inculturation can be recognised in the well-known achievements of those liturgically creative fourth-century churches within which bishops like Cyril, Ambrose, Theodore, and John Chrysostom presided. The communities these men served in the Mediterranean basin shared in common pre-Christian Hellenistic and Roman cultural strains that were the result of past military conquests. In addition, each population center also had the residual cultural features of pre-imperial indigenous local populations. Since every cultural tradition is a complex expression of true but only partial achievements of human community and meaning, each was open to new expressions of the human spirit.

Cultures are porous. Imaginative people, who lack the longevity of either culture or institutions, are ironically the pores of both. What gains entrance at a human point of permeability may eventually transform both the social community and the system of symbols by which it coheres. The Mediterranean cultures are an obvious historical illustration of this process which was operating long before the Gospel of Christ was proclaimed as a way of life. However, during the fourth century when the Gospel of Jesus Christ which had first seeped quietly into the low spots of imperial culture entered full-flood into the mainstream of public life, the creative interchanges and the new integrations which resulted had profound consequences. Nothing was the same: not the cultures, not the rites for public worship, not the peoples who came to the assemblies where the great bishops presided, not the bishops themselves.

Yet what subsequent generations of Christians know about the creativity of these churches is what was finally integrated into its common life and its liturgical assemblies. It is unlikely

8. See R. Firth, "Private Symbols and Public Reaction" in *Symbols: Public and Private* (Ithaca and London 1973) 207–240.

that what became part of the recorded tradition exhausts the range of what was conceived and even tried by imaginative believers in the effort to express what faith in the Gospel of Jesus Christ meant in the fourth-century communities. What was finally overlooked or set aside was not necessarily false or worthless. It is at least likely that at times a church closed its eyes to the blinding insight of one of its gifted members, opting for a less painful light. Creative individuals offer their gifts. Whether and why and how these are received touches on another set of social dynamics. What is perceived as confusing or dangerous will not gain entrance.

Institutional Sanction of Creativity

The 1963 Constitution on the Sacred Liturgy discloses the current formal arrangement by which any ritual creativity relative to the Roman liturgy must receive a triple warrant, at the local, national or regional, and Roman or central levels (SC 40). The arrangement reflects a practical judgment about suitable means to maintain the community of faith in the praise of God and the sanctification of diverse peoples. Even the most stable human institutions, the church among them, must have mechanisms for enabling creativity to effect institutional change or for inhibiting such an outcome. Someone must be authorised to apply the twin criteria of intelligibility ("the new form must grow organically from forms already existing") and value ("the good of the church is at stake") to the liturgically novel.

Before any formal judgment occurs at the institutional center, many informal judgments take place at its margins. The creative person communicates the gift of new form or new meaning, a personal achievement but by no means yet a public one. Others in the community must begin to entertain the creative gift with its correlative gain into the meaning of the life of faith. Aesthetic concerns are not insignificant in the initial presentation of the new form or meaning, but they are seldom decisive. In fact the creative individual will begin to recede in importance as the gift is entertained.[9] Does this attempt to reorder the world of common public meaning allow the community to see and to absorb a new vision and yet to keep a firm grasp on the common tra-

9. The work cited in note 8, at pp. 230–240 provides foundations for this discussion.

242   THE PRACTICE OF WORSHIP

dition? The community will inevitably suffer a measure of destabilisation as it is confronted with the unfamiliar. But if the new
insight originally born through the individual psyche's creative
achievement has power to reveal meaning latent in the tradition,
it will stimulate emotional, intellectual, aesthetic and moral response from others within the community. As that broadened
base of response signals a valuable augmentation of the tradition,
others will take it up, even promote it, and the social group will
have moved a step closer to sanctioning the gain as a public
achievement.

The formal sanctioning of the novel requires endorsement of
the official authorities in the community, those who are vested
with responsibility to "guard the tradition." Two human factors
can impede this step. One is the private preference or personal
sensibilities of the official judges, which leads them to respond
indifferently to one possibility, enthusiastically to another, and
with suspicion towards a third. The second factor is the tendency
of those who hold the common tradition in trust to identify its
interests with their own, so that what threatens personal or
group interests is perceived to threaten the tradition. In this
situation, the gift of form and meaning offered by the creative
member and welcomed in the community may be significantly
modified by the endorser, if it is endorsed at all, to weaken its
impact on the public life of the community and so to protect
those vested interests.

Recognition of these two obvious obstacles at the level of official judgment opens up the more complex question of authenticity or inauthenticity in the whole church's response to the
liturgically unprecedented. The fact of the existence of parish,
diocesan, national, regional, and Roman liturgical authorities
does not guarantee that judgments rendered at each level will
always work to the good of the church. Group inauthenticity is
a factor to be dealt with in any discussion of the dynamics of
liturgical creativity. It can operate at every level, posing the most
serious obstacle to lively and life-giving gains in the forms of
public worship.

Obstacles to Desirable Innovation

Earlier it was noted that a community will resist new forms
and meanings which are confusing or dangerous; the ecclesial

community is no exception. But not all novelty has such consequences. For example, much of the liturgically unprecedented
which the bishops of Latin America, Asia, and Africa are calling
for is that novelty of liturgical form which will allow a people to
express its praise of God in the many languages of its own culture: its rhythms, its colours, its code of social decorum and
hospitality, its dress, its ecological harmony with its own environment. These elements introduced into the liturgy will serve
to bond the people to the Roman Catholic Church. Such developments will not endanger a people's sense of well-being, nor
do they threaten to impinge on the well-being of the rest of the
church, unless, of course, a worshiping community lives with
the notion that worship has to do with disengagement from life.
Normally such changes are easily judged to be intelligible. But
are they the only valuable kind of innovation?

A theological consideration must be introduced. All liturgy is
the church's symbolic enactment of the mystery of Christ and
the church. It is theologically sound to celebrate the mystery of
salvation using forms which assert the dawning reign of God in
human history in all its particularity. But a peculiar creativity,
that of the Christian believer, is required to maintain evangelical
tension within liturgical assemblies so that they are not merely
mimetic of human achievement but a manifestation of what more
the reign of God promises (SC 2). Because the irruption of the
reign of God in history is dangerous, genuine liturgical creativity
cannot help but be potentially so.

Accordingly, it is not only possible but probable that certain
liturgical innovations which some see as confusing or dangerous
are also both valuable and intelligible for the advancement of
the Gospel at the end of the twentieth century. But to be open
to their value and meaning demands conversion. Yet as the Canadian theologian Bernard Lonergan notes in his discussion of
individual and group bias, certain insights are unwanted because
they lead to correction and revision.[10] A church which prefers
to repent and believe the good news selectively will protect itself
from dangerous insights operative in some forms of liturgical
innovation, favouring the harmless. Three strategies are readily
available to obstruct what is unwanted. They have to do with

10. B. Lonergan, *Insight* (San Francisco 1957); see pp. 187–193.

appeals to doctrinal orthodoxy, to power, and to human traditions.

Resistance to innovations with regard to liturgical ministers in the face of evident need is symptomatic of radical resistance to dangerous inbreaking of the Spirit of Jesus even in the church. New arrangements for liturgical ministry, once authorised, will undermine the past achievement of ecclesial order and the theology which supports it, leading to an unknown future.[11] What kind of church will it be in which the pastoral care and anointing of the sick, the witnessing and blessing of Christian marriages, the reconciliation of sinners, the celebration of the eucharist, and the formation of new Christians are recognised as the right and responsibility of the whole community of the baptised? But what kind of a church is it which fails to heal, strengthen, and nourish, to preach the Gospel, to bless, and to give thanks together because of a shortage of seminary-trained ordinands? What corrections and revisions in self-understanding will be demanded of the laity, of presbyters and deacons, of bishops, of the bishop of Rome, as these ecclesial constituents seek to open themselves to the value and truth of new possibility in the liturgical celebration of the mystery of Christ at work in the world? It is in the immediate interest of many to resist further innovation in liturgical ministry. It is not so clear that it is in the interest of fidelity to the apostolic mission of the church. Nevertheless, theological arguments can easily be joined to impede the development of liturgical ministries, forming in the name of doctrinal orthodoxy a screen against the creative insights rising in worshiping communities in every country. Liturgical innovation will require theological reinterpretation.

If theological obscurantism is one likely impediment to liturgical innovation, the high-handed use of institutional power is another. A single example will illustrate. In the 1970s growing numbers of liturgical assemblies in North America hospitably received the use of flat bread baked by a member of the assembly in occasional and even Sunday eucharists. Diocesan liturgical commissions monitored the practice quietly; the Canadian episcopal commission studied the matter theologically, historically, even scientifically. It prepared to release guidelines to shepherd

11. M. Collins, "The Public Language of Liturgy," *The Jurist* 41 (1981) 261–294.

the development, seeing in it a legitimate effort to assure that the bread of the eucharist was a convincing bread-sign, as required by the 1970 *Ordo Missae* (283). Roman curial intervention aborted the work of local and national commissions. Roman Catholic eucharistic assemblies in North America still remain hospitable to the notion that the specialness of the bread of the eucharist demands that it not be the product of assembly line host-making technology but the evident work of human hands, bread to be broken and shared as a pledge of commitment to discipleship. So the practice persists, somewhat less widespread now. However, bishops are not allowed to guide it nor to develop catechesis to interpret it; the Roman congregation expects bishops merely to suppress it.

High-handed uses of institutional power point to the delicate balance which must be maintained in the liturgical phase of the inculturation process. Inculturation theory asserts that the agents of creative appropriation of the received tradition to a cultural community are the community's own members, not those who represent the tradition's earlier achievements.[12] Where the balance of ecclesial authority—diocesan, national, and central—is not held in tension, liturgical innovations which are both intelligible and valuable will continue to be snatched abruptly from worshiping communities. Episcopal authenticity requires that bishops claim their pastoral responsibility and reintroduce tension into the balance of institutional power. Evangelical authenticity requires that worshiping communities press their claim for worship forms which give expression to life-giving insights into the dawning reign of God which is present, proclaimed, and celebrated in the liturgy.

Unfortunately, low levels of energy and commitment in worshiping communities harbor the third major obstacle to significant liturgical innovation. Significance implies that the unprecedented forms with their correlative insights reveal to the church more intimately and more powerfully the living Christ present and available for the world's reconciliation, for its conversion as well as its comfort. Each culture where the church dwells participates in a distinctive way in the social disorder which manifests the sin of the world. The Christian liturgical

12. A. Roest Crollius, in the article cited in note 7, 733.

assembly which fails to reveal the reconciling power of the reign of God is a flaccid manifestation instead of a dying Body of Christ. Such assemblies abound. In Mexico City on the feast of Our Lady of Guadalupe the powerful ecclesiastical and civil elites gather inside the basilica with US tourists to eat at the eucharistic table. Outside, thousands of peasants remain marginalised even on this patronal feast, performing ritual dances in the square to memorialise the coming of the Spanish conquistadores who shaped their world and diminished their humanity. There is no hint in either of these assemblies that anyone present believes in the power of baptism and the church's eucharist to overcome this division.

Human sinfulness generates institutions which use human differentiation as the basis for the aggrandisement of some persons at the cost of the diminishment of others. Anyone can see each 12 December in Mexico City unredeemed racism wearing the aura of sacred celebration, and no diocesan or national or central authority nor the people itself says "blasphemy" and requires authentic liturgy in the name of Christ. But one can find virtually everywhere liturgical assemblies which do the same thing, honor human arrangements that separate races, tribes, castes, classes, and the sexes, and mindlessly do so without reference to the mission and ministry of Christ and his church.

The shaping of new liturgical forms to affirm the value and dignity of each people is one level of the challenge for liturgical creativity. The reshaping of familiar forms to reveal the power of Christ to overcome actual human disorder and establish the reign of God is another. These must both happen if liturgical creativity is an expression of ecclesial authenticity. The second dimension will undoubtedly be experienced as confusing and dangerous in apparently prosperous ecclesial communities. These can take up in their defence theological obscurantism, high-handed uses of institutional power, spirtual and aesthetic delight in the familiar. Churches poorer in such resources because of a searching faith may be the weak point where the Spirit of Jesus will break through, giving an almost impervious church new ritual forms, new insight, and newness of life it does not yet find intelligible or valuable.

14

Eucharist and Justice

IN ELIE WEISEL'S NOVEL *THE OATH* WE HEAR A TALE THAT SPEAKS about the place of the service of justice in the life of the believer. The story situates us in a twentieth-century Eastern European village, one which is neither pre-holocaust nor post-holocaust, signaling the reader that a series of events which seems realistic is parabolic. In this village Christians and Jews give every evidence of being enlightened moderns. They relate well as neighbors, share a common public life, and enjoy a mutual regard. Then an apparently minor incident shows that the villagers' civility secures only a fragile peace, masking the tragic character of human existence itself, marred as it is by sin. The incident: an adolescent boy disappears from his home.

The disappearance is without explanation and initially fails to stir much interest among the citizenry. But the boy's mother, in her need to understand what is happening in her life, reaches back into her memory and finds what she is looking for, an explanation: "They have killed him; those enemies of Christ." At first the enlightened Jewish and Christian citizens consider this charge preposterous. But the boy is not found. No alternate explanation develops. And since there is nothing either to prove or to refute the mother's claim, the possibility begins to work its effect through the common memory of the whole population.

The Catholics of the town, following the mother's lead, become suspicious. True, they do not have a victim at hand, but only an unexplained absence. But they start to look for a culprit to blame for what is otherwise incomprehensible. Their imaginations are fed by anxiety and concern to contain the mysterious danger among them. The Jewish citizens, too, recognize the danger in the changing social climate. The leaders of the synagogue begin to see that it might be wise to have one person suffer to expiate the purported sin of their community and so control the Catholic thirst for vengeance.

An Hasidic teacher, Moshe the Mad, presents himself to the synagogue leaders as the potential martyr to save all the villagers from impending bloodshed. Reluctantly, his brothers agree to his plan. Moshe then presents himself to the police chief, confessing guilt for a crime widely fantasized but not established in fact. The police chief arrests him and tortures him mercilessly. But this fails to satisfy the chief's need for thoroughness in the performance of his duties. Because no body of a victim has ever been found, it first dawns on the police chief and then becomes a cherished conviction that Moshe had accomplices.

It becomes evident to the leaders of the synagogue that the imagined danger to the town cannot be abated by one man's self-gift. So the Jews prepare for pogrom, and Catholics prepare to become executioners of God's justice. What else can people do but play out the time-honored roles that have been stored in their common memory. In crisis, ritualization, not reason, promises to redress social breakdown.[1]

Moshe, temporarily released from the jail, broken and suffering, continues to try to think of a way out of the suffering for the next generations, should there by any survivors of the coming pogrom. In his search, he considers the role of the witness in the cycle of tragic Jewish suffering and then offers an unprecedented solution to the synagogue leaders:

We are going to start on an unexplored path which does not lead to the outside, to expression. We shall innovate, do what our ancestors and forebears could not or dared not do. We are going to impose the ultimate challenge, not by language but by the ab-

1. The behavior of Wiesel's fictional characters is plausible; theoretical foundations making it intelligible can be found in V.W. Turner, *Dramas, Fields, and Metaphors* (Ithaca and London: Cornell University Press, 1974) 35ff.

sence of language, not by the word but by the abdication of the word . . . . we shall testify no more.[2]

Silence will be the new response to uncontrolled human violence.[3]

Wiesel the narrator explains that Moshe had been visited in prison by the community's chronicler. He had reflected on the role of the chronicler as witness and had begun to recognize how chroniclers in every generation had chronicled the history of the people's suffering. It seemed somehow true that the fact of suffering and the chronicling of suffering were intrinsically linked. This pattern suggested a way out: the witnesses must refuse to witness, must take an oath of silence. Perhaps, then, the cycle of human suffering would be broken.

If it seemed an odd solution, Moshe nevertheless thought its very novelty commended it. "Here is one solution we have not tried." As he told his brothers in the synagogue, when the village authorities had allowed him one last conversation with them before they took him away for the last time, "If you agree, if you give me your trust, we shall resolve the problem of Jewish suffering. We shall do it without the help of the Messiah: he is taking too long."[4]

Wiesel's story only begins here, with the oath of silence by potential survivors and possible public witnesses to the impending pogrom. The impact of the oath on the life of one survivor is the substance of the tale. But three fragments of the vision which informs the novel are pertinent to the discussion of the connection between worship and ministering on behalf of justice. The fundamental vision is informed by biblical faith concerning 1) remembering as a religious act, 2) the justice of God, and 3) the role of the witness.

Each of these fragments of the biblical vision of the divine and human relationship are also operative as emerging themes in

2. E. Wiesel, *The Oath.* (New York: Avon Books, 1973) 243.

3. For a critical discussion of this theme in Wiesel, see Marie M. Cedars, "Silence Against Silence: The Two Voices of Elie Wiesel," *Cross Currents* (Fall 1986) 257–266.

4. Wiesel 244.

Roman Catholic sacramental theology. This essay will explore the theological question of the new Catholic concern for establishing greater justice in the world and its grounding in the liturgical celebration of the paschal mystery of Christ. It is Wiesel's ironic, parabolic tale that will help guide the reflection on the connection between liturgy and life which the church has overlooked too long, to its own peril and the peril of the race.

A Prefatory Note

Preliminary remarks are in order to set this inquiry within the context of the larger question whether ministering on behalf of justice is as important as eucharistic worship for the well-being of the church. The contemporary discussion has been framed in terms of post-conciliar teaching on the constitutive elements of the church. That discussion began with the 1971 Synod statement on *Justice in the World*. As Charles Murphy has indicated, the final sentence of the introductory section of the document precipitated a lively debate. The now familiar sentence reads: "Action on behalf of justice and participation in the transformation of the world fully appear to us as a constitutive dimension of the preaching of the Gospel, or, in other words, of the Church's mission for the redemption of the race and its liberation from every oppressive situation."[5]

Murphy inquires into what "constitutive" meant to those who drafted and presented the synod text, not because their intention controls its meaning but because their thought might suggest lines for further investigation and interpretation. He shows cogently that the final, officially approved text asserts grammatically that the "action" and "participation" being advocated are *"a constitutive dimension"* (emphasis added) of the Gospel. The first Italian version of the text used the definite article, reflecting the conviction of a drafting committee member that the Gospel is preached precisely by such action.

The tension in the synod text is pertinent, since more than

---

5. The complete text is available in D.J. O'Brien and T.A. Shannon, edd. *Renewing the Earth* (Garden City, NY: Image Books, 1977) 384–408. Cf. C. Murphy, "Action on Behalf of Justice as a Constitutive Element of the Preaching of the Gospel: What Did the 1971 Synod Mean?" *Theological Studies* 44:2 (June 1983) 298–310.

one Catholic concerned about social justice has voiced exasperation with the claim that the eucharistic liturgy is the "source and summit" of Christian life.[6] Some hoped to find in this synod document a corrective to what they perceived to be distortions and exaggerations about the importance of liturgy. Many found more credible in the contemporary world the belief that ministry on behalf of justice is the element which so constitutes the church of Jesus Christ that the church's authenticity stands or falls dependent on the absence or presence of such ministry in its self-definition and its life.

This reflection proceeds from the conviction **that** the ecclesial reality is constituted by a somewhat larger cluster of elements which, taken together, authenticate the church as **the** church of Jesus Christ. But these elements must be taken together; believers cannot pick and choose in the way they design a dish which pleases them at a salad bar. The viewpoint of this essay is that the eucharistic liturgy itself will lead the church, if the church learns to celebrate eucharist well, to an integrated understanding that authentic Christian life indeed demands that a local church which participates in the eucharist must also direct itself to ministry on behalf of justice. The reform and renewal of the liturgy goes hand in hand with the reform and renewal of the church.

Memory as the Memory of God's Justice

Wiesel's Moshe identifies the chronicler's task as chronicling the history of the suffering of God's chosen people. But there is something further which Moshe does not speak of that the canonical books of Moses testify to. The record of the people's suffering is inextricably woven into the history of God's own witness to human suffering. We read in the book of Exodus that at the call, "Moses, Moses . . ." the Lord declared:

> *I have witnessed* the affliction of my people in Egypt and have heard their cry of complaint against their slave drivers, so I know well what they are suffering. *Therefore, I have come down to rescue* them from the hands of the Egyptians and lead them out of that land into a good and spacious land. . . ." (Ex 3:7ff; emphasis added)

6. *Sacrosanctum Concilium*, par. 10.

In the scripture the chronicle of human suffering always leads to the account of how God set things right. This dual memory within the biblical witness has provided the basis for the Jewish people's sustained trust and hope in a God who had often acted and would act again on their behalf.

The psalms take up the theme of God as witness and redeemer and play it out in many modulations. The recurrence of the theme in the psalter, the temple hymn collection, establishes the vital connection between this matter of witnessing to the memory of human suffering and God's deeds in response to it and the business of public worship. Further, recent biblical and liturgical scholarship has established clearly that sound insight into worship is dependent upon some grasp of liturgical action as *anamnesis* or memorial in the technical sense in which that concept appears in the scripture.[7] Accordingly, any attempt to understand from a liturgial perspective why ministry on behalf of justice is among those elements which constitute the church must deal with the foundational notion of liturgical memorial.

The concept of liturgical memorial itself is grounded in a more basic understanding of remembering as a foundational reality in biblical religion.[8] YHWH, who tells Moses of the divine intent to rescue the Hebrew people from their suffering, subsequently confirms that intent by entering into a permanent beneficial relationship with the people by the gift of a covenant. Whenever the relationship deteriorates, the root cause of the breakdown is perceived to be either forgetfulness of the covenant promise by YHWH or neglect of the demands of the covenant relationship by the people. Remembering is the key to maintaining the covenant relationship. So remembrance is institutionalized in a variety of ways; liturgical institutions find their significance within this world of religious meaning.

Sabbaths and festivals, sacrifices and the reading of Torah, all

7. Cf. B. Childs, *Memory and Tradition in Israel* (Naperville, Ill: Alec R. Allenson, 1962), W. Schottroff, *"Gedenken" im Alten Orient und im Alten Testament* (Neukirchener Verlag, 1964).

8. J.B. Metz asserts that memory is "the fundamental form of expression of Christian faith," and that "Christians accomplish the *memoria passionis, mortis, et resurrectionis Jesu Christi"* in faith. Metz does not actually investigate liturgical memorial, however. *Faith in History and Society,* trans., D. Smith. (New York: Seabury Press, 1980) 90.

were directed to activate memory, that is, to overcome forgetfulness, oblivion, spiritual amnesia. The activation of memory is the activation of redemption. YHWH remembers by moving toward the people, "turning his face," toward them, intervening to bless or to correct. When the people remember, they recognize the relationship which is basic to their being and well-being; and this recognition prompts them to praise God, lament, express compunction, shed tears of repentance, or plead. But the true test of whether they have hardened their hearts or recommitted themselves and returned to God is not what they do in the temple but how they show justice and mercy to widows and orphans, aliens and strangers, and the dispossessed who live in the land.

Moshe's proposed alternative to his neighbors that they take an oath of silence, refusing any longer to witness publicly to the Jewish people's suffering, is understandable as a last resort. It is a radical response to God's apparent indifference to the voices raised generation after generation by those who have no other hope than God because hope in human help has been fruitless. Christian faith which claims that God has intervened decisively in behalf of the suffering world is incomprehensible to Moshe, because suffering has not abated with the presence of Christians. In Moshe's world, Christians are the source of human suffering.

Nevertheless, this foundational biblical understanding of liturgical events as works of remembrance which reactivate the redemptive relationship underlies the liturgical mandate of the church. When, on the night before he died, Jesus directed his disciples, "Do this for a memorial of me," he was operating within this biblical horizon. There is no reason, whatever the mixed results, to doubt that Jesus's intent for liturgical activity among his disciples was the constant reactivation of the saving relationship that his whole life had embodied. That the church has failed to grasp that saving relationship in depth is reflected in significant defects in both eucharistic liturgy and Christian life for many centuries.

While it is a Christian truism to say that Jesus's own life, death, and resurrection is the revelation of God's salvation, baptized Christians like those in Wiesel's parabolic village often seem to miss the point about what this way of salvation requires of them in ordinary life. This deficiency in understanding and acting will be considered below as both cause of and expression of deficiencies in eucharistic liturgical praxis. Accordingly, it will be argued that changed eucharistic praxis which sets out an expanded horizon of the mystery of redemption is basic to any serious new understanding within the whole church why "acts of behalf of justice and participation in the transformation of the world . . ." are constitutive of authentic living and preaching of the Gospel.

Behind this position lies the assumption that the overwhelming majority of Catholic Christians everywhere know what they know about the mystery of salvation, the mystery of the church, and their role in these mysteries from what they do or do not do within the liturgical assembly.[9] Neither occasional nor systematic instruction about Christian life and doctrine or about ministry for justice will have cogency for most believers unless that instruction sheds light on and rises from what they experience symbolically through participation in the eucharistic assembly over a lifetime.

It is always within the context of the problem of real human suffering that liturgical assemblies gather. The hard questions about salvation must be posed and understanding sought in the face of suffering. But before developing any further the relationship between the church's eucharistic praxis and its ministry on behalf of justice a doctrinal issue must be explored. Is God just? If so, what is characteristic of God's justice?

God's Justice: My Ways Are Not Yours

Paul, a first generation believer whose thinking was formed within the horizon of rabbinic Judaism and who consequently interpreted God's acts in Christ in terms of traditional rabbinic concerns, is an eloquent witness to the mystery of God's justice. While no attempt will be made to propose a developed Pauline theology of God's justice and human justification, key elements of the development of the biblical doctrine must be identified.

Although the *Jerome Biblical Commentary* warns that the Greek word *dikaiosyne*, employed in the New Testament to point to the mystery of justice, has "a broad range of meaning," contemporary English Bible translators help to delimit the range. Trans-

---

9. Theoretical foundations for this assertion can be found in C. Geertz, *The Interpretation of Cultures* (New York: Basic Books, 1973) 89–100.

lators use "right," "what is right," "holiness," and "righteous-ness," as equivalents for "justice." The concept of justice is clearly not self-explanatory. Justice is fundamentally an attribute of YHWH learned through historical experience that YHWH does justice and requires that justice be done. Justice is a primary characteristic of the covenanting God who is faithful to the promise, "I have witnessed the affliction of my people. . . . Therefore, I have come to rescue them. . . ." God expects fidelity in return. In the Old Testament, God is just both in punishing those who violate the covenant stipulations revealed through Moses and in blessing those who obey.

God's justice, so characterized, is problematic for a Job and a Qoheleth in the Bible and for Wiesel's Moshe precisely because of the apparent absurdity of the doctrine of God's justice in the face of innocent suffering and the impunity enjoyed by evildoers. The trio—Job, Qoheleth, and Moshe—are truthful witnesses to this absurdity. They are faithful witnesses to the memory of all the suffering which God never set right. It is within this frame of reference that Christian believers must come to recognize the mystery of the workings of God's justice in Jesus Christ. What is obscure becomes clearer in this light, what is absurd compre-hensible to faith. Jesus is the Just One (Acts 3:14), faithful and obedient, by all the criteria of the first covenant. Yet God allows Jesus to suffer, for this is the design of God's incredible justice.

Paul's formulation of the saving significance of this paradox comes through his creative rethinking of the covenant mystery of God's justice. The norm of God's covenant faithfulness is not simply the relationship established in Egypt and at Sinai, as-surance that the wicked will suffer and the good prosper. A new covenant is unfolding. The long-standing norm of the justice of God revealed in the Mosaic law has given way to the emergent revelation of "the law of Christ." Henceforward, it will be under-stood that the life, death, and resurrection of Christ Jesus is the true revelation of how God effects justice.

Jesus, son of God and God's obedient servant is a faithful witness that "Abba" will faithfully intervene on behalf of suf-fering and sinful humanity alike. But now it will be through Abba's chosen, his beloved child. In Christ, God will set things right and reconcile everything in the universe. But the reconcil-iation and justice God intends will not come easily. God's adopted children in every generation, those baptized into the death of Jesus in order to share also in his resurrection, will have to give their lives to honor God's will. The disciples will have to struggle, as the master did, to break the power of sin and to offer the human race a way out of its bondage to demonic forces. Jesus showed the way of God's justice: obedience to God's work of reconciling the world, born of trust, brought Jesus first to the cross and only then to glorification.

If Paul got hold of the mystery by naming this new revelation of God's justice the "law of Christ" (Gal 6:2), he is not the lone prophet of the mystery. The Johannine community captures the differences in understanding about the full justice of God through the ongoing debate recorded in the Gospel of John. At issue are contrasts between the way of Jesus and the way of Moses as Moses was customarily interpreted by the acknowledged holy men of first century Palestine. In the way of the Law, God's justice in honored through faithful observance of the Sabbath. But Jesus knows another way to honor the justice of God: "My Father is at work until now, and I am at work as well" (Jn 5:17). Jesus heals when he sees need, whatever the day. Collaborating in God's own work of setting things right takes precedence over even the unquestioned justice of Sabbath observance.

The Matthean community corroborates this unfolding mystery of God's justice. It witnesses to Jesus's teaching that believers' fidelity to God's justice must go deeper than the conventional notion that justice will be served through the norm of the law (Matt 5:20). In the church of Matthew, the just who are beloved of God and worthy of participation in the Kingdom of Heaven (25:34–40) are recognized to be those people who see human need and act to set things right.

In the contemporary theological discussion about the church's responsibility for doing works of justice, it is this justice of God revealed in Christ Jesus which is the heart of the matter. The goal of God's justice is setting all things right, making all things new, effecting atonement and reconciliation within the whole broken and sinful world. Commitment to anything less than that is a questionable commitment for the church of Jesus Christ and for each person who is a disciple of Jesus acting in Jesus's name.

Questions of strategy remain. How might things be set right in a disordered and sinful world? The "wretched of the earth" would undoubtedly be grateful to have even imperfect human justice established in their behalf. They would consider themselves justly treated if the UN Charter of Human Rights or those rights guaranteed by national constitutions were honored in their regard. Most would consider themselves blessed if unjust laws were changed—laws which put some peoples at a disadvantage even within their own societies. But the honoring of constitutional guarantees or international laws is inevitably less than the justice of God, which always intends more than the best human arrangements can achieve. God's justice offers forgiveness and mercy as part of the work of setting all things right.

It is the work of the eucharistic assembly to remember God's justice in its fullness in the face of human suffering; it does this through its remembrance of Christ Jesus. This memory of God's radical justice is the only authentic foundation for Christian acts on behalf of justice and participation in the transformation of the world. God's justice is not limited by human conceptions of what is good and fair.

The Church's Eucharist and Ministering in Behalf of Justice

In advancing the argument that eucharistic praxis is the key to the church's commitment to the justice of God, we must acknowledge the contribution of Dom Gregory Dix, an Anglican scholar, to contemporary liturgial reform through his classic study *The Shape of the Liturgy*. Dix's recovery of the archaic structure of early Christian eucharistic liturgy has made axiomatic the idea that a four-part action is basic to the church's eucharist.[10]

The four-part structure—take, bless, break, eat—is ritually elaborated in the symbolic ritual transactions which comprise the presentation of gifts, the great thanksgiving, the fraction, and the communion rite. The recovery of the structural integrity of the church's eucharist was one of the major achievements of the 1970 Roman *Ordo Missae*.[11] But the greater wonder is that the

10. G. Dix, *The Shape of the Liturgy* (London: Dacre Press, 1945) 48.

11. Par. 48 of the General Instruction on the Roman Missal acknowledges this structure; however, by joining the fraction and the communion under the single title "the communion rite," the danger is introduced of obscuring the fraction of the eucharistic bread and the pouring from the one vessal as themselves significant actions. This danger seemed to be confirmed in current praxis in the U.S. We tend to overlook in liturgy and in life the meaning of communion in the Body of Christ broken and the Blood poured out.

church's eucharistic praxis had been skewed for thirty generations or more by mutations in the archaic structure.

Dix himself had pointed explicitly to the need to look critically
at the ways the transaction of the presentation of the gifts had
developed in the East and the West, and to consider the impact
on ecclesial self-understanding consequent upon these developments.[12] Something of what Dix undoubtedly intended is reflected in recent discussions of the way in which the church's
offering for the poor gradually turned into the stipend system
for clergy support.[13] This change not only signaled the loss of
the communal liturgical act which linked the eucharist with the
service of the poor; it marked a profound disruption of the whole
ecology of eucharistic spirituality.

Presenting the offering had once been the prerogative and the
responsibility of the baptized. It was the initial movement in a
wonderful series of exchanges which climaxed in the communion
of all the church in the bread and wine become the Body and
Blood of Christ. But the rise of the stipend system and the decline
of the people's personal offering of their gifts for the eucharistic
table and for the poor bore witness to greater distortions of
eucharistic understanding. Concurrent with the rise of the stipend system and the decline of the liturgical offering, the laity's
participation in the eucharist was shrinking to the point where
the presence of the baptized was considered tangential to the
priest's celebration of Mass. In all four movements of the liturgical transactions which comprised the original shape of the eucharist, lay participation became expendable.

The stipend-governed restriction that there could be only a
single "donor" per Mass required no gathering of the church; it
did not even require the donor's personal presence. The great
thanksgiving of the whole church became a private priestly utterance, an act of personal priestly power. Ocular "spiritual"
communion at the post-consecration elevations of the host and
chalice replaced the laity's real eating and drinking from the

12. Dix 110–123.
13. M.F. Mannion, "Stipend and Eucharistic Praxis," *Worship* 57:3 (May 1983)
194–214; also E. Kilmartin, "The Sacrifice of Thanksgiving and Social Justice,"
in M. Searle, ed., *Liturgy and Social Justice* (Collegeville, Mn: The Liturgical
Press, 1980) 53–71.

eucharistic table. With no one expecting to eat and drink there was no longer need for the breaking of one loaf or pouring from a single flagon. The priest typically "communed" alone with the Body of Christ. When the laity occasionally received communion as church law required or confessors permitted, their presence came to be seen as a disruption of the eucharistic action and their communion was relegated to a position as appendage to the now-seriously-diminished four-part action.[14]

People with gnostic tendencies may be convinced that these ritual transmutations are insignificant, having little to do with either the church's sense of mission of its *de facto* ministry. Ritual theorists know better.[15] Rituals are about relationships; religious rituals are about ultimate relationships—about a people's origins and destiny and their true identity and purpose even in ordinary life. People learn who they are and who they are becoming before God by their very physical positions and their assigned roles in sacred assemblies, by what they themselves do and say, by what is said and done to them and for them, by the transactions in which their participation is either prescribed or proscribed. This learning, because it is ritual learning, is pre-conscious, not consciously available to the liturgical participants. It is nevertheless taken into their identities and is formative of the world view from which their behaviors will flow.[16] Liturgical participation provides a basis both for dialogical catechesis and for more systematic doctrinal instruction, something the great fourth century teachers like Cyril of Jerusalem, Theodore of Mopsuestia, and John Chrysostom knew well.[17]

The marginality and passivity of the baptized in all four moments of the church's eucharistic liturgy, their *de facto* expendability for a millenium, was inevitably internalized as the true state of affairs regarding both the baptized and ordained in the work of salvation. The program of revised rites of Vatican II was intended to renew the church through the reform of its liturgical

14. For a general account of this history, the best source is still J.A. Jungmann, *The Mass of the Roman Rite.* 2 vol. (New York: Benziger, 1951, 1955).

15. See R. Grainger, *The Language of the Rite* (London: Darton, Longman, Todd, 1974) ix–xii, 107ff.

16. Geertz 89–100, 127.

17. See, for example, *St. Cyril of Jerusalem's Lectures on the Christian Sacraments*, ed. F.L. Cross (London: SPCK, 1951).

praxis. That renewal will not come in a single generation. But the new possibilities for the church's being and well-being, for its identity and its mission, are not unrelated to what the church is and will be doing in eucharistic assemblies in this and subsequent generations in order to remember the mystery of the suffering of the world, the suffering of Jesus Christ, and the full justice of the one Jesus called "Abba."

Admittedly, little research has been done to establish the impact of different trajectories of eucharistic praxis on ecclesial life. Only now are theological foundations and suitable methods being proposed for sustained observation of the actual eucharistic celebration of a particular worshiping assembly and for tapping into the eucharistic meanings consciously available to those who preside and participate in these local assemblies. This preliminary work suggests that there is a great gap between the eucharistic doctrine of the great tradition and what is activated and formative in the life of faith in any given time and place.

Furthermore, in the course of this short reflection, it is impossible to address the rich tradition of eucharistic praxis in the four movements of the liturgy. At different times and places distinct ecologies of eucharistic action have prevailed; but more research is needed to understand these systems, their cogency, and their intelligibility for the churches which found the deepest meanings of their lives in them.[18] A single matter will be pursued further here in order to understand how liturgical renewal and renewed understanding of the church's commitment to works of justice are intimately connected.

Can You Drink the Cup?

The contemporary recovery of the eucharistic cup for the laity in the communion rite has the potential for great impact on the church's understanding of its participation in the mystery of Christ and of God's way of setting things right in the face of human suffering. The eucharistic cup is being singled out for attention because of the latent human and religious meanings "stored" there and waiting to be released in the church by an active recovery of the symbolic eucharistic transaction of cup

18. N. Mitchell contributes to this goal in *Cult and Controversy: The Worship of the Eucharist Outside Mass* (New York: Pueblo, 1982).

sharing. New experiences of cup sharing and new inquiry into its significance can prompt the church to integrate its emerging consciousness of its call to witness to justice with its eucharistic center.

The first obstacle to be overcome through renewed eucharistic praxis is the baptized's self-perception that they are somehow pneumatic cripples, limping along in life with a deficiency of the Spirit of Jesus. Liturgical praxis has contributed to and continues to contribute to this perception. An overdeveloped preoccupation with the spiritual power conferred at ordination coupled with devaluation or diminished awareness of the baptismal gift of the Holy Spirit have worked their effect over many ecclesial generations.[19] The charismatic renewal has served many of the baptized in reclaiming their Spirit-filled identities in this post-conciliar era. But this movement operates in an adjunct relationship to ordinary parochial life. How does the whole church move beyond the distorted and false distinctions that tell the laity they have a "passive share" in the Spirit while the ordained enjoy an "active share."

Paul maintained, "One Holy Spirit was poured out for all of us to drink" (I Cor 12:13). The image of the Holy Spirit poured out from a cup at which all gather to drink is unfamiliar, but it is part of the central Pauline teaching on the meaning of the common cup. In context, Paul sees in this drinking from the One Spirit the source of all spiritual gifts. The actual physical weekly drinking by all the baptized from the eucharistic cup will provide the strong experiential foundation needed within the church as it tries to deepen its appreciation that all are called to drink deeply of the Holy Spirit of Jesus and to open themselves to the Spirit's inebriating power and whatever consequences might flow.

Where there is no personal baptismal memory of the Spirit's transforming presence, the weekly eucharistic cup can stimulate the church's imagination. It can become the regular moment for remembering, reactivating, and sealing the redemptive truth long sunk into oblivion. The Spirit of Jesus imbibed within the as-

19. M.M. Kelleher's case study of the communion rite in a local church points out that the selective restoration of the eucharistic cup to lay liturgical ministers is being perceived as an affirmation of their having taken on a quasi-clerical status in their increased access to the altar. See *Liturgy as an Ecclesial Act of Meaning* (Ann Arbor, Mich: University Microfilms, 1983).

sembly is the same Spirit who was poured out on Jesus at his baptism and at the baptism of each believer. It is the same Spirit who conferred on Jesus his identity as the chosen one of Abba, who sent him to preach the good news of forgiveness of sin and to reveal the dawning reign of God by his acts on behalf of suffering and sinful humanity. It is the same Holy Spirit, the spirit of adoption, who has gathered the baptised to give thanks.

Paul speaks of this Spirit-filled cup as "the cup of blessing which we bless." The church's great eucharistic action arises from its awareness that all the blessings of salvation are gathered and focused in the mystery of Christ whose blood was poured out for the world's salvation. How are these blessings to be described? On the night before he died Jesus's own cup blessing disclosed what Abba was doing. God was revealing a new covenant to be sealed in the blood of his beloved child. From that time forward, the mystery of God's justice, setting things right on a cosmic scale, would be effected through "the law of Christ." This is the mystery that the way of salvation is along the path of self-giving. Every beloved child of God, born of God's spirit, would forever be asked freely to pour out their own life's blood for the life of the world. Regular drinking of the eucharistic cup in the Sunday assembly, accompanied by continued communal reflection on the meaning of the ritual act, promises to deepen the church's engagement with this mysterious blessing.

If communion in the Blood of Christ activates the memory that suffering for the life of the world is a blessing for those who drink deeply, it also stimulates consciousness of the reign of God already at hand and the joy possible among those who trust themselves to the mystery of the new covenant expressed in the "law of Christ." Again, on the night before he died, Jesus pledged that the next cup sharing between him and his disciples would take place in the kingdom (Lk 22:17). Every eucharistic communion in the Blood of Christ invites the church to faith and confidence that the communion already achieved in this broken world is only a taste of what is yet coming—full communion of all things in the universe with God, in Christ, by the power of the Holy Spirit.

Pneumatological, sacrificial, and eschatological dimensions of Christian life are packed within the sign of the shared eucharistic cup. These cannot be opened up, except abstractly, when a community is cut off from this primitive Christian ritual action. The scholastic doctrine of eucharistic concomittance operated at a level of theological abstraction, not at a sacramental level.[20] The eucharistic bread sign speaks eloquently of nourishment, but it does not bear the whole meaning of the eucharistic memorial. It is the cup, which at a human level witnesses to the human capacity for self-transcendence by the imbibing of spirits, that promises transformation and joy in the loss of self to the power of the Holy Spirit of Jesus.[21]

These are dimensions which are important for any sound development within the church of a commitment to action on behalf of justice and ministry for the transformation of the world. Unless Christian commitment to works of justice is integrated into the deepest level of Christian self-understanding through significant eucharistic renewal, the dreary alternative will be a new age of Catholic moralizing, only now generating guilt over social as well as sexual sin. Maturity of faith grounded in an integrated understanding of the mystery of Christ is necessary to sustain the new ecclesial commitment to justice. "Can you drink the cup I shall drink or be baptized in the same bath of pain as I?" (Mk 10:38) The liturgical posing of the challenge and the faith-filled response of the church gathered for public worship is at the heart of the church's spiritual growth in this regard.

Epilogue

We are going to start on an unexplored path. . . . We shall innovate, do what our ancestors and forbears could not or dared not do. . . Here is one solution we have not tried . . . . commitment to action on behalf of justice and participation in the transformation of the world based on our eucharistic communion in the Blood of Christ.

---

20. For a history of the theology of concomittance, see J. Megivern, *Concomittance and Communion* (New York: Herder, 1963).

21. P. Rouillard, "From Human Meal to Christian Eucharist," *Worship*, 52:5 (September 1978) 427–431.

15

Ritual Symbols: Something Human Between Us and God

TO STUDY LITURGICAL RITES IS TO RAISE THE QUESTION OF HUMAN mediation in religion. The early church fathers knew this. Augustine's pithy *sacramentum ad hominem* summarized the wisdom of the early centuries on the power of religious symbols to connect believers in the Lord Jesus with the great mystery at the center of their lives. Fifteen centuries later, we wonder whether we know more or less, and suspect we have lost contact with wisdom as we have taken greater control of liturgical forms. The promulgation and use of the *Directory for Masses with Children* invites some serious thought on ritual mediation of the eucharistic covenant in the Roman Catholic tradition.

Covenant and the Search for Meaning

Jesus revealed a new covenant relationship even as he faced the unknown as the beloved son who was not spared. At a meal with his disciples before he died, he took the familiar covenant enactment of his people and made it the bearer of the new covenant meaning: This cup is the new covenant in my blood. Whenever you drink it, do so in remembrance of me. Jesus, who ultimately faced the power of the living God without the mediation of the institutions of a religious tradition became himself a mediator for his disciples. He also indicated a mediatorial action, a bit of symbolic behavior that would condense all the meanings about life and death in a single action. This mediation of the new covenant through the eucharistic bread and cup remains the core of Christian liturgical action. It is the condensation of the whole mystery revealed through Jesus.

This ritual action is dense with points of references, layer upon layer: reference to the life of Jesus, to the old covenant, to the new situation revealed in Jesus, and to the experience of the community. This ritual action absorbed all the meanings of the covenant and the covenant community. It became for believers an amazing grace—something human between them and God, between them and the inexplicable demands of human existence. It disclosed a covenant and a way to enter into and seal the covenant. No longer were they left alone without understanding.

Eucharistic action for children is a curious phenomenon of our times. A covenant is carefully being shared even though childhood is not yet the time for the solitary quest for the meaning of existence: if I must die, what shall I do to satisfy my desire to live? All childhood exists in ordinary human covenant with whatever community nurtures it. It does not yet seek a covenant of ultimacy. Adolescence is filled with search for ultimate understanding about the purpose of life and love and sexuality. Adulthood must come to terms with time, loss, and mortality. Why, then a *Directory for Masses with Children?*

Without entering into the dispute over the initiation of children, it is a fact that the Directory is a significant development in the church of our times. This is evident when one considers it against the background of No. 23 among the general norms for liturgical renewal in the 1963 Constitution on the Sacred Liturgy: "there must be no innovations unless the good of the church genuinely and certainly requires them." The Directory is unprecedented in liturgical history, a fact not lost on the Roman congregations concerned.

The very existence of the *Directory for Masses with Children* constitutes an ecclesiological judgment supported by sound social psychology. Profoundly affective ritual experience of the eucharistic covenant in childhood supported by a developed religious memory and imagination will constitute part of the data of the emerging self in adolescence and adulthood. This personal awareness of covenant, once introduced in childhood, will have to be dealt with during that search for meaning which will inevitably come in virtually every life lived in this twentieth century.

Ecclesiology and the Eucharist

To keep the Directory in proper perspective, two other norms from the Constitution on the Sacred Liturgy need to be probed. Among those norms drawn from the ecclesial nature of the liturgy, No. 26 reads: "liturgical services pertain to the whole body of the church, manifest it, and have effects upon it."

And No. 34, based so the document says on the educative and pastoral nature of the liturgy, proposes: "rites should be distinguished by a noble simplicity; they should be short, clear and unencumbered by useless repetition; they should be within the people's power of comprehension, and normally should not require much explanation."

The eucharist celebrated with children, like every eucharist, manifests the church and has effects upon it. Every celebration pertains to the whole body. The theory is unquestionable. The existential tensions in the local church are sobering. Which church is manifested? What ecclesial norms are being embodied? What ecclesial structures are being reinforced in any eucharistic celebration, with or without children?

Avery Dulles' work, *Models of the Church*, has helped to identify one source of the tension which permeates much eucharistic action today. He notes that from Trent to Vatican II the prevailing model of the church was the institutional model, with hierarchical power and jurisdiction as the controlling concepts. Vatican II repudiated this as the dominant model. It did not, says Dulles, deny the institutional reality and the need for ecclesial order. It refused to endorse it as the sole or controlling model, supplementing it instead with other models of the church as mystical communion, as sacrament of salvation, as herald proclaiming the good news that shaped it, and even as the servant to the world.

Not many local churches, priest and people alike, are still unable to commit themselves to the new ecclesial situation and to abandon what the council has declared abandoned. While they may dutifully use the new liturgy, they do no more than that. They lack experience and so mistrust anything but an institutional model. Predictably, they cannot give expression ritually to a reality they do not know in any real way.

Ritual communication about the nature of the covenant community is powerful. In the language of academicians, ritual communication is a manifestation of ritual awareness—"conscious, but not too conscious." Ritual behavior grows out of the community's memory bank, lexicon, or reservoir of images and recollections about the religious ideal. No eucharistic liturgy can avoid saying something about the prevailing sense of church in the celebrating community—not simply by the words they use, but also by what they do ritually with comfort.

Consider an example of the way this works, whether for children or adults. On a major Catholic university campus only recently gone coed, there gathered for the Holy Thursday liturgy of the Lord's Supper a community made up of religious priests who sponsor the university, women and men students, and religious women of the area.

The distinctive ritual feature of the eucharist of the Lord's Supper is the footwashing in response to the proclamation of the Gospel of John. The footwashing takes the form of a structural inversion. That means simply that for a brief moment the high become low and the low high. Ritual inversion has two purposes. It affirms the more fundamental bond that unites the group prior to the role distinctions and ordering that normally obtain in the group—in this case the baptismal bond. Secondly, the ritual inversion affirms also that the role distinctions and order being suspended temporarily are accepted as ritual and necessary for the well-being of the group.

In the specific liturgy of footwashing in question, the provincial superior of the religious community of priests performed the ritual service, assisted by a deacon. This was comprehensible and congruent with the purpose of ritual inversion. Less comprehensible was the group of twelve assembled to manifest the *ecclesia*, the community of the baptized: six white adult males in their prime and six small boys, evidently their sons. Given the actual composition of the assembly, some preconscious lexicon was clearly at work for the liturgy planners, selecting and rendering visible and invisible, diminishing and augmenting to present ritually the religious ideal with which the community was comfortable. (There were no women at the last supper, were there?) The total eclipse of female presence in the ritual inversion process had the result not simply of making them structurally subordinate in the *ecclesia* which is hierarchically ordered. It made them extraneous, unwittingly, through the power of preconscious dispositions in the adult community.

How the Eucharist Speaks to Children

The *Directory for Masses with Children* says it is the catechist's task to lead children to "understand how from first communion on they may actively participate with the people of God and *have their place* (emphasis added) at the Lord's table and in the community of the brethren" (No. 12). The catechist is either supported or thwarted in each Mass where children are present. There is no "neutral" celebration without a preconscious ecclesiology. Some norms, some values, some structures, some ideal is always embodied—manifesting the local sense of church and confirming it.

Children will learn their place, and whether and to what degree there are different roles in the body for baptized and ordained, male and female by the shape of the assemblies in which they participate. They will learn, if they are involved in good eucharistic liturgy, that the community precedes the ordering of ministries within it. They will also learn that both the baptismal bond and the actual ordering of ministries are part of the ecclesial reality. If they continually participate in assemblies where the institutional forces of clerical power and jurisdiction and male exclusivism dominate, their ritual lexicon will contain only these entries.

Every eucharistic assembly will speak of the nature of the covenant community. It will do so in the mode of ritual, that is, through condensed symbolic action more powerful than any statements about ecclesial relationships. When the Directory advises catechists to lead children to "authenticity" of understanding about the nature of the church and their place in it, eucharistic catechesis is compromised by the inauthenticity manifested in the church itself. Claims of authenticity by a flagging ecclesiastical culture express themselves in eucharistic action through subtle but powerful manifestations of class distinctions, autocratic power and oligarchy. Rival counter-claims of authenticity rooted in populist culture propose *ad hoc* leadership without authority or responsibility. Theological authenticity demands bringing young children to experience the unity of a people with one Lord and diverse spiritual gifts—to a knowledge of holy order among a holy people.

The Directory endorses this theological authenticity when it states, "with the consent of the pastor . . . one of the adults may speak to the children after the gospel, especially if the priest finds it difficult to adapt himself to the mentality of children" (No. 24). The power of this proposition and its wise interpretation should not be underestimated. The experience from early childhood of a church which acknowledges distinctive spiritual gifts and orders them well in the community is capable of rocking the institution from within. A new sense of church which is not exclusively juridic institution is being communicated wherever pastoral need gives rise to practice contrary to law. A generation so formed, not by discussions about community and ministerial order but by liturgical experience embodying a renewed ecclesial sense, cannot at some future time be contained in older ecclesiastical forms.

It was said often in 1965 that the surest sign of the Holy Spirit's presence to the church in council was the hierarchy's willingness to endorse as good for the church things contrary to their own predispositions. In 1975 the existence of the *Directory for Masses with Children* with a broadened ecclesial vision is again testimony of the spirit's abiding presence to those who believe that the magisterium will countenance "no innovations unless the good of the church genuinely and certainly requires them."

The prospect of participation from childhood in a covenant community that embodies the covenant reality with great theological authenticity at every eucharistic celebration will help sustain the credibility of the covenant itself as childhood turns toward the adolescent and adult quest for ultimate meaning. The adult *ecclesia* will remain credible mediators of the covenant faith in the measure that they are grasped by it.

Ritual Awareness

Not only the ecclesial reality is at issue in eucharistic catechesis and celebration. The ecclesial fact only points the way to the relationships at the very center of the church's existence: the crucified Lord Jesus, risen and glorified at the Father's right hand, pouring out his spirit on his people. Ritual mediation of the trinitarian mystery of redemption, like ritual manifestation of the covenant people, demands some developed ritual sense. Unfortunately, both the Constitution on the Sacred Liturgy (No. 34) and the Directory seem to suggest that good ritual forms have clear and simple meanings. Nothing could be farther from the truth.

Ritual forms or ritual symbols—those molecules of rites by which things are handled, relationships expressed and events enacted—are dense with multiple meanings. Such actions function effectively as ritual symbols precisely because they continue to have the capacity to absorb and bear meanings from diverse referents. They have the capacity, therefore, to trigger the religious memory and imagination.

Ritual symbols are valued and retained in a religious community to the degree that they have power to tie it to the primordial religious experiences as the heart of the covenant relationships. A trio of airborne rabbinic students quizzing each other for a final examination on the meaning of horseradish and the appropriateness of raisins in the paste of apples, nuts, and wine illustrate the point. Secondary ritual forms may come and go in different cultural eras. Truly archaic ritual forms are not easily supplanted by new symbols. They have condensed centuries of religious experience and are no longer expendable.

This kind of ritual awareness, too, is most powerful when it is pre-conscious. Eucharistic action draws upon a preconscious lexicon of memory and imagination that recognizes profound saving power in assembling around the converting word and taking the cup of communion. Only when the religious memory bank exists does the norm apply that "rites . . . normally should not require much explanation." Eucharistic catechesis for children will develop the lexicon.

Liturgy of the Word

Since Vatican II and the introduction of the vernacular, certain false expectations about the word service in the eucharistic liturgy have become entrenched. Lacking any feeling for a ritual assembling around the converting word, many priests and people alike have come to expect either that the meanings of the word should be transparent or that the word service become an occasion for scripture study in community But ritual proclamation of the word is equivalent neither to a lecture nor to a study club. It is an occasion for acknowledging the relationship of this covenant people to the living word.

The *Directory for Masses with Children* advises, "Depending on the capacity of the children, the word of God should have a greater and greater place in these celebrations" (No. 14). The catechist or liturgist with sound ritual instincts wisely wonders: *depending on their capacity for what?* Capacity to read? Clearly not. Capacity for recognizing distinctive genres? Hardly. Capacity for language? Linguists tell us the child's language capacity is complex, and grows by exposure to unknown uses of language. The liturgical reading of a scripture text with rhythm and cadence has communication power beyond the sense of the words themselves. And children who have dealt imaginatively with TV's bionic man may be more ready than unimaginative adults to deal with Paul's first and second Adams.

Adults can and perhaps should function in the ritual role of lector. This constitutes a legitimate adult ministry. The practice of substituting or paraphrasing a text to eliminate difficult words and concepts so that beginning readers can read the covenant word implies that the goal of the word service is transmitting the words from the page in a book into sound waves familiar to children. The dominant issue is really the child's capacity for recognizing the community's relation to the living word. Children's capacity for active participation in the liturgy of the word is related to their capacity to interact with the word in their midst. Suitable catechesis will lead them to awe and fascination with the scripture as a two-edged sword, not easy familiarity with it as another child's book with which they soon become bored. Much more is involved than reading a half-dozen sentences.

Ritual Authenticity

Over the centuries the Christian people have employed a wide repertoire of ritual actions to express their relationship to the covenant word in their midst. Insofar as the church is, like Israel, a people of the book, Christians have carried the word in solemn procession, enthroned it, venerated it by surrounding it with lights, flowers, branches, movement; they have acclaimed it with shouts, echoed it in song, responded with instruments; they have proclaimed it in rhythmic cadence; they have attended to

it by taking distinct physical postures before it. They have ex-
pounded it in the homily and they have enacted it, as with the
ritual footwashing of Holy Thursday.

Not all of these ritual behaviors are within the child's "natural"
capacity. But most of these can be brought out in eucharistic
catechesis. Nevertheless—or for this very reason—authenticity
will remain the catechist's concern. What is ritual authenticity?
Is it to be found in revitalizing—or in repressing—the truly archaic ritual traditions of a people? If not in archaic ways, then
in what ways shall the relationship of the community to the
converting word become a manifested reality.

Admittedly catechists come from an adult generation which
is only now learning to discriminate between forms of ritual
authenticity centered on the covenant word and distortions of
the tradition which carried, enthroned, venerated, acclaimed and
attended to clergymen: *Ecce sacerdos magnus!* or which carried,
enthroned, venerated and acclaimed the living bread but failed
to take and eat it.

Eucharistic catechesis must take into account the fact that archaic ritual symbols of the covenant word and covenant communion are condensed expressions which refer to many things
and experiences simultaneously. Of themselves they are neither
good nor bad. The question is whether these ritual behaviors—
things done, said, handled, to express relationships—have the
capacity to tie this generation into the fundamental covenant
mystery. If they have this capacity, they remain part of a living
tradition even if they call for a behavioral repertoire that has no
parallel in contemporary cultural experience.

Ritual carrying and enthroning and acclaiming prelates has
generally ceased because the church has recognized this behavior
as an inauthentic expression of lordship, a distortion of the covenant relationship between the ministers and the people. The
disappearance of a Byzantine ritual style does not demand the
elimination of all symbolic acknowledgment of Lordship in favor
of equally absolescent rationalism. The catechist and the community are responsible together for introducing the children to
ritual behavior which is capable of expressing and bearing the
mystery of the transcedent relationships at the heart of Christian
life.

Ritual catechesis does not have as its task the identification of a single true meaning for ritual actions. The task is what the fathers of the church perceived it to be—the cultivation of the imagination and memory of the neophytes. Some ritual behaviors associated here with the liturgy of the word clearly suggest things Byzantine. But they also recall the ark of the covenant, the handling of the book of covenant found during the temple restoration, and the entry into Jerusalem of Jews, the living word of God.

Analogously, the one word proclaimed in every liturgy is the condenser of all the covenant does mean, has meant, and can mean. The relationship of this community is not to a single text, but to the covenant grace and the covenant demand expressed in it. Neither the child nor the adult believer is "conscious" at any liturgy of all possible meanings of the word for her life. Through good ritual celebration of the word children and adults alike can be conscious of the word as the power source by which they live.

Extending these reflections to the rite of making eucharist, it remains true that the archaic words, actions and interaction, have the power, for those ritually predisposed, to suggest and to unify many levels of religious experience, some receding and others emerging with greater or lesser prominence in any given ritual celebration. The footwashing rite of Holy Thursday is one way of enacting the covenant symbolically. The more ordinary way is that presented in the synoptic tradition and Paul's letter to the Corinthians: making eucharist in his memory until he comes. It is this covenant action which is the Christian answer to the question: if I must die, what can I do to satisfy my desire to live?

The impact of that covenant mystery is greatly diminished for children because they do not yet fully understand the question nor the range of answers to the question posed by their culture. Even for them the covenant symbols are capable of gathering and focusing the religious vision. In learning the traditions associated with the cup of the covenant, the cup of blessing and the cup of vengeance, and the cup of Elijah left untouched until the dawning of the kingdom, the young neophyte can absorb the meanings of hope and fulfillment associated with the eucharistic cup. In hearing of the grain which dies, the blood shed for the many, and the blood which seals the covenant the child can be introduced to the paradox of the eucharistic covenant that loss is gain. Associations with consecration as handing life over to God can come through familiarity with one's own hands raised in the *orante* posture, the bread and cup raised in liturgy, the Lord Jesus raised on the cross and raised to the father's right hand.

The Communion Ritual

The very ritual forms of eating and drinking to seal the covenant say something symbolically to the neophyte about the consequences of covenant with the risen Lord in this community. The eucharistic bread and cup left unattended with no instruction from the community about appropriate approach to the covenant food suggests that this is a group without significant moves or norms, customs or order.

On the other hand, the practice of distributing the eucharistic bread and cup by different rites for the ministers and the laity proposes to the neophyte in a powerful way the existence of two levels of covenant communion with the risen Lord—one immediate the other more remote.

Most current forms of the eucharistic communion rite make more ambiguous ecclesial statements fully appropriate to a transitional period. The continued insistence on the priest's prerogative and responsibility to place the eucharistic bread on the tongues of the baptized makes power and jurisdiction the controlling reality. The cautious use of officially deputized lay women and men to distribute the bread of eucharistic communion moves carefully toward a broader statement about ecclesial reality. Yet the simultaneous appearance throughout the land of simple, non-deputized ministers of the cup who assist the priest and community whenever need arises injects a ritual counterstatement that a new sense of church is already here.

It is not surprising that ecclesial concerns are more prominent than other doctrinal concern in this current evolution of eucharistic celebration and eucharistic catechesis. The nature of the church in all her relationships was the controlling issue of Vatican II. The ritual expression of these relationships—still being clarified in the local churches—will come not by abandoning the traditional ritual forms, but by discovering anew their power for good when used well in faith.

The *Directory for Masses with Children* makes provision not only for working *with* but also *beyond* the norms and values and structures and visions that obtain in the adult community. The church has thereby made the celebration of eucharist with children a privileged and sanctioned situation for the development and renewal of ritual forms for the eucharist of the church. Eucharistic celebrations with children are too important for either sentimentality or trivialization. If, because they fail to recognize the truth of the moment, catechists and liturgy planners make eucharist with children a sandbox for inconsequential fun and games not only this generation but perhaps countless future generations will be the losers. The possibilities of the moment are great— limited only by the theological authenticity and the religious memory and imagination of those entrusted with eucharistic catechesis and eucharistic celebration for the very young in the community.

16

Is the Adult Church Ready for Liturgy with Young Christians?

TWO PRIMARY SCHOOL CHILDREN WERE OVERHEARD IN A CLASSROOM conversation discussing their religion lesson. The teacher's objective had been to broaden the children's awareness of the needs of others. As one of the resources for the lesson, she had used a Maryknoll mission magazine. In it were photos of African children with distended bellies, suffering from kwashiorkor, a disease caused by malnutrition. Later in the morning Freddy and Brenda had returned to the reading corner and were reflecting together on the pictures.

Freddy wondered: "But how can you tell if you're starving or pregnant?"

Brenda knew: "Easy. Look with an x-ray. If there's nothing there, you're starving."

Sounding the Good News for the Young in an Alien and Alienating Land

Humor, so we're told, rises from unexpected misplaced, misdirected, or inappropriate responses to situations. But the Freddy and Brenda exchange is not pure comedy. It reflects the high level of alienation within the lives of many middle-class children in the Western world at the end of the twentieth century. Hunger is a human reality most of them have never really experienced; starvation is incomprehensible. Yet these are the grandchildren and the great-grandchildren of immigrants who were regularly in touch with human hunger—their own—just two and three

generations ago. Now children tend to be overfed. And they
have been deprived of access to the memory of the hunger of
their family as well as the human race. The story reflects another
kind of alienation: the intrusion of technology into ordinary life,
so that basic personal life processes are increasingly inaccessible
to people. Reflection on liturgical celebration for young Christians cannot abstract from this cultural reality. Adults and young
Christians alike are held captive by alienating structures in Western culture and by social institutions in the United States.

The fact is that the market in this land of plenty is full of things
for producing liturgies for young Christians. Not all of it is really
nourishing for Christian faith. It is not my purpose to provide
a theological critique of such commercially available materials;
nor to reflect on the current practice regarding children's liturgy;
nor to focus on the *Directory for Masses with Children* which has
occasioned our interest in the question of children's liturgy. My
concern is to look at the interplay between liturgy and cultures.
All liturgical events have a human cultural context which those
concerned with children's liturgy must take into account. Both
the social sciences and the traditional Christian faith can tell us
something about the limits of our present understanding of liturgy for children.

The current dominant values of American society breed attitudes of hostility which result in the exploitation and rejection
of children. Liturgical celebration and catechesis which avoid
that cultural fact are bound to estrange the young from the church.
To register this charge is not to claim that social hostility toward
the young is either new or indigenous to our culture. It is an
unfortunate human reality. Our interest must be in recognizing
its manifestations in our lives.

The exploitation of children is often for financial gain. Such
exploitation is sometimes crass, sometimes subtle, but it is pervasive in the dominant culture. While adults still respond with
outrage at the disclosure of the phenomena of pornography,
prostitution, and family-promoted sexual abuse of children, too
many have adjusted to the inevitable attacks on young people's
physical and emotional health through commercially lucrative
sales of sugar-saturated foods, alcoholic beverages, tobacco, and
other drugs. Our rhetoric laments this as a permissive society

which puts almost no restrictions on our children. It is possibly closer to the truth to call ours an oppressive society which puts almost no restrictions on the ways we burden the young. It is adults who deprive them of constructive choice and victimize their weakness and dependency for the sake of adult advantage. Sometimes parents function as protective shields; sometimes they are the witting or unwitting violators of their own young. Most often parents are victims of a culture of alienation which they unconsciously accept as inevitable.

The rejection of children in the United States finds expression in a full range of ways. Consider the obvious. It is common to find urban and suburban housing laws and rental policies which exclude couples with children and threaten eviction to those who presume to have a child after they have signed a lease. Voters regularly defeat school bond issues. Equally common is the rejection of the claims of children on parental time and attention. Rejection of such claims finds expression in the physical abuse of children, in their neglect, or in their economic indulgence. This society tends to look for resolutions of conflict through violence or through money. The results of such rejection are devastating for the young. The May 1979 *Harpers* published an essay on the accelerating rates of the suicide of children in this society.[1] Suicide, the author wrote, is the ultimate internalization of parental rejection. The child, always wanting to please parents and win their approval, takes to heart the message that one's very existence is offensive. So one accommodates to the parent's wish by self-destruction. At least, said the author, children who are physically mistreated tend to struggle for survival. Other reports indicate that an increasing number of mistreated children turn to violence. In some cases, this violence may be directed towards their peers and/or adults. In those situations where the child is both mistreated and ignored, the violence may be self-directed.

Legislators reject children when they refuse to develop legislation which will provide for adequate child care for working

---

1. Spencer Scott, "Childhood's End," *Harpers* 258 (May 1979) 16–19. The number of children who attempted suicide in 1978 has been placed at anywhere from a quarter of a million to half a million. (17)

parents. Employers do the same. Instead, the dominant society has agreed to provide and even pay for abortion, a manifestation of the social acceptability of the rejection of the young.

The society shows its hostility for the young in another way, by denying the young identity and a sense of self-worth. Our young must contend with the phenomenon of prolonged adolescence, a most bizarre time of passage, ten to twelve to fifteen years. During this time of social marginality, they learn to be consumers, encouraged toward indulgence in spending for themselves and indulgence in precocious sexual behavior. Reports from social scientists say that more than fifty percent of our young people have had sexual intercourse before they are eighteen years of age. Reports from social scientists say twice as many adolescents died violently at the end of the decade of the seventies as in the recent past, and that the death rate for 18–25-year-olds has risen significantly.[2]

Running this social gauntlet is cruel and unusual punishment. Increasingly larger numbers of the young collapse under the strain, and become socially deviant. Twenty-year-old collegians voice self-estimates and fears unimaginable to many adults: "If we didn't belong to a strict religious sect, we'd be degenerates and acid heads." Unable to face the possibility of foundering on the rock Permissiveness in their journey toward personal identity, many adolescents have impaled themselves on Authoritarianism and are clinging for their lives. But they are no closer to coming to personal identity and sexual maturity on their comfortingly secure perches. Nevertheless, large numbers are not ready to come down and take on what this society calls the normal life of an adolescent. In their confusion, many see no adults they can rely upon.

Why do I paint such a bleak picture of the current cultural situation regarding children and youth? On the basis of the evidence in published resource books on Christian celebration for the young it seems that those who are presently exploring children's liturgies have a romantic view of childhood and youth. Such a view actually denies their experience and ours. It also denies the young access to the mystery of our faith, namely that

2. "U.S. Reports in Death Rate Among Youth," *The Washington Post*, August 5, 1979, p. A10.

life's terrors and dangers are real, but our God gives life even in the face of cruelty and death. The children of the Hebrews have regularly cultivated the memory of suffering, hostility, and death.[3] Why not the children of the church?

A single book of more than a dozen commonly used resources for children's liturgy had a scenario for celebration that acknowledged and interpreted in the light of faith the concreteness of young people's experience of terror and pain.[4] "Birmingham Sunday: A Liturgy of Innocents" allowed junior-high-aged children to celebrate the memory not of Martin Luther King, but of four junior-high-aged girls, Carole, Cynthia, Addie Mae, and Denise, and all the other children of the world who have been victims of adult cruelty but who have nevertheless affirmed the power of life. A liturgy of the word let a message of hope resound through the words of a fifteen-year-old: "I see the world gradually being turned into a wilderness, I hear the ever-approaching thunder, which will destroy us too, I can feel the sufferings of millions, yet if I look up into the heavens, I think that all will come right, that this cruelty, too, will end, and that peace and tranquility will return again."

Exploitation and rejection, suffering and death, failure to show a clear path to identity and self-worth are as much a part of the cultural experience of our children as belonging and sharing and nurturance and affirmation. The focus on the latter and the denial of the former must result in a distortion of the message of salvation. Nathan Mitchell puts it succinctly, ". . . the Christian liturgy has never hesitated to speak, *simultaneously*, a language of sin and a language of healing. . . . The simultaneous presence of both languages creates a tension that makes genuine festivity possible. For unless festivity can deal with the unavoidable am-

3. The Passover Haggadah is one traditional liturgical action through which children are overtly introduced to the memory of suffering. So also, children's participation in Purim deliberately engages them in the conflict and hope endemic to membership in the covenant community that is Israel. See for example, A. Millgram, *Jewish Worship* (Philadelphia: Jewish Publication Society of America, 1971). Most recently worshipers have been struggling to incorporate the experience of Holocaust into the mystery of covenant life. See D. Roskies, *Nightwords* (Washington, D.C.: B'Nai B'rith Hillel. No date.).

4. Virginia Sloyan and Gabe Huck, *Children's Liturgies* (Washington, D.C.: The Liturgical Conference, 1970) 186.

biguity of real life—its scabs and its successes—it becomes escapist. By insisting that we acknowledge our pain—our failure and our finitude—the festivity of worship offers us the possibility of moving *beyond* it toward a vision of humanity healed and reconciled."[5]

One author wrote prophetically: "The continued use of irrelevant forms of worship for children and high school youth can only lead to confusion, boredom, and ultimate frustration, rather than to a vital faith, life, and prayer experience."[6] Confusing, boring, and frustrating are apt words to describe much of what is now in print, the products of our first decade of efforts to adapt liturgy to the faith life of the young. Perhaps what has been happening on location in communities around the country has been more profound, more tension-laden and integrating, than what is in print. If not, we must reach for that depth as our first goal in the decade ahead. Otherwise we will be in danger of missing the opportunity to engage young Christians in truly "messianic festivity" which "struggles to awaken life, to intensify consciousness in all directions." And, since pain is inescapably present to human consciousness and life, "messianic festivity" neither denies it nor conceals it.[7]

Adaptation to the needs of children and youth cannot mean adaptation to their neurotic needs for denial of sin and suffering, nor to ours. Cultural adaptation does mean asking and answering the question: Given this culture, how must we live and celebrate faith so that the young may hear the good news of the saving work of Jesus and want to participate in the work of reconciling this world to God?

Bringing Childish Fear and Fantasy to Paschal Faith

A church which intends to celebrate faith with its young must itself celebrate the paschal mystery in its fullness. The church must celebrate this mystery in ways that fit the human development of the young. If the goal is kept in view to lead the young gradually into deeper understanding of the mystery of life and death within which they live, one can begin to find

5. Nathan Mitchell, "L'Zikkaron," *Liturgy* 24 (July–August 1979) 14.
6. Maria Rabelais, *Children Celebrate!* (New York: Paulist Press, 1975) 5–6.
7. Mitchell 14.

resources for the tension-laden "messianic festivity" which culminates in the eucharistic assembly of the people of God, the fullest liturgical celebration of the one mystery.

Not all children's liturgy is eucharistic; but it should all be implicitly paschal. This is as true for children's liturgies as it is for the assemblies of the whole people of God. I am not talking about the language "paschal mystery" but about the depth of vision. Whoever lacks such depth of vision ought not to presume to exercise liturgical ministry for anyone, for this mystery is the heart of Christian faith.[8] Anything less than a profound liturgical ministry for the young is a betrayal of trust, another form of exploitation of the young at their expense.

Several years ago Nathan Mitchell wrote about the phenomenon of contemplative imagination or fantasy in the life of the very young, which itself constitutes a form of ministry within the whole church.[9] He noted that children aspire to construct a world where despite pain and danger things turn out right after all. This hope for a world more real than the world they live in creates in the human heart a readiness to hear the Good News. The child wants, says Mitchell, what adults want: a deathless world where stories are what Tolkien calls "eucatastrophes"— stories with happy endings. The Gospel is . . . the ultimate "eucatastrophe," the final fulfillment of all human fantasies about a world where things turn out right.

So, says Mitchell, the presence of children in the Christian community confronts all of us with a choice. It forces us to decide whether the fantasy that is the Gospel is true and worthy of a lifetime's dedication in love, or whether it is false, another in an infinite series of illusions about a world doomed to inglorious extinction at the hands of stupidly realistic men. If the child is right, then the world has a future and so do we. If the child is wrong, then we should "all fold our hands and wait for the end with stoic composure." The child, says Mitchell, comes to the

8. *Constitution on the Sacred Liturgy,* #5: "Christ achieved his task principally by the paschal mystery of his blessed passion, resurrection from the dead, and glorious ascension, whereby 'dying, he destroyed our death and, rising, he restored our life.' " W. Abbott, ed., *Documents of Vatican II* (New York: Association Press, 1966) 139ff.

9. Nathan Mitchell, "The Once and Future Child: Towards a Theology of Childhood," *The Living Light* (Fall 1975) 436–437.

gospel through his fantasy and that fantastic aspiration can be brought to celebration in messianic festivity.

Child psychologist Bruno Bettelheim has written about the value to the developing child of hearing again and again tales of young travelers through life: the Hansels and Gretels, the Dorothies, and the ducklings, who face the dangers of wicked stepmothers, evil kings in castles, sorcerers and witches who cast spells that block life, and dragons that threaten to destroy it. Such stories acknowledge evil and danger but show the child hope for safe passage through it.[10] Celebrations of this hope culminate for the Christian people in the eucharistic banquet. But the signs for celebration of hope are everywhere. And so are the stories of hopeful events worth celebrating. Eventually the growing child must come to appreciate the sacred significance of the biblical story and the sacred signs common to Christian celebration.[11]

To the degree that the children of the church have withheld from them in catechesis, in celebration, and in life the corporate confrontation with evil and resistance to its power by the power of God in the body of Christ, they are poorly served in their life journey in this or any other culture. Strictly upbeat celebrations create illusions. Such liturgies which lack tension and ambiguity may simply be variants on the simplistic situation comedies of prime-time television. The mystery proclaimed in Jesus is that the forces of diminishment and destruction are real indeed, but the power and purpose of God will ultimately prevail.[12]

Christians hope, says Paul, for what they do not yet see clearly. Children's liturgies which celebrate wholeness and reconciliation as present realities without attending also to children's very real experience of threats to their well-being, threats which seem not

10. Bruno Bettelheim, *The Uses of Enchantment: The Meaning and Importance of Fairy Tales* (New York: Random House, 1976).

11. For a brief introduction and further bibliography, see Jerome Berryman "A Gift of Healing Stories for a Child Who is Ill," *Liturgy* 24 (July–August 1979) 15–20, 38–42.

12. The theme of the victory of Christ over the forces of evil is deeply rooted in the rites of Christian initiation from the earliest period. For a discussion of alternative themes, however, see Gabrielle Winkler, "The Original Meaning of the Prebaptismal Anointing and Its Implications," *Worship* 52 (January 1978) 24–45.

to promise hope or resolution, are denials of the paschal mystery, not celebrations of it. Liturgical celebrations for very young Christians must be informed by a paschal vision which guides their fantastic aspirations for a deathless world toward the good news of Christ dead, buried, raised, and present among us for the world's salvation.

Coming to Maturity in the Body of Christ

In all cultures the young have to deal with the question of psycho-sexual-social identity and roles. We must remember that our version of early and prolonged adolescence is a cultural invention of a contemporary affluent Western society. A dozen years or more of social-psycho-sexual marginality is not one of the inevitably recurring structures of human existence. Much of the world neither knows nor has to deal with the luxury and the terror of requiring of its young this extraordinarily long passage to adulthood. Parents, pastors, and the adult community of the church want the outcome of this passage to be commitment to the faith within the body of the church. Yet there is an important issue at stake which the adult community has been skirting: the matter of personal-social-sexual identity within the body of Christ, which is the church.

Recent anthropological and sociological research have developed some pertinent ideas about the power of ritual activity to engage or to alienate participants in a ritual assembly. The work of social scientists in the area of ritual studies suggests that every human ritual assembly of a group makes affirmative assertions about the humanity and identity of those who are gathered.[13] It also makes demands on the persons so identified. Rituals do this symbolically and obliquely, not through direct assertion. To the degree that what is affirmed ritually is able to engage the participants, they will also be open to what is required of them

13. For an introduction to this approach to ritual analysis, see Victor W. Turner, "Forms of Symbolic Action: Introduction" in *Forms of Symbolic Action, 1969 Proceedings of the American Ethnological Society*, ed. Robert F. Spencer (Seattle: University of Washington, Press, 1969) 8–10. See also V.W. Turner, *Dramas, Fields, Metaphors* (Ithaca, N.Y.: Cornell University Press, 1974) 55–57. Also Roger Grainger, *The Language of the Rite* (London: Darton, Longman and Todd, 1974).

as members of the group. One could express the idea simply: the desirable dimension of life makes the obligatory dimension acceptable and possible. There is a correlative to this idea. If what is affirmed about the humanity and identity of those who are gathered is not engaging and desirable, the cumulative effect of the ritual action will be alienating.

The British sociologist Robert Bocock has recently studied the phenomenon of the growing alienation of many Anglicans from official church liturgy. He contends that many still look to liturgy for critical life moments: birth, marriage, death, and burial. But he notes that such participation often tends to compound confusion and not to help ordinary people to deal with the ambiguity and mystery of their human lives. On the basis of his study, Bocock suggests a hypothesis: What causes this withdrawal from the church's liturgy is the dynamic in Christian liturgical action which separates people from their own bodiliness, their own humanity, in a full range of overt or subtle ways[14] at the preconscious level. But it does occur, and it works its effect. Many nominal Christians have expressed their discomfort of a Christian church which continues to be alienated from human bodily existence. They react to this implicit denial of their full humanity by withdrawing from the assembly.[15]

The adult Catholic community—lay, religious, and ordained—lacks clarity of vision about the mystery of the human person, male and female.[16] Our assemblies reveal our corporate confusion about human sexuality and its place in the mystery of sal-

14. Robert Bocock, *Ritual in Industrial Society* (London: George Allen and Unwin, Ltd., 1974), 30–38; 147ff.

15. See Andrew Greeley, *The American Catholic* (New York: Basic Books, 1977) 136ff., for research data and interpretation which correlates with Bobock's thesis.

16. See Rosemary Haughton, "Neither Side Seems Aware," in the *National Catholic Reporter* 15 (August 24, 1979) 4, for a response to the controversy over the publication of the study commissioned by the Catholic Theological Society of America, Anthony Krosnick et. al., *Human Sexuality* (New York: Paulist Press, 1977), and the subsequent letter from the Vatican Congregation for the Doctrine of the Faith published in *Origins* 9 (August 30, 1979): 167–169. She writes ". . . the older ways of describing that landscape are no longer useful. To a young adult, to poor people, to non-Western people both languages (Aristotelean philosophy and secular humanism) are equally irrelevant because what is being described is not what they are seeing."

vation. The good news of human identity and human sexuality
as part of the creative and redemptive work of a loving God is
not clearly proclaimed in our assemblies, because we scarcely
believe it. We have a celibate male clerical liturgical assembly as
we have a celibate male clerical church. The church has allowed
the story of maleness to be told as a story of unrestrained do-
minion over the earth, including human bodiliness, for so many
generations that we have lost track of the original story of the
image. That story speaks of God's image in humanity male and
female.[17] We have forgotten that the *ecclesia* is called to witness
to the first fruits of redemption, the reconciliation which over-
comes the sin of the world. The vision of God's covenant within
all of creation gradually has given way to or been usurped by
the vision of patriarchy, and male and female reciprocity has
disappeared from the word of God. Reconciliation has become
an incomprehensible message, not a saving mystery within which
the people of God live.

Our adolescents look to the adult church to show them a full
humanity which presents models of psycho-sexual-social integration for male and female persons. Is it not possible that our
own confusion about the mystery of human sexuality is a greater
obstacle to the faith of adolescence than the confusion we have
about when to confirm? It is clearly easier and safer for us to
debate the timing of confirmation than to struggle together as a
church to grow in understanding of male and female identity
and responsible sexual behavior. Authentic rites of commitment
to a community demand that those committing themselves recognize a place and roles for themselves that are both humanly
intelligible and also manifestations of the paschal character of
Christian life. To the degree that we don't always make sense
even to ourselves as a ministering community of adults with
mature or at least maturing sexual and social identities, our young
may have no choice but to dismiss us as insignificant guides of
their journeys.

In this culture, personal adult identity is too often reduced to
a capacity for consumption and a capacity for sexual relation-

17. Rosemary Ruether gives an account of the fortunes of the "image" theme
in patristic literature. See Ruether, ed., *Religion and Sexism* (New York: Simon
and Schuster, 1975) 151–169.

ships. The young are encouraged to consume and to copulate before they have learned to interact with other persons in a full range of human relationships. But they are children in a church with a received tradition of anxiety about human sexuality. What have we to say to them? Can we tell them about a sexuality which is both creative and redemptive?

The early twentieth-century canonization of the adolescent Maria Goretti has long been recognized as an attempt to offer youth a model counter to developments in Italian society. The holy martyrs of Uganda were adolescents lauded for their deaths in resistance to homosexual abuse. But our young live in a world in which the culture of easy adolescent sexual activity devoid of commitment is perceived as normal—the real world. Does the adult Christian community offer with any clarity the possibility of mature human sexuality lived out in relationships that are rich with mystery, both painful and healing, both consuming and nurturing, both creative and sustaining? Are there really people who live for others and mysteriously become whole themselves?

Our imaginations and our energies are drained by preoccupation with the wrong human, liturgical, and theological questions when we aim catechesis and liturgical celebration for adolescence toward "confirmation" or reconciliation or vocation. Confirmation belongs to the initiatory cluster, and our adolescents have been Spirit-filled members of the faith community most often from their infancy. Reconciliation is a lifelong process, not an adolescent preserve. Vocation should follow after the achievement of a measure of personal identity with the mystery of Christ as the mystery of one's own existence.[18] What is the sacrament which discloses this mystery? It is the eucharist, but the eucharist celebrated in the fullness of the sign "body of Christ."

Our adolescents have been part of the ecclesial "body of Christ" from infancy. Only in adolescence does personal sacramentality emerge as young people gain an active capacity for sustained

18. In his essay "The Future of the Christian Family," J. Dominian identified qualities he considers basic to a Christian adulthood that is capable of relationships of intimacy. See The Way 14 (1974) 276–87.

relationships with peers, adults, and children which are marked by reciprocity and responsibility, by creative and redemptive living. Messianic festivity for the adolescent requires sensitive and honest exploration of the mystery that "those who would gain their lives must lose them." Such celebrations must help them have an image of the body of Christ which is intelligible to them at a human level: an image of a people who find in the mystery of Christ the possibility of reconciling body and spirit, male and female, rich and poor, young and old, friends and strangers. A humanly intelligible manifestation of the body of Christ must rejoice in incarnation. That incarnation must be expressed in the domestic church and the local church or adolescents will leave the Good News of Jesus as they have abandoned the "eucatastrophes" of their childhood fantasy.

The matter of a special sacramental event for adolescence is falsely formed when it is cast as confirmation or nothing. Many rites of public blessing of persons have risen in response to the reality of the actual life of the Christian people. That can happen again if we judge to be true what youth ministers are telling the whole church, that there is a pastoral need for the special blessing of adolescents at significant points on their ten- or twelve-year journey. We don't need a new sacrament nor the distortion of a liturgical action which has another meaning. We may well need public blessings of the young person within the eucharist community "at moments in her life critical for her salvation" to use a Rahnerian formulation.[19] What might those critical moments be? We need to celebrate with the young their increasing visibility as persons living out the mystery of Christ in their own lives. The appropriate setting for the celebration of the sacramentality of the ecclesial body of Christ is the eucharist.[20]

We might learn something about the ritual possibilities and the problems of such a public blessing of the young from Mexican American Catholics who have begun to revitalize a traditional celebration of the fifteenth birthday of a young woman of the

19. Karl Rahner, *The Church and the Sacraments* (New York: Herder and Herder, 1963), 41 and passim.

20. One could argue whether there should be eucharistic celebrations presided over by the bishop as the focus of unity and authority in that local church in which the young people are gaining identity in their own right.

community, the *Quinceañera*.[21] In its traditional form, the moment of blessing is also a public presentation of the girl as a Christian woman who will in due time approach Christian marriage. That content has particular historical significance which will not occupy us here. I make reference to *Quinceanera* because it presents the fact of a culturally responsive public blessing of the young within the eucharistic assembly. The adult church in the persons of parents and baptismal sponsors joins with the young woman's peers, her childhood and adolescent companions, to present her for the blessing of the church. She is singled out as a person in her own right, approaching her future in the community in the company of the many who have contributed to the fabric of her life to that moment.

We've blessed our fields, our church buildings, our church bells, and our fleets at various times and places. We did so because we believed that the stuff of mundane life—brick and mortar, clay and iron—could become by the invocation of the Spirit signs of God's saving presence in the world. Why not celebrate with hope our confidence that the young people among us are becoming salt, light, and leaven, the body of Christ, by the power of the Holy Spirit within them from their baptism?

Catechesis and liturgical celebration with adolescents must be geared towards exploring the mystery of the body of Christ in its present reality and its future possibility for their lives. Catechesis and minor celebrations prepare for public blessings by exploring the mystery of incarnation—the human person taken up into the saving work of God. Adolescent catechesis and celebration must never lose sight of the mystery of incarnation, teaching the young Christians, male and female, to be at home in and reverent with their bodies, learning the limits and possibilities of their persons.

Consulting the Tradition in the Search for Direction

Cyril of Jerusalem, one of the bishops of the early church, spoke in an Easter homily of the hidden power of the great symbols of the Christian life and worship. He encouraged the newly baptized, "Let the oil itself become your teacher. You were

21. Angela Erevia, *Quinceañera* (San Antonio: Mexican American Cultural Center. No date.).

anointed with chrism, and you have become Christs."[22] Saint Augustine of Hippo in North Africa had a similar vision of the power of the sacramental signs. In his sermon 272 we read:

> Would you understand the body of Christ? Hear the apostle saying to the faithful: "You are the body and the members of Christ." If, then, you are Christ's body and his members, it is your own mystery which is placed on the Lord's table; it is your own mystery which you receive. It is to what you are that you reply Amen, and by replying subscribe. For you are told: "The body of Christ," and you reply, "Amen." Be a member of the body of Christ, and let your "Amen" be true.[23]

Fifteen hundred years later, their words constitute good advice to the whole church in the early stages of liturgical renewal following the reform of our liturgical books. Let the signs become your teachers. Become what you are. It is your own mystery which you contemplate.[24]

It is possible to propose a concrete direction for catechetical work which heeds the advice of these early bishops, the call of Nathan Mitchell for tension-laden and "messianic festivity," and the call of the Vatican Council for greater clarity in sacramental signs for the whole church. This clear and simple direction comes from some research and theological reflection I have done over the past five years on the renewed rites. This proposed direction corresponds with the basic perspectives of the *Directory for Masses with Children*, namely that celebrations must be concrete in order to open children to the perception of the mystery of Christ.[25]

Not a few people have commented over the years that such a perspective is a need of adults. This convergence of adults'

22. E.C. Whitaker, ed., *Documents of the Baptismal Liturgy* 2nd edition (London: SPCK, 1970) 29.

23. Augustine of Hippo, Sermon 272, in Migne, *Patralogia Latina* 38 (1861), Column 1247.

24. In his essay, "The Idea of Christian Initiation," P.M. Gy notes that the fundamental understanding of Christian liturgical action involves initiation "by the mysteries" themselves, not instruction about them. See *Studia Liturgica* 12 (1977) 174–175.

25. Sacred Congregation of Divine Worship, *Directory of the Mass with Children* (Washington, D.C.: United States Catholic Conference Publication Office, 1974), #9.

and children's needs for concreteness in liturgical action comes to the fore in the *Rite for Christian Initiation of Adults*. Just as the *Directory for Masses with Children* also speaks to adults' liturgical needs, so also the *RCIA* provides a firm vision for those working with children and adolescents.

The *RCIA* sets out programmatically the basic cluster of the dominant ritual signs which occur over and over again in all of Christian life and celebration.[26] The basic tension-laden liturgical signs for messianic festivity accessible to Christian young, adolescent, and adult are the same, few in number, and to the degree that we—adult teachers of the young—are present to their mystery, these signs will indeed teach a paschal "habit of being" in the world.

What are the dominant recurring liturgical signs of the Christian people? The *RCIA* presents them as: (1) assembling; (2) signing with the cross; (3) salting; (4) proclaiming a living word; (5) laying on hands; (6) anointing; (7) illuminating; (8) plunging into water; and (9) sharing bread and wine.

How are we and young Christians to become present to the mystery of these human signs that are at the heart of Christian worship? We must explore and celebrate them in depth, in all their richness and ambiguity, in their human cultural meanings, and in their place in the story of salvation. We must explore their imaginative and significant use by the Christian people at different times and places in response to the circumstances of their lives and the quality of their faith.

Consider only signing with the cross. The *RCIA* presents this ritual action as the framing action for initiation.[27] It is the first liturgical sign with which the church meets the prospective Christian, infant or adult. It is also the penultimate sign of the process of initiation. In the joining of cross and chrism the church welcomes into the fullness of the ecclesial body of Christ the one who lives by the sign of the cross and the empowerment of the

26. *The Rite of Christian Initiation of Adults* investigated using as a working hypothesis ideas set out in Clifford Geertz, "Religion As a Cultural System" in *The Interpretation of Culture* (New York: Basic Books, 1973), and in V.W. Turner, *The Forest of Symbols* (Ithaca, N.Y.: Cornell University Press, 1967).

27. Sacred Congregation for Divine Worship, *Christian Initiation of Adults*, *The Rites* (New York: Pueblo, 1976), #83, #270.

Spirit. Only then do all participate together in the mystery of the eucharistic body of Christ.

The sign of the cross under which the Christian people live invites "messianic festivity." It is a sign of contradiction as well as a cosmic sign of wholeness which has been recognized and used as a sign of integration by peoples everywhere. The four ends of the earth are drawn together in this sign. Renaissance artists saw it as the organizing basis of the human body. It is, according to Jung, an archetypal human sign, present in life, art, and religious iconography as an expression of the aspirations of the human psyche.[28] But the cross is also an instrument of execution and a sign of destruction, degradation, and humiliation within human history. The Romans hung Jesus on a cross 2,000 years ago. Cambodians hung a twelve-year-old boy on a cross for pilfering food in the summer of 1979, and the news services made him a universal public spectacle, a sign of contradiction.

Early Christians recognized the mystery of Christ in this tension-laden sign and claimed it as a symbol revelatory of their faith. Christians have marked all manner of things with this sign. Just as people engrave serial numbers on property and brand the flesh of herds to prevent theft, just as humans have circumcised and tatooed and raised keloids on their own flesh to identify their allegiance and their belonging, so Christians have marked the sign ritually on their foreheads with oil and ashes and human touch. They have traced it on their bodies and have designed their buildings so that they could gather within the sign. All this has been done so that they could let their lives be transformed by the meaning of the cross. Artists in the Christian tradition have heightened the power of the sign by emphasizing now one, then the other of the polarities held in its balance, the fact of diminishment versus the desire for and praise of wholeness.

But the cross is accessible to young people only to the degree that memory and imagination are engaged in the creative exploration of the sign both as humanly intelligible and as a call to faith and hope. The experience of the Christian community with this sign and with each of the basic symbols acts of the liturgical repertoire constitutes an abundant and almost inexhaustible resource for opening up the paschal vision and the

28. Carl G. Jung, *Man and His Symbols* (New York: Dell, 1968) 273–276.

paschal habit of being which is the core content of Christian life and liturgy.

The late Margaret Mead warned Catholics, in an address she gave at Catholic University in the 1960s, that the American culture lacked the capacity for ritual, because Americans did not value the stuff of which rites are made. One characteristic of good ritual is redundancy, the presentation of a single reality in multiple "languages" or expressive forms. Another is repetition, the valued and sanctioned recurrence of significant tension-laden behavior.[29] Mead was indeed prophetic in speaking a word of warning and judgment that needs resounding among us again.

Liturgists for the young, like all of us in a consumer culture, tend to look for and to want to create novelty, not depth of significance. Ritual redundancy and repetition are not of themselves inherently boring unless they are the activities of boring people who lack both memory and imagination. For those who are alive to life and those who are coming to life in Christ, the capacity of the human mind to act as a great transformer of the stuff of human life into signs of salvation should not be underestimated. But people need to be tutored in Christ in order to be set free.

The athlete and the dancer first discipline themselves in order to appropriate a tradition of movement, rhythm, and order. Only then are they free to improvise and go beyond the established forms. Adults who were not themselves disciplined by and who have not appropriated the great Christian ritual symbols and biblical stories that disclose the paschal mystery are not yet free to improvise, to create and to innovate ritually to bring children to celebration.

Therefore, it was sobering to discover that none of the earliest books published on children's liturgies listed among their bibliographic resources either the *General Instruction on the Roman Missal* or any of the texts of the revised sacramental rites. Were these dismissed by catechists, rejected as irrelevant, or taken for granted? Internal evidence in books on children's liturgy suggests that their basic content has not been mastered. It is, for example, a truism among professional liturgiologists, at least

29. For a published statement of similar themes, see "Celebration: A Human Need," in *The Cathechist* (March 1968) 7–9.

ever since Gregory Dix, that the basic structure of eucharistic action is take/bless/break/eat and drink.[30] Yet only one of the dozen books consulted reflected awareness of that ritual structure of the liturgy of the eucharist and explored its meaning with young Christians.

Which brings us back to Freddy and Brenda. Look carefully: where there is no new life growing, the community may be bloated—but starving.

---

30. *The General Instruction on the Roman Missal* (#48) offers a modified version of the Dix thesis; see also Gregory Dix, *The Shape of the Liturgy* (London: Dacre Press, 1945) 48ff.